"Sleeping Beauty," a Legend in Progress

"Sleeping Beauty,"
a Legend in Progress

Tim Scholl

Yale University Press

New Haven and London

Photos of the 1890 production copyright © St. Petersburg State
Museum of Theater and Music; photos of the 1999 production by
Natasha Razina; the page of choreographic notation, courtesy of
The Harvard Theatre Collection, Houghton Library, Harvard
University.

Set in Adobe Garamond and Stone Sans types by The Composing Room
of Michigan, Inc.

Printed in the United States of America by Sheridan Books.

Library of Congress Cataloging-in-Publication Data
Scholl, Tim, 1962–
    "Sleeping beauty," a legend in progress / Tim Scholl.
        p. cm.
Includes bibliographical references and index.
    ISBN 0-300-09956-8 (alk. paper)
    1. Sleeping Beauty (Choreographic work)—History.   2. Ballet—
Russia (Federation)—History.   I. Title.
    GV1790.S55S35 2004
    792.8′42—dc22

                                                    2003017368

A catalogue record for this book is available from the British
Library.

The paper in this book meets the guidelines for permanence and
durability of the Committee on Production Guidelines for Book
Longevity of the Council on Library Resources.

10 9 8 7 6 5 4 3 2 1

Contents

Preface, vii

A Note on the Text, xiii

1 Genre Trouble, 1

2 Legends of *Sleeping Beauty* (What Becomes a Legend Most?), 30

3 Achieving Symphonism (The Soviet Ballet in Theory), 64

4 Red Auroras (The Soviet Ballet in Practice), 101

5 Bringing *Beauty* Back, 131

Appendix: Reviews of the 1890 Production, 173

Notes, 219

Works Cited, 233

Index, 241

Preface

Each of the surviving ballets of the nineteenth-century Russian repertory is unique, in part because there are so few of them. Only *Swan
Lake* includes choreography by Lev Ivanov, for example. Ivanov
choreographed in the shadow of Marius Petipa and may have possessed comparable genius. *La Bayadère* and *Esmeralda* are the surviving members of a large family of ballet melodramas set in exotic locales. *Don Quixote* represents another genre, the comedic ballet, and
like the remaining fragments of *Paquita,* reveals Russia's nineteenth-
century fascination with sunny Spain. Of the ballets composed by
Alexander Glazunov, only *Raymonda* survives.

    Sleeping Beauty continues to occupy a special place among these
works. The first and only opportunity for choreographer Marius
Petipa to realize a collaboration with composer Pyotr Tchaikovsky,
then a rising star on the stage of St. Petersburg's Imperial Theater, the
work sidesteps the nineteenth century's usual melodramatic plots in
favor of a fairy tale set in France in the reign of a monarch who bears
more than a passing resemblance to Louis XIV. *Sleeping Beauty* avoids
the drama and denouements typical of ballets of its day (to the chagrin
of its first audience) as well as the aforementioned exoticism. Instead,

the ballet's creators relied upon the parade of characters from the tales of Charles Perrault (and a surfeit of fairies) to lend the work its color and variety.

Sleeping Beauty was the brainchild of Ivan Vsevolozhsky, the director of Imperial Theaters, who championed Tchaikovsky's work (he commissioned *Nutcracker* and *Queen of Spades* as well as *Sleeping Beauty*). An aesthete and Francophile, Vsevolozhsky crafted the libretto for *Sleeping Beauty* and designed its costumes. Frequently reproduced, Vsevolozhsky's designs conjure a fanciful fairy-tale world as they exude a wit and elegance few professional designers for the ballet have managed since. Much of the continued fascination with the first, 1890, production of *Sleeping Beauty* is thanks to Vsevolozhsky's evergreen designs.

The visual record of the 1890 *Sleeping Beauty* also speaks to the ballet's uniqueness. Sketches, photographs, models—even costumes—from 1890 have survived. Yet it was a curious cache of notations of the Petipa choreography that prompted the Maryinsky (former Kirov) Ballet to undertake the reconstruction of the ballet's original production in 1999, more than a hundred years after the ballet's premiere. A St. Petersburg dancer and pedagogue, Vladimir Stepanov, devised a system to notate choreography in the waning years of the nineteenth century. As Marius Petipa faced retirement, the Imperial Theaters adopted Stepanov's system to preserve the balletmaster's legacy, until the 1917 Revolution refocused the Russian ballet's priorities on the new. When Nikolai Sergeyev, the controversial regisseur of the Imperial Ballet, left Russia the following year, he took the archive of ballet notations (for some two dozen ballets and the dances from as many operas) with him. Sergeyev was instrumental in transferring important parts of the Imperial Ballet legacy to the West; his stagings of the Russian classics in London, for example, established the Royal Ballet's classical repertory.

Meanwhile, in the city once known as St. Petersburg, and in a theater formerly known as the Maryinsky, Soviet balletmasters essayed their own versions of *Sleeping Beauty*. Fyodr Lopukhov premiered his staging in the State Academic Theater of Opera and Ballet in Petrograd in 1922; Konstantin Sergeyev showed his post–World War II redaction of the ballet in Leningrad's Kirov Theater in 1952. By the late 1990s, when the theater was again known by its prerevolutionary name and the city was again called St. Petersburg, the Maryinsky Ballet decided to reclaim another portion of its history: a reconstruction of the 1890 production of *Sleeping Beauty*, with sets and costumes built from the original designs and choreography revised from the choreographic notations recorded in the theater a century earlier (the notations had since found their way to the Theatre Collection of the Harvard University Libraries).

In 1999, as in 1890, the production of *Sleeping Beauty* proved controversial, and the questions it raised motivated me to write this book. Why, for example, in a city, a theater, and a ballet company that revered its past, should a return to that past—even partial or incomplete—arouse such debate? That question led me back to 1890, and to productions of the ballet staged in the theater since. If I first attributed the uniqueness of the ballet to the features I have detailed above, which any student of dance history could recite, I began to see the centrality of *Sleeping Beauty* to the history of Soviet/Russian ballet: how the ballet shaped Soviet ballet history, and in turn, how the vicissitudes of that history molded the Tchaikovsky-Petipa ballet. What began as a study to investigate the 1890 production and its impact in 1999 became an investigation of the ballet's survival over the course of an arduous century.

In his monumental study of the Tchaikovsky ballets, Roland John Wiley shows that *Swan Lake* was a ballet "in progress" as he examines the many amendments to it in its earliest productions. It struck me that *Sleeping Beauty*, a work that underwent surprisingly few new productions in its first century, represented something quite different, and my title derives from the centrality of stories to *Sleeping Beauty*, including the abundance of legends and myths that still swirl about it. Narrative concerns have been at the center of discussions of *Sleeping Beauty* from 1890 to the present. The first viewers were shocked that the ballet was based on fairy tales; the ballet's extensive use of pantomime remained problematic throughout the twentieth century. Vsevolozhsky concocted his ballet from the tales of Charles Perrault, yet the stories at the heart of the ballet run deeper, to the richer mines of myth. Given the ballet's saturation in stories, it is no surprise that the ballet has generated myths and legends of its own over the past century. The 1999 production rewrote many of these, hence the controversy.

Behind the history of *Sleeping Beauty* lurks a larger story: a narrative of creating autonomy for dance. One could argue that the dance had been liberated in the nineteenth century as it gradually broke away from the opera and took its own place on the lyric stage, with its independent repertory and, in St. Petersburg, separate "ballet evenings." The Diaghilev ballet surely affirmed the ballet's independence and made that fact known in Europe and the Americas— perhaps more obviously than in Russia. Yet the Soviet-era history of *Sleeping Beauty* is also the story of carving out a place for dance among the academies, canons, and bureaucracies that grew with the new state.

My aim in writing this account of the first hundred-odd years of the history of *Sleeping Beauty* in St. Petersburg has been the stated goal of all historians: to set at least a part of the record straight. I take issue with many Soviet-era accounts of the period in question even as I remain grateful for and indebted to the enormous contributions to the history of Russian and Soviet dance made by such historians as Yuri Slonimsky and Vera Krasovskaya. I quote *Music and Musical Life in Soviet Russia,* Boris Schwarz's masterful study of Soviet music, on the sensitive subject of the ideological pressures that Soviet music writers and musicologists faced: "They had no choice but to heed the Party line, to produce hackwork in praise of Soviet realism and propaganda literature against Western Music and musicians." Nonetheless, neither Schwarz nor I believe the process was one-sided, that power flowed in only one direction. Schwarz notes that when it came time to advance the careers of ideologically supple hacks, for example, "critics had to be found to praise them . . . and they were found" (255–56).

Sergei Vikharev and Pavel Gershenzon, the two persons most responsible for reviving the 1890 production of *Sleeping Beauty* in 1999, have promised to detail their reconstruction of *Sleeping Beauty:* the editorial choices made in the reworking of the ballet's choreography and the reconstruction of its visuals. I leave discussion of the details of 1999 production to them. The aim of this book is broader: to chart the trajectory from 1890 to 1999 and to examine the commonalities that link the two epochs. Russia was emerging as a world ballet power in 1890. The years that followed saw Russian soloists replace Italian guests on the stage of the Maryinsky and the rise of the Diaghilev ballet in Europe decades later. In 1999 the Maryinsky Ballet was emerging once again from relative isolation. Well aware of the Russian ballet's glorious past, the troupe was anxious to test its prowess on world markets. If the 1890 production of the ballet did much to announce the Russian ballet's first wave of international fame, the 1999 production naturally revisited a number of issues the first production of the ballet raised, notably questions of genre (was ballet indeed a "high" art and had it always been so?) as well as the status of the ballet as a national art form.

St. Petersburg productions of *Sleeping Beauty* are the focus of this study. British *Sleeping Beauty*s, and the role they have played in the development of a very different national dance culture, are the subject for another book—one that I leave to scholars of British ballet.

A series of fortuitously timed leaves from Oberlin College allowed me to witness the planning, production, and premiere of the Vikharev *Sleeping Beauty* in St. Petersburg at various junctures from 1997. A Fulbright teaching and research grant to the University of Helsinki gave me needed time to write. I must thank the faculty, staff, and students of the Theatre Research Department at Helsinki University for their kind hospitality and the chance to explore the many issues raised by the new production of *Sleeping Beauty* in a semester-long seminar, a dream assignment for any dance historian. The Slavonic Library of the Helsinki University Library remains one of that city's great treasures and Irina Lukka is the collection's heart and soul. I am grateful to colleagues, librarians, and the staff of all three institutions. The fine staff of the Finnish Dance Information Centre merits special praise.

Makhar Vaziev and his assistant Pavel Gerhsenzon were gracious hosts at the Maryinsky Theater, and I am indebted to both of them for the access I enjoyed on many visits. Anna Shoulgat and curators at the St. Petersburg State Museum of Theater and Music provided archival photographs for this volume graciously and efficiently despite their collection's temporary move. Librarians at the St. Petersburg Theater Library also provided able assistance, though it was Maria Ratanova who unearthed many of the reviews of early productions of *Sleeping Beauty* and provided superlative collegial support.

Dance lovers around the world owe their debt of gratitude to the Harvard Theatre Collection for maintaining one of Russian ballet's most precious archival legacies and making it available to researchers and would-be restagers. Annette Fern and her staff have assisted Sergei Vikharev, Gershenzon, and me on numerous occasions.

Elena Monastireva-Ansdell and Tatjana Honkanen assisted with the translations from Russian. The translations from Akim Volynsky's notoriously difficult Russian would not be included but for Irina Klyagin's expertise and gracious assistance.

Elizabeth Blayney, Dolsy Smith, Sarah Combellick-Bidney, Katie Scodova, Brianna Tindall, and Margaret Ryan each provided invaluable support as interns in the OCREECAS office. A number of people read early versions of the manuscript, and I am grateful to all of them, but especially to Steve Rugare. I must also thank the two friends who insisted on the worthiness of the project over lunch in the courtyard of the former Stroganov palace in St. Peterburg.

Most of all, I, and many lovers of ballet around the world, owe an enormous debt of gratitude to Sergei Vikharev and Pavel Gershenzon. Without their courage, persistence, expertise, and many headaches, none of us would have come face-to-face with a production that continues to fascinate more than a century after its first premiere.

A Note on the Text

It has become formulaic in volumes that include transliteration of Russian names to stress that the author has followed a more or less scientific system, except in cases where names familiar to Western readers would be less recognizable. I bend to the will of editors who prefer the familiar spellings "Tchaikovsky" and "Diaghilev" to correct transliterations of those names (Chaikovsky, Diagilev). I use transliterated names of Russian newspapers in the text: *Novoe Vremya* rather than "new times," *Pravda* rather than "truth." The majority of dance writers in late nineteenth-century Russia wrote anonymously or used pseudonyms. Where authorship is known, the author's name is given.

In 1890, the early reviewers of *Sleeping Beauty* bemoaned the inconsistencies in the names of characters and dances in the ballet (some French, others Russian). The first-act set piece called the Garland Dance in the West is known as the "peasant waltz" in Russian and sometimes referred to as the "valse villageoise" in 1890 sources. I use standard Anglo-American terms for the ballet's set pieces (Garland Dance, Rose Adagio, etc.) to avoid further confusion. The names of the ballet's third-act characters derive mostly from Perrault, and I use standard English-language translations of those names (Cinderella instead of Cendrillon) whenever possible. The names that yield least to translation—the fairies in the ballet's Prologue—derive not from Perrault but from Vsevolozhsky, and apart from the Lilac Fairy, I leave the names of the remaining fairies in Vsevolozhsky's French: Canari, Violente, Miettes qui tombent, Candide, Fleur de Farine (also Coulante), and Carabosse.

It should also be noted that in Russia, scenes are numbered consecutively through the work, so that the hunt scene (Act II, scene 1, in Anglo-American terminology) is scene 3 in Russian. I use the Western system of numbering scenes within acts, but the reader may encounter the Russian designations in the appendix.

Prerevolutionary dates are given old style; Soviet-era dates are given new style.

Unless otherwise noted, all translations are my own.

Chapter 1 Genre Trouble

Like many stage works now regarded as classic, *Sleeping Beauty* received a decidedly mixed reception at its premiere in 1890. Sharp differences in critical opinion revealed new faults developing in the terra firma of Russian ballet. Ironically, given that *Sleeping Beauty* came to be regarded as the quintessence of late nineteenth-century Russian ballet, a number of the ballet's first critics were certain that *Sleeping Beauty* marked the decline of the art form. And these general condemnations had little to do with the choreography, which was mostly appreciated when noticed at all. Instead, writers noted that the ballet's music, visuals, and narrative all marked significant departures from Imperial Ballet practice. Many of the ballet's original critics were not certain that *Sleeping Beauty* was a ballet at all.

Sleeping Beauty drew these issues into relief at a time when the presence of foreign dance troupes on Petersburg stages (after the prohibition on private theaters had been lifted in 1882) began to allow for a direct comparison with the visiting troupes and dancers (mostly Italian) then appearing in St. Petersburg. The Imperial Ballet could scarcely be considered a national enterprise, with foreign balletmasters, composers, teachers, and visiting artists, yet the distinctions Petersburg critics perceived between the local and guest performances boosted nationalist pride in the Russian ballet.

Dance writers in nineteenth-century Russia mostly belonged to the cadre of inveterate dance fans known as "balletomanes."[1] Conservatism and connoisseurship characterize their writing on the ballet, and their interest in the ballet was proprietary: they saw themselves as defenders of a tradition they "owned."[2] In general, these writers opposed *Sleeping Beauty*'s music as well as its thin narrative and regarded the ballet's elaborate visuals with deep suspicion. When they perceived imitations of Western European ballets in the production of *Sleeping Beauty,* they expressed their outrage and concerns for the ultimate decline of the Russian ballet.

A more progressive set of critics saw things differently: they endorsed the ballet's music and its plot, hailing both developments as potential solutions to the Russian ballet's perceived difficulties. Where the balletomane-insiders expressed a proprietary interest in an art form they perceived as national and superior, these outsiders (mostly music critics) expressed their interest in the development of an art form they viewed within a much larger context: contemporary performing arts traditions in Russia and in Western Europe.

Reactions to the production of *Sleeping Beauty* suggested two very different scenarios for the future of Russian ballet. *Sleeping Beauty*'s blend of "high" and "low" generic traditions, its unprecedented juxtaposition of "symphonic" music with visual and choreographic elements borrowed from lower dance genres posited two possible outcomes: the ballet could take its place among the high arts (alongside the opera and the symphony) or remain true to itself (if not exactly "low") and maintain the status quo. *Sleeping Beauty* raised an important new question: Were Russian ballet's interests best served by merely maintaining national superiority or should the art form entertain more cosmopolitan hopes for the future?

In this book I will examine the mutual interdependence of this very important ballet and the art form for which it came to function as an exemplar: *Sleeping Beauty*'s role in shaping the history of Russian and Soviet ballet over the course of a century, and how the history of the art form, especially in the Soviet Union, influenced the evolution of *Sleeping Beauty.* In this chapter I will detail the beginning of that process, examining the tensions that greeted the Petipa-Tchaikovsky-Vsevolozhsky ballet in 1890.

Of the ballets of the Russian nineteenth-century repertory, the 1890 *Sleeping Beauty* possesses the fullest documentation. In addition to the choreographic notations in the Sergeyev Collection, Russian researchers preparing for the 1999 reconstruction of the ballet made use of an abundance of photographs (made on stage as well as in photographers' studios), machinists' instructions, light plots, Vsevolozhsky's famous costume designs, original costumes, sketches of the sets, at least one model (the hunt scene), and conductor Riccardo Drigo's notes in the original performance score.

The written record of the ballet's first production falls into two categories: journalistic accounts and memoirs. I cite sixteen accounts of the ballet, from the perfunctory to the detailed, that appeared in Russian newspapers and periodicals in the weeks surrounding the ballet's premiere, as well as reviews of subsequent Russian productions. Ironically, the *Sleeping Beauty* reviews from the late nineteenth century devote the least space to the ballet's choreography. Information about the dancing generally focuses on the execution and interpretation of leading dancers, and discussions of the choreography follow a similar pattern: the choreographer is similarly judged on the "execution" of his craft. Originality and invention play a role in the evaluation of the balletmaster's contribution, though the reviewers' tendency to judge the dances "appropriate" or not suggests the relatively narrow range of expectations these reviewers held for the choreographer and the art form at the end of the nineteenth century. The 1890 reviews of *Sleeping Beauty* circle consistently around four issues: the music, the plot, the visuals, and the ballet's genre. Compared to the column inches devoted to these, the choreography receives scant attention.

THE MUSIC

The single most divisive aspect of the new *Sleeping Beauty* proved to be the one element that guaranteed the ballet's livelihood in more tumultuous times: the ballet's music. The commission of a serious native composer (in place of the usual foreign house composers) signaled a departure from Imperial Theater routine and was widely discussed in reviews of the new ballet. A few of these writers mention Tchaikovsky's earlier attempt at ballet composition, the ill-starred premiere of *Swan Lake* in Moscow in 1877, though none attests to familiarity with more than that ballet's music.

The polarized response to *Sleeping Beauty* in the press divides rather neatly between the balletomanes (and those who faithfully report their position) and critics chiefly interested in the ballet's music. Mikhail Ivanov, the music critic of *Novoe vremya,* suggests that Tchaikovsky's contribution to the ballet attracted a wider public as well as a more diverse group of reviewers: "*Sleeping Beauty,* a ballet novelty, whose music was written by Mr. Tchaikovsky, is now the most important event in the musical theater. Mr. Tchaikovsky attained such a level of popularity after *Eugene Onegin*, even among a public indifferent to art, that he forces it to take an interest in all his new stage works" (22 January 1890). Several newspapers sent two critics (dance and music) to the performance. Those writers mostly limited themselves to their respective specialties, though Konstantin Skalkovsky, Ivanov's colleague at *Novoe vremya*, summarized balletomane reaction to the music in his review: "Our music critic will make a more detailed and competent judgment of Mr. Tchaikovsky's music. We will note only that the music is melodious, easy to listen to, elegantly orchestrated, and pleased the public, which called for the composer several times. In places, as in the prima ballerina's variations, the rhythm is not sufficiently distinct, which is very disadvantageous for the performer. Of course, a too-marked rhythm imparts vulgarity to music, but is necessary in dances. They gain in their illustrative quality and hold the public's attention in the appropriate place" (5 January 1890). Skalkovsky's relatively diplomatic assessment of the music's unsuitability paled before the admonishments of the *Peterburgskaya gazeta* critics. The bastion of balletomane opinion, the newspaper was edited and published by dance critic, historian, and ballet librettist Sergei Khudekov. "Concerning Mr. Tchaikovsky's music, its orchestration shines, it is always elegant and transparent . . . but . . . but . . . for the ballet it is nonetheless far from suitable. In the audience they called it either a symphony or a melancholy. There are several numbers, especially in the last scene, that caress the ear . . . but in general the music didn't satisfy the balletomanes" (4 January 1890). A subsequent review in *Peterburgskaya gazeta* provides a fuller account of Tchaikovsky's failings. The author frets that Tchaikovsky is attempting to be "original," to say something new. The reviewer allows that this is natural for any artist, but that Tchaikovsky's innovations in external form come at the expense of musical thought.

> Why, for instance, did the composer need such dense colors and the massive orchestration for the depiction of Aurora's Christening, the first scene, which is superfluous in the ballet—both to the narrative (is there a christening in the tale?) and to the music. Judging from the music, one might guess that it was something about Macbeth and his witches.
>
> Isn't this like weaving a spider-web with a rope? In ballet one awaits music that is more or less transparent, light, and gracious, that speaks to the fantasy of the plot. Instead, *Sleeping Beauty*'s listeners find themselves under an influence that nearly borders on the sensation that follows some sort of "good" act of *The Ring*. Operaticism,

and especially symphonicism in the ballet—when they have no dramatic content whatever (in contrast to Mr. Ivanov's *La Vestale,* for example)—too rich and heavy, are armor in costume's place.[3] (16 January 1890)

The reviewer's charges of "operaticism" and "symphonism" in *Sleeping Beauty* suggest a further problem with the music (and one to which most writers only alluded): not only was the music insufficiently rhythmic, it was encroaching on the hostile (and higher-genre) territory of the opera and the symphony. The review in *Peterburgsky listok,* which compares Tchaikovsky's "failure" to that of Ambroise Thomas, whose ballet *La Tempête* had premiered in Paris six months earlier, reveals the peculiar balletomane anxiety vis-à-vis these higher genres:

Concerning the music of such a venerable composer like P. I. Tchaikovsky, it proved in the most positive sense that the most talented *opera* maestro may be unsuccessful as a *ballet* composer. In this case, P. Tchaikovsky suffered the same fate as the great French artist-composer of many wonderful operas, Ambroise Thomas, who wrote the music for the ballet *The Storm.* We attended the premiere of *La Tempête* in the Grand Opera in Paris last summer. The ballet suffered a fiasco, thanks primarily to Thomas' music, which turned out to be completely unsuited for dance, although it was very rich with the beauties of a serious symphony. Almost the same occurred a few days ago in the Maryinsky Theater. The difference being that P. Tchaikovsky's music for the ballet wasn't a failure in the end (and it couldn't be, since there was not *ballet*). But like Thomas' music, it didn't suit dances. Our famous composer isn't the guilty party here: nature grants that every artist is given "his" special purpose. Minkus, Pugni, and Delibes couldn't have arranged such an opera as *Eugene Onegin.* And Tchaikovsky couldn't cope with the demands of ballet music. None of this, by the way, prevents the first three or the last from being great musical artists in his own line and genre. (5 January 1890)

Ivanov's *Novoe vremya* review and another, unsigned review in *Nuvelist* enjoin this discussion of contemporary ballet composition, broadening the debate to include ballets in operas. The *Nuvelist* writer first gives a historical overview:

It has been several years already since the theater administration changed the former order of things regarding the composition of music for new ballets. Before, there was a special post in the theater—the "composer"—who was obliged to write music for all the ballets that appeared on the state stages without exception. This position, which even now still seems to exist in Moscow, was occupied by Pugni for the last thirty or forty years and after him, by Minkus. Both are experienced in their craft and

undoubtedly talented, especially the latter. But the choreographic routine in which
they were supposed to vegetate, the job of inevitably writing one or even two ballets
every year, could not help but weigh heavily on their fantasy and on their very attitude to the work. Mr. Minkus, who, together with Delibes, wrote one ballet for the
Paris stage (*La Source,* it seems), should have known of the new tendency in ballet
music, a tendency that was revealed in France and that took on a serious aspect that
even the music for such a wonderful ballet as Adam's *Giselle* doesn't evoke. Mr.
Minkus remained faithful to the traditions that have already ruled on the Petersburg
stage more than a half century, traditions that accorded music a distinctly second
place and demanded nothing of music but light tunes, with rhythms mostly marked
by a bass drum. He has several wonderful ballets, in which his talent speaks vividly,
but there is no doubt that he nonetheless has remained outside the movement evident among the ballet composers of France. (3)

The writer contrasts this "new wave" of ballets composed in France (including
the ballet numbers in the operas of Meyerbeer and Rossini, and by Russian
composers Glinka and Rubenstein) to the "lousy models" provided by recent
Italian ballets. "French composers, with Delibes in first place, first showed that
even for the ballet one could write music that was accessible to all, comfortable
for the choreographer's goals, and together with that, such music that any developed musician could sign on to" (4).

Ivanov, in *Novoe vremya,* shares the opinions of the *Nuvelist* writer—to such
an extent that one suspects they are the same author. Like his colleague (and al-
ter ego?) at *Nuvelist,* Ivanov sees the future of ballet music in recent French ballets and in dances composed for Russian and European operas: "Meyerbeer,
Gounod, Glinka, and many other opera composers gave us more than a few
models of excellent ballet music in their operas that have nothing in common
with the ballets of the past. The new generation of composers who write music
for the ballet should have followed, and have followed, their example, using
means to achieve a symphonic genre of music. Of course, the music of one is
more successful than that of the other, and one shows talent and the other is
boring. But the direction remains unavoidable, and the ballet composers of
other countries are joining the movement begun in France (Delibes, Lalo,
Salver, Thomas, and others) and in Russia" (22 January 1890).

According to the *Nuvelist* writer, Tchaikovsky's ballet was not the first "symphonic" ballet to be heard on the imperial stages. The "French" tendency was
already "fully realized in M. Ivanov's *La Vestale.*" Produced in 1888, with music
by *Novoe vremya* critic Mikhail Ivanov and a libretto by *Peterburgskaya gazeta*
publisher Khudekov, the composer was "forced to endure a great number of re-

proaches from the balletomanes for his 'boring symphonies' and the like": "*La Vestale* was the first of our ballets in which the composer completely and consciously tread new ground in ballet music and made extensive use of the symphonic genre. Mr. Drigo's *Talisman,* which followed *La Vestale,* in part in its plot, and in part thanks to the nationality of its author, markedly stepped back from this principle, though it already had little in common in character and instrumentation with the old ballets. In *Sleeping Beauty* Mr. Tchaikovsky followed the same path as Mr. Ivanov in *La Vestale* and, like his forerunners, drew the same reproaches from the balletomanes: of symphonicity and the unsuitability of his music for choreographic purposes" (4). The most curious feature of the *Novoe vremya* and *Nuvelist* reviews is that both say essentially the same things. In addition to their endorsement of French opera music over Italian, both authors regard Minkus the master of ballet music (though Ivanov claims to know this only by hearsay), both mention Minkus' bass drum, both discuss the abundance of waltzes in *Swan Lake,* both esteem *Sleeping Beauty* highly, both recognize the Prologue and Act I as the strongest components of the ballet, and both discuss the transformations of the Lilac Fairy's theme. The two reviews even note the influence of Glinka's enchanted kingdom music from *Ruslan and Ludmila* on Tchaikovsky's music for the slumbering kingdom. Of course, Ivanov could scarcely have signed his name to the *Nuvelist* review: he accords himself too high a place in the history of Russian ballet composition as the student whose composition anticipated the innovations of the master.[4]

Another Tchaikovsky supporter, music critic Herman Laroche penned the most reasoned account of Tchaikovsky's music for *Sleeping Beauty.* His essay appeared in *Novoe vremya* two weeks after the ballet's premiere as a "musical letter from St. Petersburg." Laroche's review touches on a number of sensitive issues the ballet raised: the absence of drama in *Sleeping Beauty,* the prevalence of foreign (French) motifs in the ballet, the use of children's tales generally, and finally, the ballet's place amongst other arts. Essentially, Laroche's essay covers everything but the music, which he treats in more detail in an essay that appeared in the 1893–94 *Yearbook of the Imperial Theaters.* Laroche maintained that *Sleeping Beauty* made Tchaikovsky's name famous in circles that had previously known only Pugni, Minkus, Herbert, Schneitzhöffer, and Adolphe Adam.

> All these composers—at times capable melodists, at times virtuosos of counterpoint—regarded the composition of ballet music with a biased striving for salon lightness, for the rhythmic expressiveness of ballroom dancing. The ballets of the adroit and learned Pugni were especially full of this affected vulgarity that in its turn,

had an oppressing effect on the tastes of the balletomanes. It would be a mistake to think that lovers of ballet watch without listening. I know people who play arrangements of ballets on their pianos at home, like we play symphonies. If they didn't actually listen, then France would not have had the ballets of Lalo and Delibes, or ballet numbers in the operas of Auber and Meyerbeer. The fame of the second act of *Life for the Tsar* would not have thundered here. It's also true that the audience that hears ballet music in *operas* is not the same public (or not quite the same) that overfills the hall on ballet days. It's true that this special ballet audience listens with less attention, speaks more noisily, and is probably more forgiving of wrong notes. But they nonetheless have their favorite effects, motives, and their tradition of forms and instrumentation. The composer of *Swan Lake* already had occasion to do battle with those habits. The composer of *Sleeping Beauty* overcame them, as if jesting. (1895, 91–92)

Laroche goes on to detail what is hinted at in the above paragraph: the question of genre, of "light" music. His discussion suggests that for all the reproaches of "symphonicity" directed at the composer and his ballet, there were also those who saw a capitulation to a lighter genre in the composer's turn to the ballet. "The ability to compose dances is not the same as the ability to compose light music. It's not difficult to imagine a ballet score with dance rhythms, but only that. The ideas themselves and the harmonic trim are cumbersome, like Robert Schumann or even something heavier. One such work is Lalo's *Namouna,* which I heard some twelve years ago. But in general one could say that a similar style in ballet represents either a lack of taste or intentional extremism. Nowhere, apparently, is this simple truth so necessary to bear in mind than in Russia, where anything light is marked *poshlost.*"[5]

As the date of *Sleeping Beauty's* premiere receded, reviews of the music, in particular, became more conciliatory. By 16 January, even *Peterburgskaya gazeta,* the bastion of balletomane opinion, reported that "it is possible that in our day, ballet music is undergoing a new phase in its development." The *Nuvelist* writer recognized that time was on the side of the music critics' faction: "It has come to the point that all the lamentations of the old balletomane will be in vain" (4). Indeed, Alexandre Benois' recollection of his first and subsequent hearings of the ballet seems to epitomize the larger trend: "I went to the second performance of *La Belle au Bois Dormant* and left the theatre in a rather hazy state, only feeling that I had just heard and seen something that I was *going* to love. . . . The more I listened to the music, the more I seemed to discover in it greater and greater *Beauty*" (1941, 123–24). Six years after the premiere, Pleshcheev acknowledged gradual acceptance of the music: "The music of P. I. Tchaikovsky, who possesses the secrets of contemporary orchestration, is melodic, beautiful, and heard with pleasure. After the first performance, Messrs. Balletomanes maintained that this music, with its 'symphonic combinations,' was quite unballetic, and that in places, the rhythm was insufficiently distinct, etc. But with each hearing it was liked more and more. Soon all were in ecstasies over the music, and *Sleeping Beauty* attracted an audience that was scarcely 'balletic'" (306). By 1908, *Sleeping Beauty*'s place in the repertory was more than secure, and critic Valerian Svetlov could poke fun at his predecessors: "How times have changed! After the first performance, which was met by a despondently cold response from the audience, the press delivered this appraisal of the inspired work: 'the plot is not very poetic, banal, and unworthy of the Petersburg stage; the production is nothing more than a museum of props.' There were reproaches of the music, which was 'boring,' monumental, incomprehensible, and 'unfit for the ballet'(!). And now? Now it is the most valuable pearl of the repertory" (18 February 1908).

The debate over the ballet's music—the most divisive of the first controversies surrounding *Sleeping Beauty*—was thus the first to subside. Paradoxically, the relative sophistication of music (to the dancing) would soon suggest a marker against which the development of the ballet could be judged, for better or worse.

FOREIGN TALES

If the balletomanes objected to Tchaikovsky's score mostly on the grounds of its "symphonicism," their objections to the ballet's subject matter covered a range of condemnations. Most found the plot lacking in even rudimentary action, some objected to the use of children's tales as the subject for a ballet, and nationalists objected to Perrault's tales because they were French. Once again, opinions divided mostly along party lines: the music critics, Ivanov and Laroche (the Tchaikovsky party), took pains to justify the use of fairy tales in the ballet, even foreign ones. The balletomanes' criticisms, though scathing, hardly presented a unified front.

Although ballets based on children's or "wonder" tales (to use Vladimir Propp's more exact term) seem more the rule than the exception today, their introduction in 1890 sparked controversy. The least biased among the ballet connoisseurs objected to the use of Perrault's tale(s) because they lack a suitable, dramatic plot and could not motivate dancing. The critic of *Peterburgsky listok,* for example, contrasted *Beauty* to favorite old ballets such as *Esmeralda* and *Catarina*—ballets in which dances are purportedly linked to the action and "arise from the content of the ballet" (5 January 1890). "In *Sleeping Beauty* there is nothing of the sort. The line of action doesn't *illustrate* the dances at all. The dances are neither here nor there, and in the majority of cases come as an unexpected surprise, like a hair that fell into the soup. Thus the viewer who hasn't read the libretto in advance or who isn't familiar with the plot won't understand anything at all" (5 January 1890). Dmitry Korovyakov, the critic who provides the most thorough description of the ballet's visual components, appreciates the opportunity for fantastic and period costumes that fairy tales suggest but expresses misgivings concerning the story these visuals dressed: "At the beginning of this article, we said that the tales of Perrault and the strength of the poeticity of their descriptions offer good material for the externals of the production. But their internal content, the lack of complexity, the simplicity, and childlike naïveté, cannot feed the fantasy essential for the creation of the program of a grand ballet of this type, to which our audience has become accustomed over the course of many decades" (*Novosti I birzhevaya gazeta*, 5 January 1890).

Peterburgskaya gazeta displayed considerably less restraint in its criticism of the ballet. The first two of the newspaper's accounts of the ballet attacked the ballet for its use of fairy tales. "The plot and dances are missing!" the writer exclaimed. And children's tales are "simply, shortly, sweetly . . . for children." The writer continued: "A fairy tale! A fairy tale in the full sense of the word! The pantomime finds itself in an unprecedented absence! . . . Don't even look for any sense! All of Perrault's tales are mixed up, thrown into one pile, and the new ballet doesn't produce any one impression as a result. It is a heap of a whole string of wonderful pictures, with marvelous decors, luxurious costumes—a kaleidoscope that blinds the viewers. It is indeed a fairy tale—a fairy tale for children and old men who have returned to a childish state . . . but a ballet, as we understand it? No! It is the complete decline of choreographic art!" (4 January 1890). The same newspaper continued its assault the following day, under the heading "The Balletomanes' Grief": "In this supposed choreographic work there isn't any sort of plot. It is summed up in a few words: they dance, fall asleep, and dance again. They wake up and once again start dancing. There is no peripeteia, no development of the plot, no interest to seize the spectator, to force him to follow the play's action" (5 January 1890).

Several of St. Petersburg's dance writers recognized something universal in Perrault's tales, but they took issue with the version of those tales used—more specifically and tellingly, they objected to the French redaction of the story. On the day of the ballet's premiere, Khudekov previewed the work in his newspaper with a brief, xenophobic commentary on the ballet:

> Ballet-féerie! . . . A new word, used for the first time on our bills. For the record, this word "féerie," a *foreign* word, ideally suits the new ballet, whose plot is taken from the *foreign* tales of Perrault.
>
> Now if the content of the ballet had been drawn from Afanasiev's rich collection of Russian tales, then the ballet wouldn't have the name "féerie," but either "tale" or "magic tale"! . . . The above-named collection includes a nearly identical tale: the "Sleeping Tsarevna." There could be costumes and decors—and all of it Russian! . . . There hasn't been a Russian fairy tale on our stage for a long time, despite the fact that the Russian fairy-tale world provides the fantasy of the librettist and the ballet-master alike a vast material! . . .
>
> The first performance of *Sleeping Beauty* is set for tonight. We love everything "Russian," and say this solely in view of the fact that if the designated plot was selected, then wouldn't it be better to make a program on the same subject from *Russian,* and not foreign tales! (*Peterburgskaya gazeta,* 3 January 1890)

The newspaper continued its assault the following day, beginning once again with the ballet's program: "In a fairy tale everything is possible. Even the illiteracy in the cast list and the mixing of languages—French with the local dialect—is allowed. It seems to us, that if you take the titles of the personages from Perrault, then you should stick to that system. Or you end up with quite a mess. One name remains French and the other is translated into Russian. For example, the Lilac Fairy (in Russian) and *Prince Fleur des pois* (in French); the Breadcrumb Fairy (Russ.), and *Fée Violante* (Fr.); Cinderella (Russ.), etc." (4 January 1890). The review continues for several paragraphs, substituting translated Russian names for Carabosse, Aurora, Désiré, and so on, affecting the naïveté of the unsophisticated viewer (whose rights the balletomane writers purported to defend).

The "Tchaikovsky party" focused on other positive features of the fairy tale. Ivanov endorsed the fantastic elements that fairy tales could supply the ballet: "In my opinion, fairy-tale plots are appropriate for the ballet in their fantasy. They suit the choreographic art better than most others, more readily compelling belief in the reality of the phantasmagoria that the ballet presents. For every ballet is not only conventionalized, but also fantastic. . . . Why chase the tale from the realm of choreography, even if there was no drama in the most recent one? A fairy tale can also have its meaning, sometimes even a highly instructive one" (*Novoe vremya,* 22 January 1890). Ivanov also addressed the nationalists' criticisms of the foreign plot: "It would be possible to discuss the relative preference of the French tale over the Russian, but such a remark wouldn't carry much weight. Does it really matter where ballet plots are ladled from? The content is important, and not the external form in which they are expressed" (*Novoe vremya*, 22 January 1890).

Laroche took up the question of the fairy-tale plot and the question of nationalism in both his discussions of *Sleeping Beauty*. His response to balletomane chauvinism has become classic: "One could say . . . that the local color is French, but the *style* is Russian" thanks to the internal structure of Tchaikovsky's music (*Moskovskie vedemosti*, 17 January 1890).[6] In addition to several fairly obvious motivations for creating a French-themed ballet (Petipa's nationality, the French traditions in the ballet), Laroche sees the French color in the ballet as just another ballet stylization, not unlike balletic excursions to Scotland, Spain, Assyria, or Japan. For Laroche, no matter what the nation or people depicted, an element of the local nonetheless emerged: "Just as Mendelssohn-Bartholdy's ancient Greeks are German Greeks, Goldmark's *Die Königin von Saba* are Viennese Jews, and the Hindus in Delibe's *Lakmé* and Massenet's *Le Roi de Lahore* are second-empire Parisians, so the folk-tale forms of the ancient Aryan epic were transformed into French forms by national assimilation and transmission and underwent yet another transformation by the pen of a Russian musician. They took on a new nationality, and became a Russian variant" (*Moskovskie vedemosti*, 17 January 1890).

Like the balletomane's objections to the music for *Sleeping Beauty*, their criticisms of the fairy-tale plot—and its foreign origins in particular—highlight anxieties concerning the nationalism of the art form. The ballet (as part of the Imperial Theater system) had not participated in the flowering of national art that Russian music, painting, and literature experienced in the second half of the nineteenth century (or the growing reputation that Russian music and literature had begun to enjoy in Western Europe). Yet the Russian capital was fast becoming part of a European ballet market at the time of *Beauty*'s premiere, with soloists, visiting troupes, and ballets from other national traditions appearing on the city's stages. Their presence allowed for direct comparison with other national schools and traditions, and though comparisons of ballerinas were not typically in Russia's favor in the 1880s and 1890s, the visiting troupes revealed the general standard of the Imperial Theaters to be much higher than those of visiting troupes. Nonetheless, their visits fed a nascent nationalism evident in anxieties surrounding *Sleeping Beauty*'s "foreign" plot.

DECORS

No art critics stepped forward to volunteer their opinions on *Sleeping Beauty,* though the visual components of the ballet received as much attention in the press as its music. The production was expensive, reputedly consuming one-fourth of the theater's annual production budget.[7] Happily, the unprecedented financial outlay was visible on the stage: the Russian word *róskosh,* for "luxury," or "splendor," peppers the reviews of *Beauty.*

Dmitry Korovyakov, writing for *Novosti i birzhevaya gazeta,* provided the most detailed coverage of the ballet's visual components. He reported that Perrault's fairy tales had fallen into good hands and that the production of the ballet "turned out magnificently" (5 January 1890). "Much taste and artistic talent was spent on the production of the new ballet," according to Korovyakov, though he admits that the luxury of Vsevolozhsky's costumes was taken to the extreme: "Silk, velvet, plush, gold and silver embroideries, wonderful brocades, fur, feathers, and flowers, armor and metallic adornments—it was extravagant and unstinting, with money lavished on the adornment of even third-rate characters" (ibid.).

Korovyakov noted Matvei Shishkov's "completely accurate" depiction of the esplanade of Versailles in the ballet's last act (Shishkov also designed the apotheosis), and lamented that the theater's comparatively shallow stage reduced the effect the scene might have created on a deeper stage. The reviewer also mentions Heinrich Levogt's palace scene (Prologue) and the designs of Ivan Andreev and Mikhail Bocharov (for Act I, Bocharov also designed Act II) but deemed these sets not "especially successful" as compared to these men's earlier work. Konstantin Ivanov's design for the sleeping castle (end of Act II) pleased the critic more, especially the transformation from a cobweb-draped, dusty hall to a bright, cheerful one. After a long description of the ballet's costumes and sets, the writer admits that "to speak of the new ballet one must speak most of all about its physical production, which really does predominate" (ibid.).

Only Korovyakov, of *Beauty's* first critics, attempts to explain the aims of the ballet's visual designers: how the costumes and sets reflect the passage of time, how the decors and stage machinery are used to produce the ballet's transformation scenes. His discussion also includes criticisms: "We should admit, that from the point of view of scenic effects, and the wonders of the machinists department of our ballet stage, neither the panorama nor the transformations satisfied us" (ibid.). The famous panorama scene gave "a weak illusion" already

Prologue, 1890 production. Maria Anderson (left) as Fée Fleur de farine with an unidentified page.

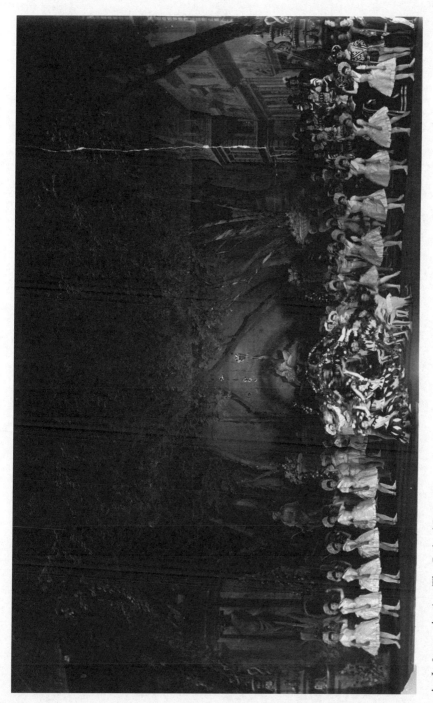

Act I, 1890 production. The Garland Dance.

Act I, 1890 production. The Rose Adagio. Two princes stand at left of Carlotta Brianza, as Princess Aurora. A third supports her, and the fourth poses at her right. Aurora holds the spindle.

Act II, 1890 production. Panorama. Maria Petipa, as the Lilac Fairy, and Pavel Gerdt, as Prince Désiré, stand in the boat.

Act II, 1890 production. Aurora's bedchamber. The sleeping kingdom awaits the kiss that will wake Princess Aurora. Maria Petipa, the Lilac Fairy, stands at right.

Act III, 1890 production. The cast of the wedding scene. Several soloists are visible at the front of the group, including (left to right, front row): Prince Fortuné and Cinderella, the four "jewel" fairies (diamond, gold, silver, sapphire), Princess Florine and the Blue Bird, Prince Désiré and Princess Aurora, and Little Red Riding Hood. The Lilac Fairy (a stand-in for Maria Petipa, who danced Cinderella in Act III) and the White Cat are visible on their sedan chairs at the rear of the stage (left and right, respectively); Fée Canari is between them, in her cage.

Apotheosis, 1890 production. Princess Aurora and Prince Désiré stand beneath the central arch at the rear of the stage. The Lilac Fairy and Carabosse stand in the clouds. Participants in the Act III entrée of the ballet stand at the front of the stage.

seen in other ballets, including *Humpbacked Horse* (1864), and the growth of the forest struck the reviewer as somewhat primitive: a simple matter of raising, rather than lowering cut drops. The awakening of the sleeping kingdom, moreover, took too long on a too-darkened stage.

Most writers found the ballet's visuals overwhelming, but their objections are neither as virulent or unified as those to the ballet's music. (In the words of the *Peterburgsky listok* critic, the ballet's unconventional narrative had turned the balletomanes into question marks, but the visual splendor transformed them into exclamation points.) Skalkovsky's response to the ballet was quite typical: he appreciates the skill and artistry that brought the production to the stage but still finds the splendor of *Sleeping Beauty* excessive. "The production of the ballet is extraordinarily luxurious. The costumes, well drawn and inspired in part by Doré's illustrations to Perrault's tales, are elegant. . . . The costumes' materials are even too luxurious, perhaps. Made from silk with gold and various other trimmings, they seem heavy for the ballet. . . . Of course, the ballet demands splendid productions, and economy has no place here, since a spectacularly produced ballet will endure a greater number of performances, draw a better box office, and soon pay for itself. But there is a limit to luxury that the very nature of the art form stipulates" (*Novoe vremya*, 5 January 1890).

If *Peterburgskaya gazeta* had begun to reconcile itself to the ballet's music several weeks after the premiere (in allowing that the ballet music might be entering some "new phase in its development" [16 January 1890]), for example, the paper had not yet warmed to the other features of the work. The same review concluded: "It is only unfortunate that such music is linked to such a banal, unpoetic, plotless work as *Sleeping Beauty,* which is a museum of props, and nothing more!" (ibid.). Skalkovsky suggested a new title for the work: *Sleeping Beauty, or the Triumph of the Art of Sewing* (*Novoe vremya*, 5 January 1890). *Peterburgskaya gazeta*'s first response to the sets and costumes quoted the balletomane's responses to the production: "The costumes are really good! The sets, very nice . . . but what's the sense of it? They didn't skimp, but with money you can make any sort of set you want!" (4 January 1890). The newspaper came to life on the issue of the costumes days later, sensing scandal:

> Although the luxury of the costumes in *Sleeping Beauty* has been noted by all, some of these costumes nonetheless present great inconveniences. Here is a fact . . . Carlotta Brianza was barely in a condition to finish the ballet. . . . In the pas de quatre of the last act, during the turns, the artist scratched her whole right arm above the elbow on Gerdt's costume, to the point of drawing blood. The straps of the costume, which seem to cover the cuirass, are unthinkable for the cavalier of a ballerina. . . .

Mlle. Brianza suffered even more, and more perceptively, when a lock of her luxuriant hair, suddenly torn from her head, fell on these straps. . . .

Then she almost fainted. Attention should be paid to such an inconvenience on
M. Gerdt's costume. (6 January 1890)

Two days later, supremely pleased with itself for drawing the impertinence to
light, the newspaper reported that the offensive costume had not been
changed, but the choreography had been reworked instead. The incident encapsulated the balletomanes' worst fear: that dance now existed solely for the
costumes.

Although *Sleeping Beauty*'s sets and costumes were enjoyed even by those
who feared the ballet's imminent decline, the splendor of the production (like
its origins in a children's fairy tale), pointed irrefutably to a new threat, and one
that the balletomanes considered the enemy of "true" choreographic art: the
féerie.

THE FÉERIE

Discussions of *Sleeping Beauty*'s visuals furnished proof, for many writers, that
the Petersburg ballet had chosen the wrong path, that *Sleeping Beauty* really was
a féerie—an elaborate visual spectacle with a fairy-tale plot—as billed. Russian
writers used the term imprecisely to describe lower-genre, Western European
ballets introduced to Russia by visiting troupes (mostly Italian) after the ban on
private theaters was lifted in Russia in the early 1880s. They used the French
term even though the most influential of the visiting troupes performed works
of a quite different theatrical lineage, the Italian *ballo grande*.[8]

Although the Russian ballet's defenders were certain of the féerie's debilitat-
ing influence on local choreography, the itinerant troupes introduced several
Imperial Theater stars to Russian audiences. Two years before creating their
roles in *Sleeping Beauty*, for example, Carlotta Brianza and Enrico Cecchetti appeared in Luigi Manzotti's dance spectacular *Excelsior,* which ran on two St. Petersburg amusement park stages simultaneously. Antoinetta Dell'Era, who
would later star in *Nutcracker* (the next Petipa-Tchaikovsky ballet-féerie),[9] debuted on a private Moscow stage the same year (Krasovskaya 1963, 286).

A relatively new theme lurks behind discussions of the so-called féeries: an
ardent nationalism that affirms the Russian ballet's superiority. The féerie was
not only "low" (operetta to the ballet's opera), it was foreign, and the *ballo
grande*/féerie confusion highlights the rather generalized foreignness associated
with those genres. The fact that these Western entertainments first appeared on

commercial, suburban, popular stages suggests both their subversive potential and their challenge to the genre hierarchies of the imperial stages. The balletomanes critics responded accordingly, adopting a conservative position intent on defending the imperial stages against incursion from the foreign, lower genre. They compared the féerie to the operetta and judged the genre similarly unsuitable for the empire's leading lyric stage.

Even Marius Petipa, who should have known the difference between the French and Italian genres, and who freely borrowed from new Western European trends (including the féerie) in his own compositions, waxed xenophobic when interviewed days before the premiere of his ballet *Bluebeard* in 1896.[10] Petipa gave an interview to *Peterburgskaya gazeta* (2 December 1896) in which he accused Manzotti and the Italian school of "ruining the ballet." Petipa added that *Excelsior* was "not a ballet, but a féerie" (1971, 123). Ironically, Petipa's *Bluebeard* was billed as a "ballet-féerie in 3 acts and 7 scenes, with apotheosis" (1971, 385). It was Petipa's fourth féerie (after *Magic Pills, Sleeping Beauty,* and *Nutcracker*), though many earlier Petipa works billed as "ballets" in the 1880s and 1890s qualified the term: "fantastic ballet" or "magic ballet."

Whatever the fantastic or magic elements incorporated in Petipa's own ballets, Russian objections to the Western European ballets focused on a few key distinctions. In the chapter on dance in Italy, 1880–1905, in his comprehensive (and unfinished) history of dance, Khudekov sees innovations in Manzotti's spectacles and notes their affinities to the political-allegorical ballets of the eighteenth century but ultimately characterizes *Excelsior* as a "tawdry, glittery féerie." Khudekov notes Manzotti's shift in emphasis from the prima ballerina, and the usual pas and variations made for her, to mass dances that might best be characterized as "groupings" or "movement combinations." The role of visuals and stage machinery increased inversely to the diminution of the soloist's display, according to Khudekov, who saw the massing of dancers, movement, and color, and the surprise transformations these produced, as the chief attraction of Manzotti's ballets (1915, 355).

Like Khudekov, other balletomanes of the 1880s and 1890s objected to the féeries' mass choreography, its simplistic structure, and the genre's exploitation of visual effects. They also decried the féeries' popularity. Writing of Petipa's revival of *Le Roi Candaule* in 1891,[11] I. F. Vasilevsky wrote:

> In the past, solo performances were especially valued and featured; they alternated with small corps de ballet groups for sake of diversion and to give the leading ballerinas a rest. Now the ballet has obviously given way to the influence of the brilliant féerie. The féerie, which serves as a compromise between choreography as art and the

democratic mood of Western Europe's demand for theater, will serve as its own indication of tastes and demands at the end of our century. In many ballets the masses
now take center stage, hurling their effects in your face. Masses fill the stage, they act,
they dance and form a variety of grandiose, pretty, figural constructions. The whole
ballet production depends on an experienced and firm general command, to the artful and disciplined bearing of the masses. Male and female dancers are deployed in
whole platoons. Second-rate performers have no need of independence or individu-
ality. They form squares, triangles, stars, and circles. Given the abundance of masses,
marches, processions, and festive assemblages, waltzes and marches will, and do, pre-
vail in the scenic development of ballet. The male or female soloist runs out, and for
the moment, diverts the audience's attention from the masses. (1891)

In much the same way that Petipa might criticize the féerie, then imitate its
most spectacular effects, the balletomane critics were not averse to the new
genre's production values. Vasilevsky describes two of *Le Roi Candaule*'s sets.
The first, an "Eastern" bath, included a pool and fountains; the second, depicted a plein air, nighttime palace scene. Vasilevsky was particularly impressed
with the latter as it featured electric lights placed to give an illusion of false re-
cession, amplifying the stage's perceived depth. The author recommends that
this effect should be incorporated into the theater's standard repertory of "*illusion en grand.*"

Petipa's first féerie, *The Magic Pills* (1886), was a "direct order" from the theater's directorate, according to Krasovskaya, and was meant to combine
"dances, singing, and comedy" (1963, 289–90). This populist rejoinder to Wagner's total art work was built around the text of a French play that had once
been in the repertory of the Alexandrinsky Theater, *Les pilules du diable,* with
actors from that theater taking lead roles.[12] Petipa designed elaborate choreography for three interpolated dance scenes. The first of these took place in the
cave of a sorceress and was distinctive for its original lighting and the refinement of its groupings, according to Pleshcheev (258). In the second ballabile,
dancers dressed as cards brought various card games to life. (Pleshcheev called
this an "allegorical representation of [card] games in dances" [259].) Vasilevsky,
who was mostly critical of the influence of the féerie, nonetheless found the
card party the height of chic: "Even the color of the ballerinas' hair corresponded to the card suits: the spades were blondes, the clubs were brunettes,
the hearts had golden coiffures, and the diamonds were light blondes. It would
have been impossible to go any farther in ingenuity, smartness, or piquancy"
(1886). The man responsible for such chic was none other than Vsevolozhsky,

according to Vasilevsky, who reported that the costumes held "allegorical meanings" and were designed individually.[13]

The kingdom of laces scene served as the féerie's finale. Essentially a national-character dance closer for the ballet, Petipa invented dances for Venetian, Belgian, English, Spanish, and Russian "lace." Children from the school—gold and silver lace—joined in the finale. Pleshcheev deemed this scene the best of the three; the costumes, he noted revealed a "great deal of taste and were striking in their magnificence" (259). Vasilevsky lavished praise on the scene, which invited comparison to the féeries of Western Europe: "The whole scene is a fantastic grotto of lace. The flies, backdrops, and the ceiling are all lace, tender, soft, and radiant, masterfully coordinated and lit by a slightly trembling electric light, at times light pink and at times, bluish. The eyes squint from this truly 'sweet' and subtle aesthetic pleasure. And in this wonderful frame, no less than one hundred pretty female dancers, with only head, feet, and hands visible in clouds of all sorts of (authentic) laces, that serve as their costumes. I saw stagings of ballets and féeries in Paris and London that were blinding in their splendor, but must admit that the 'Kingdom of Laces' is above the competition" (1886). This early Petipa foray in the féerie genre suggests a series of divertissements thrown into a mostly unrelated story, much like the ballets of Manzotti Petipa excoriated in the Russian press.[14] What is more, the obsessive visual detail of Petipa's card game suggests the massing of color typical of Manzotti's works.

Direct comparisons to works such as *Excelsior* or Petipa's *Magic Pills* reveal *Sleeping Beauty* to be rather far from the popular Western genre despite certain similarities. If the visual splendor of *Beauty* recalled the Italian spectacles, Petipa's ballet lacked dancing masses. Only the peasant waltz (with its "*tricolore*" costumes) could be said to resemble a scene of a Manzotti ballet.[15] And if *Beauty*'s transformation scenes were elaborate and expensive, they could scarcely be called glittery or cheap. It is worth noting that the most withering indictment of the féerie on the imperial stage—the 3 January 1890 review in *Peterburgskaya gazeta*—appeared before the work's premiere and responded to the designation on the programs, not to the ballet itself.

Still, the balletomane critics were intent on censuring *Sleeping Beauty* as a féerie. The critic for *Peterburgsky listok,* who stated his preference for ballets in which the dances arose directly from the plot, put it simply: "The first condition for the ballet to be a *ballet,* and not a féerie with dances, is that: (a) that the dances correspond to at least the basic needs of the choreography and (b) that these dances must necessarily be a *direct consequence* of the ballet's plot" (5 January 1890). Understandably exasperated by the third day of his newspaper's coverage of the new ballet, Khudekov declared *Sleeping Beauty* something even less: "*Beauty* should not be called a ballet-féerie, but a diorama and exhibit of costumes and props. But not a *ballet* in the sense that Noverre and other pillars of the art understood the term" (5 January 1890).

Skalkovsky, who had suggested "The Triumph of the Art of Sewing" as a second title for *Sleeping Beauty,* understood the long-term economy of an expensive ballet production. Nonetheless, he also cautioned of the dangers of the new genre:

> Of course *Sleeping Beauty* will bring full houses, attract an audience, and interest the public in its spectacle, but as it already represents a transition to the féerie, it will force real connoisseurs of choreographic art to sigh. Though their number, alas! is shrinking everywhere.
>
> For the latter, the greater or lesser magnificence of the production is a secondary concern. They look for aesthetic enjoyment in ballet. . . . An enormous number of supers in expensive costumes and various transformations are, in essence, only a grand *balagan.*[16] It will bring box office revenues, especially in the capitals, where there are millions of potential audience members, but this sort of spectacle has no permanent audience, no circle of educated connoisseurs. (5 January 1890)

Skalkovsky provides a context for the ballet's decline, and, in good fin de siècle fashion, places the blame on democratization: "This direction is not noticeable only in the ballet. In the opera today bel canto is not valued, but the size of the orchestra and number of acts are. Steam machines are brought in to change the scenery and double basses are counted by tens. In plays no one pays attention to the lines or their delivery, and the play has no success if the actresses don't spend five or ten thousand rubles beforehand on their outfits. Such is the influence of the democratization of art" (ibid.). Korovyakov seconded Skalkovsky's concern that *Sleeping Beauty* was bringing about the decline of the Russian ballet tradition: "If the ballet will *only be a spectacle,* a varied kaleidoscope of costumes and decors, then no production splendor can purchase its emptiness, lack of content, and the tedium that inevitably takes hold of every 'adult' by the end—let alone the aesthetically developed spectator. At risk of seeming a purist in art, we cannot help but lament the path chosen by the theater's directorate in lowering the artistry of our ballet" (*Novosti i birzhevaya gazeta,* 5 January 1890).

Despite this rather widespread and unified opposition to the féerie, as the term was understood in Russia in the late nineteenth century, some saw potential in the form. The prolific playwright Alexander Ostrovsky, who served as head of the repertory department of the Moscow Imperial Theaters in the 1880s, wrote of the need for lighter genres to fill the "large hole" in his repertory planning and balance the "serious" plays in the repertory: "They usually give old ballets like *Humpbacked Horse* for such a public. Of course, children like to see magnificent decors, and the bottom of the sea, and dancing crucian carp and oysters, and a whale. But when they get home, they tell the nanny in a whisper that some sort of shameless women were dancing with bare legs and arms" (185). Ostrovsky's 1885 letters to a potential collaborator could have confirmed the ballet conservatives' worst fears: he saw the need for a spectacle modeled on English Christmas pageants, something "between the féerie and the operetta" (173): "The ballet is really in decline now. The dances remain art worthy of a serious stage, but the monotony of pantomime has gotten old and seems somehow silly. The féerie should replace the ballet. It has everything: dances, singing, and comedy. For holiday performances—when the audience goes to the theater not for intellectual nourishment, but for entertainment—these spectacles, with their luxurious productions, should be very appealing" (179).

Laroche saw different potential in the féerie. Writing of *Sleeping Beauty*'s music, he constructed oppositions of music and dance genres: "Choreography and music, the tone poem and the ballet, the symphony without a program and the féerie: all of these realms are very close to one another, and they all drift in the common element of the vague and the spontaneous" (1890). In opposing the féerie to the ballet, and linking the former to the symphony rather than to program music, Laroche predicted the ballet's potential as a modernist art form. Where Ostrovsky saw the féerie's entertainment potential, Laroche sensed the dance's potential to join "purer," nonprogrammatic art forms, to aspire to the condition of "pure" music.

It is scarcely surprising that the newspapers do not identify the one person who was, in all likelihood, most responsible for the introduction of the féerie to the imperial stage. Director of Imperial Theaters Ivan Vsevolozhsky reprised his role in *Sleeping Beauty* and designed the costumes for the card party in *The Magic Pills* the following year. Vasilevsky noted only the costumes' "allegorical meanings," their individualized designs, and their "brilliance and taste" (1891). Whatever praise the writer felt obliged to lavish upon the director's efforts, the "mosaic quality" Vasilevsky notes in Vsevolozhsky's designs for the card party recall the effect created by the play of color groupings in *Sleeping Beauty*'s Garland Dance. Several of the Imperial Ballet's subsequent productions likewise suggest the general influence of the féerie and *ballo grande*—and the hand of

Ivan Vsevolozhsky: the Kingdom of Sweets in *Nutcracker,* for which Vsevolozh-sky once again designed costumes; the return to Perrault in Petipa's *Bluebeard;* and the "allegorical" ballets Petipa staged in the Hermitage Theater in 1900, when Vsevolozhsky was director there.

Of all the reviews of *Sleeping Beauty,* Laroche's musical letter navigates the main arguments surrounding the production with skill and insight. His visit to the ballet likewise prompted some of the most perspicacious writing on the general state of the ballet in 1890.

> Just as there is nothing more pervasive, accessible, and loved than poetry, there is nothing so closed in on itself, specific, and unpopular as ballet. . . .
>
> Compare the number of opera theaters with the numbers of ballet theaters; com-pare the number of ballet-goers in our own Maryinsky Theater with the number of operagoers, and you will see that choreography, at least in our time, constitutes a dis-tant, unattractive, and uninteresting realm, that has become relatively inaccessible and incomprehensible to the nonspecialist as a result. . . .
>
> Choreography itself, as experts, or some of the experts say, is in decline, and has yielded to pantomime on the one hand and the féerie on the other. But music for it has gone from the previous banal "motifs," loud and monotonous, to the choicest, most elevated style. (1890)

Laroche's comments reflect the odd position Russian ballet found itself in 1890, confronting a choice between the high and the low, the elevated and the banal. The ballet's old guard preferred to maintain the ballet as it was, with the genius Petipa creating ballets whose dances would arise naturally from (melo)dramatic narratives. These men were hardly averse to the magnificent production *Sleeping Beauty* enjoyed, though they remained suspicious: it smelled of the féerie, and the ballet's dull libretto confirmed their worst fears. Foreign tales written for children scarcely seemed an appropriate inspiration for a national ballet. Particularly as comparisons to other national schools and idioms became possible and the perceived strengths of the Russian tradition be-came increasingly apparent.

By contrast, the "outsiders" were anxious to see the ballet develop in accor-dance with their understanding of dance and theater traditions in Western Eu-rope as well as in Russia. Their comparatively cosmopolitan perspective was less tied to notions of national supremacy. Like their balletomane colleagues, the music critics concerned themselves with the ballet's place in the aesthetic hier-archy of the day and regarded the second-rate music that typically accompa-nied the dancing as the most serious bar to the ballet's ascension to the status of a legitimate high art. Laroche, for example, sees some advantage in elevating the musical level of an art form, especially one widely perceived to be declining. Predictably, given the softening of the oppositional to Tchaikovsky's music, the progressives won this battle, though their victory proved Pyrrhic. The reliance on music to justify the ballet's existence would, over time, threaten the dance once again with second-class status.

Chapter 2 Legends

of *Sleeping Beauty*

(What Becomes a Legend Most?)

Fairyland is the place where the action of a ballet can most easily be
developed. . . . For a ballet to be at all convincing, it must be entirely
unrealistic.
—Théophile Gautier, *La Presse,* 11 July 1837

One criticism of *Sleeping Beauty* remained as relevant in 1999 as in
1890: the charge that the ballet has no action. In 1890 Khudekov complained, "they dance, fall asleep, and dance again" (*Peterburgskaya
gazeta,* 5 January 1890). The dance writers of Khudekov's era displayed
a marked preference for swashbuckling tearjerkers, though a few of
Beauty's first critics defended the fantastic plot: "Why chase the tale
from the realm of choreography, even if there was no drama in the
most recent one? A fairy tale can also have its meaning, sometimes
even a highly instructive one" (*Novoe vremya,* 22 January 1890). By
1999, critics saw other virtues in *Sleeping Beauty's* story. As Arlene
Croce noted, "no libretto ever had less suspense and more wisdom."

Perhaps because *Sleeping Beauty* is as popular as its plot is thin, writers have long searched for deeper meanings in the work, with the pre-
dictable result that a considerable mythology has sprung up around

the ballet. Western scholars have long maintained that the ballet served a diplomatic function—a theatrical homage to France, with whom Russia would soon be allied, thus providing *Sleeping Beauty* a myth of origin. Soviet scholars demonstrated less interest in explaining the ballet's birth, though their recounting of the Vsevolozhsky-Tchaikovsky correspondence that initiated the work encircles the letter exchange with a nimbus normally reserved for immaculate conceptions. For Soviet researchers, Ivan Vsevolozhsky's legendary Francophilia and his status as a professional courtier (he reported directly to the minister of the imperial court) seemed sufficient motivation for an expensive stage work celebrating French monarchical succession. Rather than construct myths of origin, these scholars focused on the ballet's ideological metamorphosis, from the first restaging of the ballet in 1914 to the first Soviet production of the work in 1922 and 1923, culminating in the 1952 Konstantin Sergeyev production.

The most perceptive insight into the workings of *Sleeping Beauty's* story may be found among the earliest reviews of the ballet, though that wisdom has been all but ignored by later writers on the ballet. Music critic Herman Laroche saw narrative implications in the work far beyond Charles Perrault and France. He grasped the story's basis in myth and compared Aurora's sleep to that of (Wagner's) Brunhilde (1890). The comparison is telling, as much for Brunhilde's connection to tales and the knowledge they hold as for her long sleep and awakening. From her earliest incarnations in myth, Brunhilde is a storyteller who personifies the vitality of the stories that surround *Sleeping Beauty.* If the literature on the ballet has mostly shied away from Laroche's imaginative mythic reading, both the ballet and its critics have persisted in generating myths of their own.

Claude Lévi-Strauss wrote of myth's power to transform and engender new versions. Sprung from the fertile soil of myth and legend, *Sleeping Beauty* demonstrates the power of myth to cross generic divides: the fairy tale becomes a ballet that spawns legends and tales of its own. And the 1999 revival of the 1890 ballet demonstrated the surprising vitality of these stories: although the production had lain dormant for over a century, it retained a powerful hold on the imaginations of dance audiences and dance professionals alike.

ENTENTE CORDIALE

One of the more evergreen of myths surrounding *Sleeping Beauty* concerns the political role the ballet allegedly played. According to this theory, the ballet served a diplomatic function, to either celebrate or further the cause of the Franco-Russian alliance of 1891–94. Lincoln Kirstein alludes to this theory in his book *Movement and Metaphor: Four Centuries of Ballet,* where *Sleeping Beauty* is termed "*La Belle au bois dormant:* Romanov Ballet de Cour": "The implied comparison of the Romanov to the Sun King's court, on the heels of a Franco-Russian alliance was not unpleasing," writes Kirstein (175). In more recent scholarship, Janet Kennedy writes, "In the context of this rapprochement between Russia and France, the Louis XIV style of *Sleeping Beauty* appears almost natural," and details the "graceful diplomatic compliments" that Russia and France paid each other in the 1890s (149). Sally Banes follows this line and speaks of a "treaty being negotiated as the ballet was being made" (42). But *Sleeping Beauty* was a product of the late 1880s, not the 1890s (it had its premiere on 3 January 1890). Those who see a political meaning in *Sleeping Beauty* and allude to a relation between the ballet and the "entente cordiale" between Russia and France ignore one of the most notable aspect of the famously complex production: the nearly two years it took to bring *Beauty* to the stage.

Vsevolozhsky wrote his much-quoted letter to Tchaikovsky on 13 May 1888, a time when Franco-Russian relations were considerably strained. A diplomatic snafu two years earlier resulted in the withdrawal of France's ambassador to Russia and the corresponding recall of the Russian ambassador from Paris (Michon, 12). Loans issued in France in December 1888 to float Russia's armaments debt marked the start of substantial French investment in Russia and a turning point in Franco-Russian relations. Nonetheless, diplomatic relations did not warm until months after *Beauty*'s premiere. In fact, French and German sources speak of Russia's continued interest in diplomatic relations with Prussia, not France, as late as 1887 and 1888 (Michon, 28). George Kennan recounts the frustrations of French statesmen in 1890: "they felt that they had gone out of their way on more than one occasion, voluntarily and unilaterally, to oblige the Russian government, and had thus built up a certain political credit on which they should, at some point, be permitted to draw" (33). Clearly, this was not a Russia anxious to seduce the French with theatrics. According to Kennan, two events finally drove Russia into the diplomatic embrace of France in spring 1890, months after the ballet's premiere: Bismarck's retirement and the lapse of Russia's (secret) Reinsurance Treaty with Prussia (19–20).

Accounts of Vsevolozhsky paint him as an anxious courtier, yet the court, in early 1888 or early 1890, would not have been especially charmed by the ballet's Francophilia or anxious to exploit the ballet's foreign policy implications. It is worth remembering the cool response of Alexander III to the ballet ("very nice") greatly injured Tchaikovsky: "His Majesty treated me very condescendingly. So be it!" (quoted in Poznansky, 505).[1]

Late in his career Petipa frequently prepared small ballets, divertissements, and bagatelles for imperial delectation: to celebrate marriages, a coronation, or important embassies. In 1897, for example, the first two acts of *Sleeping Beauty* were shown at a fantastic outdoor spectacle arranged on an island in a lake at Peterhof to honor the Austrian emperor's visit. Special performances also marked the visits of the king of Siam, the emperor of Germany, and the president of the French Republic that same year. Nonetheless, these court ballet performances—with international rather than local significance—began only in 1897, according to Soviet ballet historian Mikhail Borisoglebsky (43–44). These onetime works might be staged in the court theater of a suburban imperial residence, the ballroom of a grand duchess' Petersburg Palace, or some other small, often temporary stage. Because their transfer to the Imperial Theaters would have necessitated extensive reworking of decors and choreography (to adapt both to a new stage), most of these ballets remained nonce works and never joined the repertory. Nonetheless, the profligacy of the last Romanovs and their love of theater has led to wild speculation in diplomatic as well as dance histories. Kennan writes that *Sleeping Beauty* had a "private dress rehearsal attended by the imperial couple in the palace theater at Tsarskoe Selo" (xviii). The Romanovs did attend the ballet's dress rehearsal on 2 January 1890, the day before the ballet's premiere, but Kennan's suggestion that the enormous production traveled to the palace in Tsarskoe Selo one day before the ballet's premiere and back again (in the middle of winter) is amusing indeed.

The shift in political winds—from Prussia to France between 1889 and 1890—was too abrupt to organize a ballet to mark the political turnabout. In fact, the theatrical event most directly effected by the changing political barometer was not the premiere of a Franco-Russian ballet, but the visit of a German opera troupe. The Richard Wagner Theater performed four very successful cycles of the operas in Russia in 1889, but attempts to schedule returns visits in 1890 and 1891 "had to be abandoned," according to Rosamund Bartlett (47): "The signing of the Franco-Russian Alliance was partly responsible for rendering conditions 'less favourable' to Wagner in the 1890s, according to Mikhail Stanislavsky: 'It was impossible even to mention German, German people and German art. . . . Our young people were gripped by Franco-Russian enthusiasm and tried to show their patriotic feelings by an assault on the Germans sitting peacefully with a mug of beer in the Zoological Gardens. In those conditions it would have been utter quixotry even to dream of repeating the experience of 1889 and give another series of Wagner performances'" (48).

Thus, as Tchaikovsky was writing *Sleeping Beauty* in 1889, the Romanov court (including Alexander III and the tsarina, who broke her usual prohibition of attending performances during Lent) (47), were hearing the first Russian performances of Wagner's *Ring* in Russia. Obviously, neither they, nor the Ministry of the Imperial Court or the Directorate of the Imperial Theaters anticipated the sudden turn of diplomatic events or the anti-German and pro-French sentiment that would accompany it. *Sleeping Beauty's* appearance in 1890 was felicitous, even prophetic, but could not have been planned.

FAIRIES, WICKED STEPMOTHERS, AND WAGNER

Had Vsevolozhsky wished to impress the tsar in 1888–89, he might have planned a ballet based on Germanic myth rather than French fairy tales. In part (and one suspects, unwittingly), he did just that. In building his libretto around Charles Perrault's *La Belle au bois dormant* (1697), Vsevolozhsky not only adapted a portion of Perrault's tale and set the ballet in Perrault's era, he invited other Perrault characters to help celebrate Aurora's wedding in the ballet's third act. The setting (late seventeenth-century France) evokes an appropriate allegory for the ballet. It speaks to the birth of the ballet, with Louis XIV as its patron and practitioner, and to the gilded court and the manners of the day. Yet Perrault was but a link in the chain of a legend that stretches back to *The Saga of the Volsungs,* the Old Norse saga recorded in the thirteenth century that proved so important for Richard Wagner in the creation of his *Ring des Nibelungen.*

A central event in the Norse saga reveals the embryo of the *Sleeping Beauty* legend: Sigurd, the dragon slayer (Wagner's Siegfried), encounters a great fire, a rampart of shields, and a man lying asleep in full armor: "First he removed the helmet from the man's head and saw that it was a woman. She was in a coat of mail so tight that it seemed to have grown into her flesh. He sliced through the armor, down from the neck opening and out through the sleeves, and it cut like cloth. Sigurd said she had slept too long. She asked what was so strong that it could slash through her coat of mail 'and rouse me from sleep'" (Byock 67). The outlines of our tale are already legible: the sleeping woman, the hero come to rouse her, and the usual folk-tale "test" he must overcome to reach her, the

Act II, 1999 production. The Vision. Veronika Part as the Lilac Fairy, Svetlana Zakharova as Princess Aurora, and Viktor Baranov as Prince Désiré.

protecting fire. The woman's martial attire tells us that she is a warrior; when she recounts the story of her somnolence, we learn that Odin had stabbed Brynhild with a "sleeping thorn" and told her to marry (ibid.).

Petipa's Aurora and Wagner's Brunhilde are the same character, though their paths to the modern era diverge significantly. Still, the woman that Sigurd discovers, in outgrown battle drag, bears scant resemblance to Aurora. The daughter of a powerful king, Brynhild is renowned for her beauty and wisdom. Clearly, the nineteenth-century lyric stage divided the spoils: opera, with its words, seized upon Brynhild's wisdom; the ballet took what it could better display: the character's beauty. Brynhild's monologue furnishes an apt analogy to her character's fate in the musical theater:

> Now shall you choose,
> As you are offered a choice,
> O maple shaft of sharp weapons.
> Speech or silence,
> You must muse for yourself.
> All words are already decided. (70)

Speech and wisdom well suited the opera, leaving silence to the ballet—as well as beauty. Aurora is a top-model with a powerful father, a wise godmother, and few thoughts of her own. Yet she is not without reminders of her former self. In Vsevolozhsky's telling of the story, Brynhild's wisdom passes to the Lilac Fairy, who dons a martial uniform when the time for the crucial awakening has come. Marina Konstantinova has compared the Lilac Fairy's guise in Act II to depictions of Minerva, the goddess of wisdom (23, 95), and many writers have noted the symbolism of the small effulgences of flowers that partially conceal the Lilac Fairy's martial guise: the lilacs that bloom from her helmet and mask the long spear she carries symbolize wisdom in Russian folklore. Like Brynhild, Lilac counsels a wandering prince (Désiré is also her godchild in this version) before she sends him on his quest. Brynhild's wisdom, long banished from the ballet's corridors, returns to rescue Aurora in the modified military gear of the Lilac Fairy.

Studies of *Sleeping Beauty* tend to focus on the librettist's adaptation of Perrault. Yet the ballet's fidelity to the earlier incarnation of the tale, the Norse legend, is as striking, as are the ballet's references to the nineteenth-century's most famous treatment of the Volsung Saga—Wagner's *Ring*. As Laroche was quick to note, "The fairy tale, despite its prosaic form, often contains the most ancient and most genuine myths. And by the way, *Sleeping Beauty*, with its main theme corresponding to Brunhilde, guarded by fire, is one of those countless manifestations of the earth taking its rest in the winter and waking from the kiss of spring. Siegfried and Prince Désiré, in this sense, are the same person" (1890). Laroche leaves Aurora out of this comparison invoking Brunhilde, Siegfried, and Désiré. The mind-body split of Brunhilde's formerly unified persona cannot be summarized so neatly. Yet Aurora and the Lilac Fairy are as closely related to Brunhilde as Désiré is to Siegfried.

Although Russia would become a hotbed of Wagner-mania in the early 1900s, Vsevolozhsky, as director of Imperial Theaters, resisted the German composer's works to the end of his tenure at the Maryinsky. Sergei Volkonsky, Vsevolozhsky's nephew and replacement in the directorate, reports that his uncle loathed Wagner (1992, I, 147).[2] No sooner had Volkonsky succeeded his uncle in 1899 than *Tristan und Isolde* entered the Russian repertory.

In *Wagner and Russia,* Rosamund Bartlett describes Tchaikovsky's more complicated and ambivalent attitude toward Wagner: "Tchaikovsky's feelings about Wagner . . . were complex. There was much he did not at first understand in Wagner's music (as his articles about the *Ring* demonstrate), but his almost obsessive desire to hear the composer's works, and discuss them in his writings—a habit maintained until his death—together with his late enthusiasm for *Parsifal,* combine to show that one should not be at all categorical about characterising his antipathy to Wagner. As often, it is a case of reading between the lines" (3–4). Tchaikovsky despised the atmosphere surrounding Bayreuth and the pretense of Wagner's music-dramas, but he admired aspects of Wagner's compositions and liked some of what he heard, including "Ride of the Valkyries" (Wiley 1985, 36). Moreover, the Russian composer regarded the *Ring* "one of the most significant events in the history of art" (Bartlett 41). Bartlett writes that Tchaikovsky "continued to take an active interested in the composer after his visit to Bayreuth, and seized every opportunity to attend performances of his works during his frequent trips abroad" (42). Whatever mixed feelings Tchaikovsky and Vsevolozhsky harbored concerning Wagner's operas, their ballet shared a common ancestor.

PERRAULT AND BASILE

In much the same way one group of commentators has fixated on possible political meaning in the 1890 production of *Sleeping Beauty,* many dance historians have long speculated on the functions and attributes of the fairies in the ballet's Prologue. The peculiar enigmatic names, the attributes these fairies bestow upon Aurora, and the choreography of their dances have been the subject of much conjecture in writings on the ballet. (The third-act fairies, with names like Gold, Silver, Sapphire, and Diamond, appear to be self-explanatory. Neither their symbolism nor their variations are frequently discussed.)

The names of the ballet's fairies are Vsevolozhsky's invention. In *From the Beast to the Blonde,* Marina Warner discusses fairy tales as the wares of women, who have passed them across continents and through generations. The act of writing the tales down, of conserving them for posterity, has more often been the work of men like Perrault in France or the Grimm brothers in Germany. In this regard, Vsevolozhsky was one of a series of fairy godfathers—literary stepfathers, actually—who adapted this universal women's tale to suit the needs and mores of his audiences.

The fairies enter the tale in Perrault's telling, a relatively late (seventeenth-century) addition to a legend traceable through Giambattista Basile, the Arthurian prose romance *Perceforest* (first printed in 1528), *The Saga of the Volsung* (written in the thirteenth century), and *Arabian Nights.* In Giambattista Basile's version of the tale ("Sun, Moon, and Talia," 1634) wise men and astrologers are invited to the castle to foretell the princess' fate. Charles Perrault substitutes fairies for these wise men but grants them neither names nor identities; they are distinguished only by the gifts they give the child. In Perrault, all the fairies that could be found in the kingdom (seven, Perrault adds parenthetically) are invited to serves as godmothers to the little princess. Each presented her a gift ("as was the custom of fairies in those days"), and each was rewarded in advance with a massive gold case containing a knife, fork, and spoon of fine gold, decorated with diamonds and rubies.

No one thought to invite the old fairy. She had not left her tower in more than fifty years and was presumed dead or enchanted. Like Vsevolozhsky's Florestan, Perrault's king attempts to make peace when she arrives by offering her an empty case (a reproach of infertility, as we will see later). Meanwhile, as six of the young fairies present their gifts (beauty, wit, grace, the ability dance, to sing, and to play music), the seventh hides behind the curtains; she has heard the old fairy mumbling, fears the worst, and hopes to save the situation. As in Vsevolozhsky's libretto, Perrault's good fairy appears to counteract the old fairy's curse: the princess will not die from the spindle wound, but merely sleep for one hundred years, until a king's son awakens her.[3]

Like Perrault before him, Vsevolozhsky concentrates the attribute of Basile's wise men on one particular fairy. Perrault's good fairy anticipates trouble even before she is called in to remedy the situation; her vigilance anticipates the Lilac

Fairy's augmented role. After putting the palace to sleep, she causes vegetation to grow to cover the castle, providing Vsevolozhsky an opportunity for the ballet's first transformation scene.[4]

Vsevolozhsky invents names for Perrault's fairies (Candide; Coulante, Fleur-de-Farine; Miettes qui tombent; Canari qui chante; Violente; La Fée des Lilas; Carabosse), but their appellations do little to clarify the exact nature of their respective gifts and attributes. The fairies give Aurora gifts to form her character (tenderness from Candide, wisdom from the Lilac Fairy, for example), but there is much asymmetry among names and attributes: Candide, Coulante, and Violente suggest temperaments; Canari is a bird; Lilac a flower. Wheat flour (Coulante's qualifier) and bread crumbs must be related, but perhaps not to the rest of the group. The 1999 costumes built from Vsevolozhsky's designs revealed new relationships among the fairies and new levels of meaning to one writer: "The solo of the Wheat Flour Fairy [Coulante] is followed, of course, by the Breadcrumbs Fairy—who has mice appliquéd on her tutu, wanting their share of crumbs. Who's next, but a bird, the Canary Fairy. In Vsevolozhsky and Petipa's kingdom, even the crumbs connect. And when the big bad fairy Carabosse storms the party, moving with humpbacked menace, it's a black cat that adorns her cape. The cat-and-mouse in the costumes is just another of the eternal circles in this *Beauty*" (Jacobs 26).

Not surprisingly, given the complex, asymmetrical relationships among these characters, many productions have attempted to flatten the variance among them, to give them grammatically agreeing names (all nouns: beauty, tenderness, eloquence, grace, temperament) or associate them with flowers, birds, or colors. Lilac and Carabosse typically escape these ploys; their inclusion in the group demonstrates the impossibility of relying on a simple scheme to regulate Vsevolozhsky's fairies.

Whatever the fairies' enigma, they remain disposable characters in the ballet. They return only to enliven the parade in Act III and decorate the set in the apotheosis. More to the point, Aurora has little need of their gifts in the course of the ballet. (No one thinks to grant Aurora free will; her duties are scripted until her wedding.)[5] In highlighting the roles of the Lilac Fairy and Carabosse (the embodiments of good and evil in the ballet, on whom the outcome depends), Vsevolozhsky continues the tradition of attenuating the characterizations of the first five fairies in the ballet.

If Sigurd and Brynhild serve as archetypes for Désiré, Aurora, and Lilac, the character of Carabosse has less to do with the god Odin, who imprisoned Brynhild, than with the outcome of the marriage plot that shapes the ballet. Marina Warner sidesteps the usual Freudian and Marxist interpretations and groups the Sleeping Beauty tale among those of wicked stepmothers: "The Sleeping Beauty's enchanted sleep or Rapunzel's magic imprisonment may not represent the slow incubation of selfhood, of consciousness of the Other and even sexual fulfillment. Rather, it may stand for the dark time that can follow the first encounter between the older woman and her new daughter-in-law, the period when the young woman can do nothing, take charge of nothing, but suffer the sorcery and the authority—and perhaps the hostility—of the women whose house she has entered, whose daughter she has become" (219–20).

In Perrault's version of the tale as in Basile's, the setting shifts from the princesses' milieu to the princes' once the two are married, and the stepmother character extends the narrative well beyond the wedding that crowns the ballet's happy end.[6] Basile's sleeping princess, Talia, remains in the woods until summoned to the abode of her prince (who is actually a king, and married) by his wife, who wishes to burn Talia on a pyre, butcher the children Talia has borne him, and serve them to him for supper. In Perrault, Basile's barren harridan is the prince's mother, not his wife. Yet this infertile wife/mother character is the archetypal wicked stepmother figure Warner sees in such tales as "Cinderella," "Beauty and the Beast," and "Snow White" (218–26).[7] Vsevolozhsky ends his Sleeping Beauty story with a wedding but augments the older fairy's role to compensate for the missing mother-in-law. His solution proves structurally correct: Carabosse is vanquished before the wedding, and the absence of any mother-in-law at the ballet's end bodes well for the requisite happy end.[8]

BRUNHILDE'S MANY GUISES

We have seen how the opera and the ballet divided Brynhild's persona for their separate ends, how the ballet's Aurora embodies her beauty, and how the opera's words better suited Brunhilde's wisdom. We have also seen how a woman's wisdom remains integral to the Sleeping Beauty story, even though the function shifts among various characters: from Brynhild in the Saga of the Volsungs, to the wise men in Basile's tale, to the wisdom of the youngest fairy in Perrault. Vsevolozhsky's wise persona is the Lilac Fairy, godmother to both Aurora and Désiré. There is a whiff of incest in their pairing, another echo of the ballet's strange German cousin: the *Ring*.

Catherine Clément groups the women in the *Ring* according to a Freudian scheme: Erda, Fricka, and Brunhilde represent the mother, the sister/wife, and the daughter, respectively (147–148). Brunhilde is the eldest of the eight Valkyries Wotan has sired; the remaining seven function collectively. The similarity to Vsevolozhsky's fairies is clear: Lilac's long skirts, her staff, and her authoritative presence suggest age and experience; the other fairies are clearly subordinate to her. In the French tale the youngest fairy fulfilled this function, counteracting the curse of the eldest, then racing back to the kingdom to put the inhabitants to sleep. Vsevolozhsky inverts Perrault's hierarchy, and the result is closer to Wagner than to Perrault.

Brunhilde is Wotan's daughter in Wagner's operas, but she also protects Sieglinde, the expectant mother who gives birth to Brunhilde's future beloved, Siegfried. Brunhilde's challenge to Wotan involves a curious assortment of matriarchal duties: she goes to battle on behalf of the father of her future lover (Sigmund), then ferries his sister/wife (Sieglinde) to a protected forest near Valhalla. Wotan punishes Brunhilde for her betrayals by reducing her to the status of a more or less ordinary woman (albeit surrounded by fire). Later, when Siegfried uncovers Brunhilde, he calls out to Sieglinde, his dead mother. Brunhilde's mother/daughter identities intertwine as hopelessly as Sieglinde's sister/wife confusion.

Vsevolozhsky's libretto calls for a similar back-and-forth reading through time and place, much as Lévi-Strauss cautions us to read myths diachronically and synchronically: to probe both the origin of a myth as well as variants of other, contemporaneous tellers, then to explore motivations for the changes.[9] Like Brunhilde, the Lilac Fairy differs from her fellow fairy/Valkyries in that she plays the role of the mother as well: in keeping with the characteristic dualities of the Brynhild character, she is the godmother of both Princess Aurora and Prince Désiré. (Theirs is an arranged marriage in every sense.) The common mother, over more than a century, lends the ballet its hint of Wagnerian incest. (Aurora is old enough to be Désiré's great-great-great-grandmother.)[10] Yet in keeping with the ballet's obsessively positive projection of the Volsung/Wagnerian saga, Lilac has no fall from grace; her work is done once Désiré and Aurora agree to marry.

Clément reads Wotan's habit of incest as a quest for knowledge, the search for the key to one's origins (156–57). And knowledge is central to her reading of Wagner's tetralogy: Brunhilde, as in her earlier incarnation as Brynhild, possesses great knowledge, then loses it when punished for disobedience by her father. Wotan briefly considers making Brunhilde ordinary, forcing her to spin, but relents and puts her to sleep.[11] In *Sleeping Beauty*, knitters (more mobile than spinners) arrive to foreshadow the crucial moment in the ballet, just before Carabosse arrives to present a spindle to Aurora. Bumbling and cheerful in the ballet, the knitters nonetheless recall the fates (Wagner's Norns) and foreshadow the act's tragic denouement: the "death" of Princess Aurora, by spindle, at her birthday party.

The usual Petipa proprieties are observed in Act I: the dances move from low genre to high, from folk dancing in wooden shoes (the knitters), to grand ballabile with props (garlands, flowers, children), to the summit of the ballet's academic choreography, the adagio for Aurora and her four cavaliers. Along the way, we are left to gauge the immense distance this gulf spans, not only from folk/character dancing to high academic technique, but also from the spinners lowly social station to Aurora's regal state. The knitters' scene is one that is frequently cut from the ballet. Yet this seemingly innocuous set piece has its place. The knitters represent Brunhilde's threat—of ordinariness and spinning—a warning that appropriately precedes the ballet's most dramatic scene.[12]

Aurora's public fascination with the spindle (she has never seen one) represents as serious a breach of protocol as Brunhilde's disobedience. (Indeed, Florestan's participation in the ballet centers around this single event.) In the refined world of *Sleeping Beauty*, where slight deformations of classical steps suffice to signal Aurora's incipient death, any link to the world of the ordinary (gossiping, knitting women) threatens to destroy the cozy order of Florestan's kingdom as well as the warrior-princess way of life.

Warner notes Propp's inability to distinguish between the functions of the princess and that of her father in his analyses of the folktale:

> It is significant that when the Russian folklorist Vladimir Propp analysed the wonder tale, he broke the form down into seven spheres of action, to which correspond different functions of the dramatis personae: the villain, the hero, the donor, the helper, the princess and her father, dispatcher and false hero. . . .
>
> When it came to the princess, Propp could not sever her function from her father's, but treated them as belonging to a single sphere of action: "The princess and her father cannot be exactly delineated from each other," he wrote, thus disclosing, unwittingly, the strictly patriarchal character of the traditional marriage plots, the steps by which the narrative moves, the dynamic of the contract made according to her father's wish. (238)

Warner also notes Propp's failure to examine the other axis of these relationships: "Propp did not analyse the wonder tale's function from the point of view of a mother, did not probe the structure for the inverse rubbing of the father-daughter design: the mother-son'" (238). In *Sleeping Beauty*, the mother-son

Act I, 1999 production. The knitters beg forgiveness of King Florestan.

pairing is entirely positive. Carabosse takes over the mother-in-law function in the ballet; the queen is seen only as Aurora's mother. No wonder that the four potential "sons" in the ballet's first act disappear like the fairies. And while the queen sleeps, Lilac selects a son-in-law for her.

If Désiré's is a case of love at first sight (Aurora has no agency here), Petipa provides the prince a very important visual clue to his future in the vision scene. Appearing as a vision in Act II, Aurora's responses to the prince's entreaties are minimal; she slips away. Although shortly after her entrance, Aurora runs to Lilac and balances on the fairy's staff as Désiré looks on. The two women reveal Brunhilde's divided persona to Désiré/Siegfried in this stage picture. Both clutch at Brynhild's spear: Lilac in pseudomilitary drag, Aurora in white with a haloed tiara, ever the virgin daughter. In this split image, Désiré sees the past and the future of his potential bride. Lilac stands in for Aurora as she sleeps, then disappears when Aurora has awakened. Once Aurora has revived, it seems that Brynhild's superego is left in control.

Obviously, the librettist(s) of *Beauty* sanitized their version of the Volsung story. Lilac is never demoted; Aurora is never asked to spin or pine for a hero who has left her, like Brunhilde, who becomes a quite ordinary wife for a time. In *Beauty,* there is only the slightest hint of incest (through the godmother). There is no consuming fire, no murders, no gold to muck things up. The wall of fire that surrounded Brunhilde becomes a choking garden, easily breached.[13] Nor will Aurora be responsible for the destruction of the gods, for immolating herself and her father, as in the opera's final and decisive ring of fire.

As Clément writes, "it is the daughter who inherits the sons' real power, and who ends the story of the family" (162). As Warner reminds us and Propp demonstrates, the daughter and the father are inextricably linked in the folktale. And this truth dovetailed perfectly with the practice and predilections of the nineteenth-century ballet: Carlotta Brianza and Maria Petipa held clout at the box office; it was the women in Petipa's theater who guaranteed the success or failure of a production. Even if *Sleeping Beauty* is really "about" Désiré (as the plot of *Giselle* is obviously more concerned with Albrecht and his redemption than with Giselle), and even though Pavel Gerdt was much admired, the cavaliers of his day lacked the box-office virility of the women they supported onstage.

What is more, those who use the fairy tale to argue for Aurora's passivity (sleeping while waiting for her man to come) might look more closely at Désiré. His refusal to hunt with his courtiers scarcely paints an idealized portrait of an engaged prince. In his encounter with Lilac (and then Aurora), he appears decidedly naive, asserting agency when the prize is before him but obviously lacking imagination. The prince's passivity echoes the court's inability to act when Aurora discovers the spindle and the four suitors' inability to capture Carabosse as she flees. In *Beauty,* as in the *Ring,* the plot turns on the daughter; the sons and fathers are spectators in their own play, much like Alexander III and his son, the future Nicholas II, who sat watching the ballet. If *Sleeping Beauty* held any political message, it was a directive to the young tsarevich (twenty-one at the time of the premiere): choose your queen well.

THE PETIPA GRAND BALLET DONE IN MYTH

Lévi-Strauss wrote that myth has the power to express opposing realities simultaneously, encompassing the incompatible.

> The fundamental opposition, the source of the myriad others with which the myths abound . . . is precisely the one stated by Hamlet, although in the form of a still overoptimistic choice between two alternatives. Man is not free to choose whether to be or not to be. A mental effort, consubstantial with his history and which will cease only with his disappearance from the stage of the universe, compels him to accept the two self-evident and contradictory truths which, through their clash, set his thought in motion, and, to neutralize their opposition, generate an unlimited series of other binary distinctions which, while never resolving the primary contradiction, echo and perpetuate it on an ever smaller scale. (1981, 694)[14]

I have written elsewhere on the importance of the romantic ballet's structure for Petipa, a choreographer well aware of that era's ballet traditions and limitations, and who created a "grander" style of ballet in Russia from the romantic ballet's binary structure (1994, 5–12). Essentially, Petipa and his librettists found ways to extend the ballet beyond the two acts of romantic ballets such as *Giselle* or *La Sylphide.* Both those ballets contrast first-act romanticized locales (the middle European countryside in *Giselle,* the Scottish countryside in *Sylphide*) with supernatural second acts. The Petipa ballets that have come down to us mostly preserve this formula (local color, followed by a scene in which the hero has a vision of the heroine, now dead), though the choreographer extends the ballet beyond the dualistic, two-act structure, stretching his ballets to as many as five acts culminating in a wedding or celebration comprising a variety of dances and dance styles. Yet Petipa's grander spectacles never replaced the simpler ballets of an earlier era: Petipa staged *Giselle* in the Maryinsky as late as 1887 and followed with *La Sylphide* in 1892.

The late 1880s, the years of *Sleeping Beauty*'s genesis, were the years of Virginia Zucchi's triumphs on the Russian stage. The Italian dancer, renowned for her acting and pantomime abilities, made her mark dancing the great melodramas in the repertory of those years: *Esmeraldā, Daughter of the Pharaoh,* the mute in the opera *La Muette de Portici.* Laroche regarded the widespread criticism of *Sleeping Beauty* a natural response from a public engrossed in balletic tearjerkers: "You don't like ballets from children's tales and you don't want the ballet to smack of the féerie, even such a well-structured, elegant féerie, harmonious in its richness, as the one served to you in the Maryinsky Theater. And even as you worry about the ballet, you wish it success. You know how easily this enchanted garden could lapse into the state of a forgotten greenhouse, rarely visited and poorly tended. Perhaps you hope to save it by introducing elements of a bloody drama. Zucchi, in *Esmeralda,* doesn't let you sleep, and the masterful representation of the young woman, crippled by torments, strikes you as the last word in choreographic progress" (1890, 4).

Laroche noted that the ballet was less equipped to treat "real" subject matter than the opera, though the dramatic theater could do this better than both. The fairy tale, on the other hand, "despite its prosaic form, often contains the most ancient, authentic myths" (1890), and myth seemed, to Laroche, the province of the ballet. Zucchi's art struck Laroche (and, he argued, Tchaikovsky) as something alien to the ballet:

> "What are these children's tales to us? Couldn't they really think of anything a little smarter for the ballet?" That's what people ask who have *their* ballet, *their* ideal of dramatic truth in pantomime in mind. Given that this happened in 1890, I can, without any unusual courage, state that that ideal was Zucchi. The brave and charming Italian turned all our heads precisely in the last half of the 1880s. She didn't dance like the others, without a smile, but utterly in her own way. And she chose plots that allowed her originality to shine in all its splendor. The sober truth is that contemporary Italy is now crazy about *verismo,* just as we were thirty years ago. Zucchi is *verismo* translated into the language of dance. Therein lies her strength, and also, perhaps, her weakness. Tchaikovsky didn't quite fall in love with Zucchi, mostly because her realism was at odds with his relationship to dance . . . , counter to all his ballet fondnesses and traditions. In other words, his ideal was classical. He remained, or wished to remain, a ballet classicist to the present day, despite the fact that he had to write music for a ballet-féerie, and not for a string of clever classical solos. Zucchi's weakness, I willingly admit, lay in the fact that the contemporary direction of ballet strives for the certainty of verbal speech—an occurrence that parallels what we see in contemporary instrumental music. In ceasing to be an "abstract play of sounds," music-poetry offers an analogy to ballet-poetry. Pyotr Ilyich wasn't far from music-

poetry; he was attracted to its climes already in his youth, and in his middle period, and toward the end of his work. He simply couldn't stand realism in the ballet.

In contrast to opera, which is capable of representing contemporary, everyday, middle-class existence, the ballet is destined to carry us to the kingdom of the fantastic and the impossible, the incomprehensible and the inexpressible. The incomprehensible and the inexpressible—in its primordial creative expression—is myth. (1895, 88–89)[15]

The manufacture of closing acts for ballet melodramas reveals no small amount of contrivance on the part of their librettists. *La Bayadère,* for example, features the usual final act wedding, but the spurned heroine Nikia, now dead, returns as a spirit to disrupt it. In *Daughter of the Pharaoh,* the heroine has to be returned to the surface of the Nile from its depths, to which she had earlier plunged in desperation. These could scarcely be called "realistic" ballets, though as in *Giselle,* the supernatural enabled the story's continuation, the life after death of the heroine. These plots suggest not only the importance of the heroine's death in the nineteenth-century ballet, but also the importance of having it both ways: the dead heroine nonetheless participates in subsequent acts.

If *Sleeping Beauty* lacked the drama of the melodramas it joined in the repertory, it signaled a new alternative to the usual workings of the ballet plot. Neither comedy nor drama, it offered the structure of the tragic ballet without the unpleasantness. Aurora was provided the usual requisites: a modified mad scene, the opportunity to appear in a vision, and a wedding celebration. And if histrionics disappeared from *Sleeping Beauty,* something more profound replaced the heightened emotions of the melodrama. Laroche wrote: "One of the most truthful works of the human spirit, the most faithful to life, is myth. If only it is an authentic, 'real' myth, and not a fake, a later fabrication, or thought-up on purpose" (1890, 3). Laroche assured his readers that *Sleeping Beauty* was a real myth and stressed the beauty, the didactic potential, and profundity of these tales.

The turn to myth allowed Vsevolozhsky and Petipa to stage the nineteenth-century ballet's Holy Grail: a depiction of the ballerina's death, appearance as a vision, and also as a bride—and all in one ballet. The dead girl only sleeps, and the supernatural is a part of the depicted world, not a second- or third-act imposition. By incorporating all three elements, they created the most perfect of the nineteenth-century's ballet plots. Yet if the libretto allowed the ballerina a more multifaceted role, the heroine they created was not without precedent. In turning away from the passions of Zucchi and her vehicles, they returned to an earlier model: the ballerina as cipher. Aurora "speaks" only in the ballet's first act, asking to put off the decision to marry and insisting on her safety: "I sing, dance, and make merry, but I never work" (libretto). This small scene echoes a motif in *Giselle,* though with shifted emphases. In Marian Smith's translation of the ballet's 1840 libretto, Giselle's mother cautions: "I am sure that if this foolish thing died, she would become a Wili, and dance even after her death, like all the girls who love dancing too much! . . . Berthe then, to a lugubrious music, seems to depict an apparition of dead people returning to the world and dancing together. The terror of the village girls is at its height. Giselle alone laughs, and responds gaily to her mother that she is incorrigible and that, dead or alive, she will always dance" (231). Once again, Vsevolozhsky has preserved the function of the romantic heroine (her love of dancing) but shifted the emphasis away from dark prophecies. (Giselle, unlike Aurora, does not recover.)

The use of myth in *Sleeping Beauty* led naturally to an emphasis on abstracted characterizations, to characters that reveal themselves through their dancing, rather than through danced acting. In *Giselle,* the shift is simple: from "peasant," pseudo-folk dances in Act I to the light dances of an apparition, the fleeting poses over Albrecht, and the escapes from his grasp in Act II. In *Sleeping Beauty,* the third act provides an opportunity for the continued development of Aurora's character. The coltish dances of the twenty-year-old Aurora give way to fleet dances in the vision and the mature poise the dances in Act III imply.

The mythic dimension of the characters in the new ballet likewise shift attention from the individual star performer and his or her dramatic gifts to the technical side of the creation of the role. And the wisdom of that decision soon became apparent. Aurora was more easily replaced than Esmeralda or the Pharaoh's daughter. Matilda Kshesinskaya, the Russian dancer whose career signaled the eventual replacement of Italian ballerinas with local talent, recalls the Petipa's hesitance in granting her Zucchi's old roles until she had "suffered" (Kshesinskaya 43), yet Aurora came almost automatically to the technically gifted Kshesinskaya, a mere three years after the ballet's premiere. (Kshesinskaya would wait until the end of the decade to dance the Zucchi vehicles.)[16]

The shift to a more abstract ballet with more abstract dancing was not lost on Laroche. In his discussion of the kinship of music and myth, he contrasts program and symphonic music, and the ballet to the *féerie:* "Choreography and music, the symphonic poem and the ballet, the symphony without a program and the féerie: each these realms is very close to one another and all of them float in the same indeterminate, spontaneous element" (1890, 4). Laroche places the féerie alongside the symphony, the "purer," more abstract of the two genres. In posing the simple comparison, Laroche initiated a larger discussion of the interrelationship of dance and music that would occupy Soviet dance historians and musicologists through most of the twentieth century.

NEW MYTHS OF *SLEEPING BEAUTY*

> With *Totem and Taboo* Freud constructed a myth, a very beautiful one at that. But like all myths, it doesn't tell us how things really occurred. It tells us how men need to imagine that things happened in order to attempt to overcome the contradictions they experience in their lives.
> —Claude Lévi-Strauss, *Conversations with Claude Lévi-Strauss*

Preparations for the 1999 revival of the Petipa production of *Sleeping Beauty* brought new legends surrounding the work to the fore. These were not stories from any sagas or tales, but homegrown myths, legends privately distilled and widely disseminated. Like the unofficial gossip webs and the nets of readers linked by the samizdat press in Soviet times, these ballet tales thrived where reliable information was lacking. Although as we will see, they were sparked and abetted by "official" information.

The chief controversy surrounding the Maryinsky reconstruction of the Petipa *Beauty* came down to wrangling over Petipa and Sergeyev. Curiously, the debate concerning Marius Petipa's 1890 version of the ballet versus Konstantin Sergeyev's 1952 staging took a back seat to controversies surrounding a different Petipa and a different Sergeyev. The Petipa in question was the choreographer's daughter, Maria, who created the role of the Lilac Fairy. And the Sergeyev was not Konstantin, but Nikolai, an unrelated namesake who was regisseur of the Petersburg ballet from 1903 to 1917. This Sergeyev was part of the team that notated the choreography of ballets in the Imperial Theaters repertory at the turn of the century, then took the notations with him when he emigrated from Russia in 1918. Essentially, the controversy in St. Petersburg in 1999 swirled about Maria Petipa's shoes and Nikolai Sergeyev's papers.

Many of those who were opposed to the reconstruction—including many interested parties who worked in the theater, the ballet school, and the conservatory—cited photographs of Maria Petipa costumed as the Lilac Fairy to point up everything that was wrong with the idea of reconstructing the original 1890 production of *Sleeping Beauty*. The famous studio photographs of Maria Petipa as the Lilac Fairy shows her in the long costume from the ballet's second act. Wearing a plumed helmet, she holds a staff and sports heeled slippers,

Act II, 1890 production. The Vision. Left to right, Maria Petipa as the Lilac Fairy, Carlotta Brianza as Princess Aurora, supported by Pavel Gerdt as Prince Désiré. At left, the Lilac Fairy's attendants in the boat. Aurora stands in a "shell" at the center of garlands.

proof enough, for some, that this Lilac Fairy didn't "dance"—at least not on pointe. Those opposed to the reconstruction saw no value in returning to a production in which the Lilac Fairy "didn't even dance on pointe," and thus had no solo variation.

The notion that the Lilac Fairy had only one costume or guise suggests a certain poverty of imagination concerning the Imperial Ballet and its ballerinas. The production stills and the costume designs for the production show that Vsevolozhsky also designed a tutu for the Lilac Fairy's entrée in the Prologue— one of three costumes the Lilac Fairy wore in the ballet. The Sergeyev notations are clear: they include two variations for the Lilac Fairy in the Prologue. One labeled with Maria Petipa's name, the other unassigned. Roland John Wiley described these in his book *Tchaikovsky's Ballets* in 1985 (169). Yet the major Russian-language work on *Sleeping Beauty* (Marina Konstantinova's *Sleeping Beauty*, 1990) does not mention them. Soviet dance historians did not peruse the Sergeyev Collection in the Harvard Theatre Collection or typically have wide access to recent Western publications. Nonetheless, the production stills and studio photographs in St. Petersburg's Theater Museum did not trouble them either.

The choreography for the Lilac Fairy—and her variation in the Prologue in particular—remain central to the debates surrounding the ballet and its choreography. Changes to that variation represent the first known amendments to Petipa's choreography for the ballet. And in 1999, the decision to return to the choreography and the pantomime notated for the Lilac Fairy in the Sergeyev manuscripts proved the most controversial element of the new/old production.

Resistance to Petipa's conception of the Lilac Fairy's role arose from the built-in peculiarities of the character the choreographer and his daughter created. If, in homage to Vladimir Propp or Antti Aarne, we wished to construct a typology of characters from the nineteenth-century ballet, to classify these characters according to their function in the ballets, we would see that the characters from *Sleeping Beauty* readily fit the standard groupings. The prince on his quest is like all the other Siegfrieds and Solors, waylaid on the road to true love. Aurora, the love object, is distinctive only in her refinement (earlier Petipa heroines, like Kitri, Nikia, and Esmeralda, rely on traces of demi-caractère dancing and local color to enliven their characterizations) even though she endures the requisite "death," appears in a vision, and revives for the ballet's final act, fulfilling all the usual structural demands. The Carabosse figure appears in various guises in each of Tchaikovsky's ballets: von Rothbart in *Swan Lake* and Drosselmeyer in *Nutcracker* (he is kindly, but a sorcerer nonetheless). The unifying quality of all the nineteenth-century ballet's undesirables is age, and often infirmity: the fop Gamache in *Don Quixote* (obviously too old for the youthful Kitri), the Chief Brahmin in *Bayadère*, or Doctor Coppelius. Even the role of Myrtha, the head Wili in *Giselle* is frequently assigned to an experienced dancer—one who used to dance the lead.

The character with no counterpart in this crazy quilt of ballet personages is the Lilac Fairy, and her failure to conform to the usual distribution of roles and functions in the ballet has troubled ballerinas and balletmasters since her debut. By the time Petipa created *Sleeping Beauty,* it was not unusual for his ballets to feature two leading female characters. (Nikia and Gamzatti in *Bayadère,* Medora and Gulnare in *Corsaire,* Kitri and the Queen of the Dryads in *Don Quixote,* Esmeralda and Fleur de Lis, to name the most familiar.) There is an observable division of labor in these pairings: the heroines are all exotics (Indian, Greek, Spanish, Gypsy), whose dancing incorporates elements of national dance (or at least, the nineteenth-century ballet's version of it), though

Prologue, 1890 production. Maria Petipa (right) as the Lilac Fairy with Lyubov
Vishnevskaya, a member of her suite.

each displays her prowess in academic choreography in the vision scene (when tutus substitute for genre costumes). The secondary heroine is a classical dancer, though she may also indulge in a bit of local color. Nikia's and Esmeralda's rivals furnish prime examples; they are also higher-borne than their heroines.

The Lilac Fairy fits none of these patterns. With only one variation, replaced early on in the ballet's history, the role scarcely tempts ballerinas. Nor does it fit the usual pattern of secondary roles. Given that Aurora functions as a kind of apogee of academic dancing, Lilac could scarcely be a classical foil to Aurora in the same way Odette complements Odile, Gulnare contrasts Medora, or Gamzatti upbraids Nikia.

The Lilac Fairy remains a folktale character with no precedent in the ballet. She more closely resembles her counterparts from wonder-tales, who appear to the hero in the time of need, usually granting him some charm or talisman to allow him to complete his quest, though Lilac is a doting donor (Propp's term). Rather than give Désiré a charm and send him on his way, she walks him through the stages, quite literally: revealing Aurora to him, taking him to find her, instructing him to kiss her.[17]

Lilac essentially walks onto the ballet stage from a folktale and that fact has resulted in no small confusion over her role and her function in the ballet. From the first reworking of Petipa's ballet in 1914, choreographers were eager to regularize her role, to bring Lilac into line with expectations for a Petipa second ballerina. By 1952, Lilac had forgotten most of her mime dialogues and her spells: as Aurora is taken into the castle at the end of Act I in Konstantin Sergeyev's production, Lilac dances about the set, as though relieved that the stage had finally cleared for her.

Given the sacral role of Petipa's ballet in the history of Russian dance, changes to the choreographic text understandably necessitated elaborate justification, and the histories of Russian ballet anxiously obliged. As was often the case in the writing of Soviet histories, vilification provided the path of least resistance, and the confusion surrounding Lilac's function in the ballet intertwines with the calumnies invented to slander Maria Petipa, who created the role. Almost every study of the ballet tells us that Petipa's daughter didn't dance, that the Lilac Fairy's role was strictly a mimed performance. Writing in 1990, for example, Marina Konstantinova describes the Lilac Fairy's role in the ballet's Prologue: "As is well known, Maria Petipa, performing the role, didn't dance a variation. . . . She entered the stage in a long chiton, decorated with flowers, with a magic wand in her hand (a sign of her power), and in a fantastic headpiece. She really looked like the fairies' schoolteacher" (72).

Konstantinova, who contributes an otherwise fine monograph to the literature on *Sleeping Beauty*, goes on to explain that that it would have been inappropriate for Lilac, who was more Valkyrie than fairy, to dance a variation. Konstantinova is the first writer since Laroche to hint at Lilac's true genealogy; her reading is provocative and sensitive, but the evidence contradicts her reading and those of many other historians.

How did generations of dance historians forget that Maria Petipa danced? Several sources from the 1960s and 1970s (published after Krasovskaya's 1963 history, which makes no mention the strange provenance of the variation) repeat half-truths long since accepted as fact. In the introduction to Lopukhov's *Sixty Years in Ballet* (1966), Yuri Slonimsky reveals Lopukhov as the author of the variation then generally believed to be Petipa's "in Moscow and Leningrad, in London, and in Paris—literally everywhere" (19). He quotes Elizaveta Gerdt:

> I well remember Maria Mariusovna Petipa in the role of the Lilac Fairy, from when I appeared as a child in the waltz in the first act of *Sleeping Beauty*. She was already far from young then; her heavy torso was in sharp contrast to her delicate, beautiful legs in heeled slippers. She never was a classical dancer, and never danced on pointe (this I know from my father). And that's why the variation in the prologue was dropped. At that point and later, the Lilac Fairy was a mime role. When I was already almost a ballerina, and took the role after L. N. Egorova (this was in about 1910 or 1912), I asked Lyubov Nikolaevna to show me the variation. From her, I learned that the variation was staged by Fyodor Vaseilievich Lopukhov at her own request. (19)

Elizaveta Gerdt (1891–1975), the daughter of Pavel Gerdt (1844–1917), the ballet's first Désiré, makes a peculiar expert witness. Five years younger than Lopukhov, Gerdt graduated from the Theater School in 1908, the year after Maria Petipa officially retired (at age fifty). Could Gerdt have witnessed or recalled more than Lopukhov? Slonimsky cites a letter he received from Gerdt (9 March 1963) as his source, then relates how, upon learning of the letter, Lopukhov admits that the variation is his own (in a letter dated six days later, on 14 March 1963). Rather than questioning the choreographer's decision to rechoreograph Petipa, Slonimsky praises Lopukhov's deception, complimenting the choreographer's skill in inserting a variation indistinguishable from the rest of the choreographic text in style and quality (20). In his own text, Lopukhov adds: "Petipa, who assigned the part of the Lilac Fairy to his daughter, was obliged not to choreograph a variation for her: Maria Petipa didn't dance classical roles. Because of that, the suite of dances didn't have a finale—neither musical nor danced" (226).

In the compilation of Petipa materials published in 1971, Lopukhov wrote: "I was selected to partner the heavy M. Petipa, the Lilac Fairy. The fairy's poses were especially earth-bound, and the support work corresponded. Petipa didn't set a variation for the Lilac Fairy. The wonderful music was sacrificed to its interpreter, who already couldn't do classical dancing" (191). One year later, Lopukhov published his memoirs and elaborated on his account of the first production of *Beauty:*

> After the fairies' variations comes the Lilac Fairy's variation, the one Petipa didn't choreograph and that it came to me to choreograph. In my time, carefully analyzing the work of Petipa and finding absurdities in the role of the Lilac Fairy that didn't fit the general sense of the ballet, I went to Pavel Gerdt for an explanation. . . . This is what I heard: "You are correct in your conjectures. But Maria Mariusovna wanted the role of the Lilac Fairy. And she was better accepted in the higher circles than her father, the venerable Petipa, who at that time was already expecting either his overthrow or a quiet removal." Not only was Maria Mariusovna not an accomplished classical dancer, she was simply out of place in classical roles because of her thin, macaroni legs, and her luxuriant bosom. (91)

The main details of the vilifying legend are clear here. This tale pits a beautiful but untalented socialite (we are left to wonder if Maria was lazy or simply a bad dancer) against her father, the genius who, according to Lopukhov's reporting, feared his own dismissal. (This at a time when the director of Imperial Theaters was entrusting the choreographer with a production that reputedly exhausted one-fourth of the St. Petersburg theaters' yearly production budget.) In 1971, Lopukhov wrote that Maria Petipa was "heavy" (191). He continues this bodily assault in the speech attributed to Gerdt: she had skinny legs and an ample bosom. The abundant photographic record of Maria Petipa in a variety of roles, both classical and otherwise, fails to support Lopukhov's claim.

Lopukhov does not bother to justify the contradiction in these two accounts: if Petipa needed to be supported in the ballet's Prologue, she was obviously dancing on pointe. Thus, the role was not a "walking" one as he suggests, but a "classical" one, at least in the Prologue. One gains a clearer sense of Lopukhov's interest in the role, however, in the passage that follows:

> In 1914 Lyubov Egorova asked me to choreograph the Lilac Fairy's variation for her appearance in a performance at Krasnoe Selo.[18] Later, this variation was used in the Maryinsky Theater, by Elizaveta Gerdt, daughter of Soloist to His Imperial High-

ness, Pavel Gerdt. This was done at Gerdt's request, when his daughter was given the Lilac Fairy's role. Pavel Andreevich felt that this variation functioned as the exposition of the role. But he hid the fact that I made the variation, and told the directorate, that it had been choreographed by Marius Petipa, who had to cut it, since Maria Mariusovna couldn't manage it. Gerdt understood that if he said anything about my authorship of the variation, that Nikolai Sergeyev, of course, would not have allowed it. From that time, my variation has been performed and accepted as Petipa's composition, which is very pleasant for me, because I regarded and still regard Petipa's work in *Sleeping Beauty* as wonderful. The variation I made really does function as the exposition of the Lilac Fairy's role. (1972, 91–92)

Sergei Vikharev discussed Lopukhov's assertions in an interview shortly before the 1999 production premiered: "The whole deception was to avoid the vigilance of Nikolai Sergeyev, who was guarding the authenticity of Petipa's text. It answers the question 'Did Nikolai Sergeyev make any capricious changes to Petipa's ballets?'" (Vaziev et al. 1999, 21).[19]

Historians have coped with the anomaly of Lopukhov's variation in their own ways, though most follow the example of Vera Krasovskaya, who, in adapting her text for a 1972 English-language article on *Sleeping Beauty* (after Lopukhov's accounts of the variation had been published), conflates all the versions, as though variants in the solos didn't matter: "After this [Canari's variation], the majestic, luminous peace of the waltz of the Lilac Fairy. A fragrant bush flowered in its flowing tempos as the dancer's arms swung open. Covering the stage with a clear, calm pattern of movements, the Lilac Fairy crowned with her dance the abundant gifts of her friends" (1972, 27). Krasovskaya's description of the choreography is sufficiently vague to apply either to the Maria Petipa version (never mentioned in her history) or to Lopukhov's. Although Wiley discusses the existence of the two versions of the variation, he follows conventional wisdom in asserting that Maria Petipa's variation required little point work (1985, 169), though in the Vikharev reconstruction, based on the same manuscript source, the dancer spends most of the variation on pointe.

A 1908 review of Anna Pavlova's debut as the Lilac Fairy adds to the confusion in these histories. "Miss Pavlova II was a charming Lilac Fairy. This role has no dances except for one small and difficult variation, which she performed with the great elegance she is known for" (*Peterburgskaya gazeta*, 18 February 1908). "But what variation did Pavlova dance?" Konstantinova asks: "Until 1907, the only performer to dance the Lilac Fairy was Maria Petipa. Obviously she danced the role as her father had staged it, in other words, without a 'difficult variation.' Tamara Karsavina [also] debuted in the role in 1907, and Svetlov, describing her variation in the Prologue, mentions entrechats-sisses and pirouettes—movements that could not have been in the original. It must be that both Pavlova and Karsavina danced a different variation than Petipa's. Vera Krasovskaya has suggested that Petipa himself could have staged a variation for these ballerinas, even to different music" (141).[20]

Konstantinova and Krasovskaya are right to suspect a second variation. The variation for Maria Petipa reconstructed from the notations in 1999 does not include entrechats-six or pirouettes. The other variation notated in the Sergeyev manuscripts resembles the choreography danced by the Royal Ballet and includes a number of difficult pirouettes but no entrechats.[21] Sergei Vikharev dates the recording of the notations to the period from 1903 to 1907 (Vaziev et al. 1999, 19); thus, this second variation in the collection is possibly the one created for the new dancers in the role in 1907—though there is no reason to suspect that new music was used. More to the point, there is no evidence to suggest that Maria Petipa didn't dance, only evidence to suggest that she did: the notations, photographs of Petipa in the Prologue, Vsevolozhsky's costume designs, even Lopukhov's assertion that he partnered Maria Petipa.

Yuri Slonimsky, born in 1902, and a ballet-goer already in the 1910s, remembered the role slightly differently in 1956 than in 1966 (above): "Petipa's choreography for the Lilac Fairy lacked virtuoso technicality. We shouldn't attribute this to the limitations of the role's first performer, Maria Petipa. She played a secondary role. The deciding factor was the desire to vary the movement characteristics of the large number of personages in the ballet. The extended, 'singing' movements given the Lilac Fairy had their origins in the music, which suggest plastique. The music didn't allow for a virtuoso-technical Lilac Fairy" (206). Slonimsky does not suggest that the Lilac Fairy didn't dance, merely that her role was not a bravura one. Yet Slonimsky, like the historians that came after him, fails to make a distinction between the variation Petipa created for his daughter, the second variation in the Sergeyev notations, or the Lopukhov version, created sometime between 1912 and 1914. And although most historians of Russian dance cited Slonimsky respectfully, they failed to heed his caution regarding Maria Petipa. The problem of the Lilac Fairy's choreography continued to be lain at the heeled slippers of Maria Petipa.

When asked to comment on Lopukhov's written statements about Maria Petipa and the Lilac Fairy, Vikharev summarized: "You can understand him: he didn't just add something somewhere or another, he allowed himself to redo Petipa's choreography, to take a variation Petipa had created out of the Prologue, and put his own in its place. Of course, he had to justify this the rest of his life" (Vikharev). As Lopukhov's justifications for his choreographic amendments to *Sleeping Beauty* suggest, changes to Petipa's classic could necessitate no small amount of explanation, and the histories of *Sleeping Beauty*, the Russian ballet of the period, and Maria Petipa's role in it are full of them.

Mikhail Borisoglebsky's *Materials for a History of Russian Ballet* (1939) (written at the height of Stalin's Terror) remains one of the most curious compilations of information relating to the history of Russian ballet. The strength of the volume lies in its biographies of Imperial Ballet dancers (including information regarding ranks, salaries, and roles). Borisoglebsky's authorship of the work reflects either a collective or a medieval understanding of that term: his entry on Matilda Kshesinskaya, for example, is borrowed verbatim from the unpublished and uncredited manuscript of D. I. Leshkov.[22]

The volume's description of the role of Maria Petipa is confusing, to say the least. The entry begins by calling Petipa "one of the most important ballerinas of Russian ballet" (279), then slips into a kind of yellow journalism atypical of the volume. In explaining that Petipa did not want to enroll his daughter as a full-time student in the ballet school, the author explains: "Surovshchikova, the mother of the future ballerina, didn't want this either, knowing full well of the miserable life of the girl students: the foul conditions in the dormitory, the humiliating fault-finding and punishments, the unavoidable participation in 'secret romantic adventures,' etc." (279). After describing the attention Maria received as the daughter of the chief balletmaster, Borisoglebsky continues: "For her success in class, in secret from her mother and father, she begged permission to gambol for a time with the 'girls' in the dormitory, where she had a course in the 'second science,' which covered the worldly fortunes of the female dancers, love and lovers, the servility of poor admirers, and the extravagances of wealthy fans, and all sorts of tales about so-and-so who got this, and how to set oneself up" (279). After suggesting that Maria's successful debut as a dancer was preordained, thanks to the good offices of her father, the author goes on to describe her qualities as a dancer: "Maria Petipa's two outstanding qualities as a dancer—her temperament and her plasticity—always won over her audience. A happy 'stage fate,' a beautiful figure, and the support of her famous father made her an irreplaceable performer of character dances and a first-rate ballerina with a varied repertory" (279).

It is not clear how these three qualities (luck, figure, and a famous father) could conspire to produce a first-rate ballerina, particularly when the author goes on to describe the range of roles Petipa danced: genre scenes such as Cinderella in *Beauty*, dramatic roles such as Paquita, and leading roles in grand ballets (in *Roi de Candaule,* for example). Even Borisoglebsky admits that Maria Petipa had no equal as a character dancer; though he writes that the success went to her head. The writer outlines the main scandals of Maria Petipa's life as though these supplanted her dancing in importance early on, despite that fact that his account of her successes over the course of a very long career suggests otherwise:

> She lost her desire to continue her classes in the school, and didn't find it necessary to perfect her dancing, and only thanks to the insistent demands of her father did she infrequently appear before the old Johansson. Not long after her debut on the stage, she addressed herself to the realization of the classes in the "second science" she once attended. Her cohabitation with D. F. Trepov, the son of the famous Petersburg governor, resulted in a son, whom the tsar's aide-de-camp Kh. P. von Derfelden recognized as his own, and secretly married M. Petipa abroad. Trepov offered the son 25,000 rubles as a baby present. The mother, naturally, squandered the money, and the son, when he reached majority, demanded from her not only the money but also the interest. M. Petipa's ties with Trepov served as a topic for a boulevard novel, published in the *Petersburg Gazette,* which caused the artist much grief. M. Petipa had no shortage of scandalous affairs, and because of her, the talented artist of the ballet, Sergei Legat, committed suicide. (280)

Legat's personal crisis, precipitated by the aborted dancer's strike during the 1905 Revolution, made him a martyr to the incipient Bolshevik cause, and that event certainly occasioned the first blow to Maria Petipa's reputation in Soviet sources. (Her old-regime connections—including her father—didn't help.) Maria Petipa is not even allowed a graceful exit from the pages of Soviet ballet history: "In 1926, M. Petipa emigrated to Paris, where she died after two attacks of paralysis, a raving lunatic" (280).[23]

Borisoglebsky's entry on Maria Petipa is scarcely typical of the tone or purpose of his volume. The volume's plagiarized entry on Matilda Kshesinskaya, the former lover of Nicholas II and a ballerina who frequently abused her considerable power in the theater, treats this most controversial figure in the history of late-imperial Russian ballet fairly, almost sympathetically. The mendacity reserved for Maria Petipa served the ongoing cause of discrediting the dancer, as it enabled others to justify the liberties taken with her role.

The hostility, the yellow journalism, and the pettiness directed at Maria Petipa may be found in at least one other entry in the volume: the biography of Nikolai Sergeyev. Several sets of motifs run through the account: the first concerns his failure to perform military service, the second focuses on the amount of money Sergeyev received for his work. The remainder of the account sets out to document Sergeyev's tyranny in the treatment of the company's dancers, his fawning to his superiors, his general stupidity and unsuitability for the position of regisseur of the ballet. (Like Maria Petipa, Sergeyev failed to take the striking dancers' side in the 1905 "revolution" in the ballet, and Soviet writers never forgave him.) According to Borisoglebsky, Sergeyev was almost indifferent to the ballet and only interested in consolidating his authority and power:

> In order to avoid military service, Sergeyev managed to obtain for himself a job as the assistant to the teacher of the Stepanov system [of dance notation] in the theater school (76). . . .
>
> In 1901, finally free of the draft, Sergeyev began trying to demonstrate the enormous importance of his work. . . . He soon got the directorate to start praising Stepanov's system . . . and they gave Sergeyev two assistants. . . . Exploiting the system of Stepanov, a person who was doubtless talented, Sergeyev achieved a great deal for himself. Though it's true that he didn't really have a grasp of the system, but only bragged of his knowledge of it, and advertised himself as the most educated specialist choreographer (76). . . .
>
> Sergeyev became the dictator of the Petersburg ballet and, terrorizing the company, chased away half of the talented artists. None of the former students of the school ever had such power or such a horrible influence on the development of Russian choreography (77). . . .
>
> It is clear from the archives that Chekrygin and Rakhmanov [Sergeyev's assistants] notated several ballets. . . . But where these manuscripts are now located is unknown. The directorate wasted about 10,000 rubles on this project, never counting the cost paid out to the notations' only enthusiast: Sergeyev, who understood almost nothing about the notation of dances, but merely "philosophized," and sprinkled his speech with incomprehensible terminology (77). . . .
>
> Sergeyev rehearsed all the ballets as though from the famous notations . . . but in fact, the artists, who knew all the choreography of the ballets being revived perfectly well, only repeated what they had learned from the real balletmaster of those ballets, Marius Petipa. (79)

It would be difficult to imagine the attacks on Maria Petipa as part of a conspiracy to discredit her solely as a justification for changing the Lilac Fairy's choreography in the 1930s (as we have seen, that campaign would wait until the 1960s and 1970s). Yet the pillorying of Nikolai Sergeyev occurred against a rather different backdrop. From 1921, when he staged *Sleeping Beauty* in London for Diaghilev, until 1939, when the same ballet was restaged for the Sadler's Wells Ballet (and Borisoglebsky's study appeared), Sergeyev staged a number of Russian ballets, from notations, in Europe and England: *Giselle, Coppélia, Nut-*

cracker, and *Swan Lake.* In other words, as Soviet productions began to diverge from their Petipa stagings, and Sergeyev purported to stage these same works authentically in the theaters of the capitalist West, his work represented a very real threat to Soviet claims of the uniqueness and authenticity of their nineteenth-century ballet inheritance ("his" notations, whenever discussed in Soviet dance writings, were reviled).

Borisoglebsky summarizes Sergeyev's work in the theater as the "darkest moment in the history of Russian ballet in the first quarter of the twentieth century" (79). But when the Borisoglebsky account of Sergeyev's career is read together with the entry on Maria Petipa, a common theme emerges: the elder Petipa cowered before them both. "[Marius] Petipa was ending his brilliant career darkly and helplessly. Once the all-powerful dictator of the finest ballet theater in the world, the famous balletmaster had become the humble servant not only of Vsevolozhsky, but of many of his colleagues. He trembled before Sergeyev, turned to the Legat brothers for support, placed his hopes on Shiryaev, and didn't allow himself even to raise his voice at guilty ballerinas" (43).

Petipa's diaries from 1903, for example, reveal an occasionally cranky man of advanced age, but one who nonetheless rehearsed, choreographed, and followed box office receipts as one might watch the stock market.

> 23 April 1903: It's enough to live to 85, still with a good mind, eyesight, and legs. After that, you have to go to that world. . . . I was at the Director's with Khoroshchenko and Drigo about *The Magic Mirror* for next season. Great! (Petipa 1971, 76)

> 19 January 1904: They're rehearsing *Sleeping Beauty* in the theater. I won't go to the rehearsal. They don't inform me. . . . My wonderful artistic career has come to an end. 57 years of service. And I don't have the strength to work anymore. By the way, on the 11th of March I'll be 86. (90)

As Petipa notes, he had worked for more than half a century in the Imperial Theaters. He certainly respected the authority of his superiors (the directorate, the court), but it would be an exaggeration to suggest that he kowtowed before them, particularly near the end of his life. Marius Petipa becomes an extremely malleable persona in Soviet histories of Russian dance. Although never discredited out of hand, his accomplishments and service were discounted with surprising regularity—even as his ballets continued to comprise the backbone of the Soviet repertory. Thus, Borisoglebsky portrays Petipa as an impotent, cowardly courtier even at the time of *Sleeping Beauty*'s composition: "The old man Petipa . . . as though firing the last remnants of his strength, managed to create not only *Sleeping Beauty* to please Vsevolozhsky, but also *Raymonda* to the brilliant music of Glazunov. Toward the end of his career he managed to draw closer to Lev Ivanov and by collaborating with his [Ivanov's] undervalued talent, staged one of the most wonderful ballets from the end of the last century: *Swan Lake*" (Borisoglebsky 44). *Sleeping Beauty* is number 55 of the 75 ballets choreographed or staged by Petipa in Russia listed in the 1971 catalog of Petipa's works (Petipa 1971, 377–88). Borisoglebsky's attempt to portray Petipa as a dying man and failed artist in 1890 is as unconvincing as his depictions of Petipa as a cowering, sycophantic figure in the history of Russian ballet.

To read the separate portions of Borisoglebsky's history against each other is to see how poorly these separate distortions of history correspond to one another: we are meant to understand Petipa as a washed-up choreographer even before the composition of *Sleeping Beauty*, yet the power his daughter and Nikolai Sergeyev allegedly exerted over him is meant to suggest a shameful disregard for an artist and superior. This disrespect is but another piece of the puzzle of political guilt assigned to the two Soviet émigrés retroactively in Soviet dance histories: Maria Petipa's final, fatal quarrel with her lover Legat, and Nikolai Sergeyev's alleged abuses of his colleagues (whatever their rank), his alleged lust for power and money, his draft-dodging, and his emigration, which would scarcely endear either of them to Borisoglebsky's readers, Soviet or otherwise. If the myth of Marius Petipa's artistic impotence could not take hold, those invented for his daughter and Nikolai Sergeyev certainly did. In Soviet dance histories, the creator of the Lilac Fairy's role became a real-life Carabosse, and Nikolai Sergeyev became the most reviled personage in the history of Russian ballet.

Sergeyev's reputation, still a controversial matter, was not helped by Ninette de Valois' memories of Sergeyev in her memoir, *Come Dance with Me*. On the subject of Sergeyev's work with de Valois, Beth Genné has written: "De Valois' recollections of the rehearsals make it clear that Sergeyev was very far from meticulous and because neither de Valois, Lopokova, or Lambert could read his notes, there was really no way to check his accuracy. It soon became abundantly clear that Sergeyev played fast and loose with the reconstructions: 'He'd learned notations, so he must have had the knowledge,' De Valois told me, 'but he went haywire when he was producing things. There were never two days done the same way!'" (Genné 140). Whatever her frustrations with Sergeyev, de Valois employed him for eight years, between 1931 and 1939. With characteristic brevity, Balanchine characterized Sergeyev quite differently in his interviews with Solomon Volkov: "Lopukhov always complained a lot about Sergeyev, he called him incompetent. I don't think that Sergeyev was incompetent, he was simply uninteresting" (167).

As Laroche had noted in 1890, myth lay at the heart of *Sleeping Beauty,* and the mythmaking that surrounded ballet continued in the Soviet era, as the work was pressed into official service. We have seen how the slander of Maria Petipa and Nikolai Sergeyev was used to further the legend of Fyodr Lopukhov, for example. But the Soviet arts bureaucracy found it necessary to prop up—or beat down—more than individual reputations. In the years following the 1917 Revolution, the very existence of "Soviet" ballet was questioned. To save the ballet required that myths be spun to the size of ideologies. Nor were Maria Petipa, Nikolai Sergeyev, Ivan Vsevolozhsky, and the Lilac Fairy alone at the vortex of stories that sprung up around *Sleeping Beauty.* The contributions of Petipa and Tchaikovsky remained so central to the history of Russian/Soviet dance that elaborate ideological edifices would be constructed to shape their proper images as well. Accordingly, the construction and dissemination of the seemingly innocuous term "symphonism" became a scholarly cottage industry in the Soviet era. Discussion of that term leads us from the troubled waters of myth and legend into the far murkier realm of ideology.

Chapter 3 Achieving Symphonism

(The Soviet Ballet in Theory)

There must be sufficient attention to action in the new ballet. And that action must be a captivating, realistic plot, and not a silly fairy tale you can't read without being bored.
—Anatoly Lunacharsky, 12 May 1930

WHAT IS TO BE DONE
(WITH THE BALLET)?

If the 1890 *Sleeping Beauty* marked the creative apogee of nineteenth-century Russian ballet, the system that brought that ballet to the stage was fast approaching obsolescence by the turn of the century. Even before two revolutions questioned the validity of "Imperial" Theaters, progressive dance-makers, dance writers, and dance-goers had begun to refer to the Petipa ballet as the "old" ballet. For a time, the "new" ballet was little more than a set of aspirations for the art form, but a recognizably different body of new works soon took shape; notably, the Duncan-influenced works of Michel Fokine and the Stanislavsky-influenced works of Alexander Gorsky. In truth, Russian ballet was undergoing a sea change in the first decade of the twentieth century as vestiges of the Petipa era began to disappear: Vsevolozhsky left the Imperial Theaters in 1899, Petipa was unceremoniously retired in 1903; Vsevolozhsky died in 1909, Petipa in 1910.

Ironically, as those who led the Russian ballet to new creative heights in the 1890s were dying, the Russian ballet was enjoying its first brush with international fame. The Diaghilev ballet's Paris seasons would, for a time, transform the Maryinsky Theater from the Russian ballet's Mecca to a kind of offsite facility, a factory producing dancers for careers in Europe and the Americas. With St. Petersburg serving mostly as a staging area for more exciting developments happening elsewhere, the old ballet sauntered on much as it had before.

Questions of succession and the future of the Russian ballet loomed large in the Imperial Ballet at the turn of the century, and the 1917 Revolution made the old uncertainties more urgent and complex.[1] Neither "old" nor "new," the next phase in the history of Russian ballet would be Soviet. And Sovietization brought three distinct new pressures to bear on the art form. First, state ideology would play an increasingly prominent role in the creation of new works and the construction of the repertory, until the ballet, like other arts, found itself a ward of the Stalinist state in the 1930s. State control did protect the ballet from a second new threat: pressure from the extreme left, whose suspicion of the ballet's class origins might have led to the art's demise. The gradual closing of borders and increasing isolation represented a third new problem for the young Soviet ballet, particularly as large numbers of those associated with the Russian ballet's most illustrious era were now working abroad and the vast majority would not return. By 1917, this diaspora helped established ballet as a viable art form beyond Russian borders. The émigré ballet metamorphosed rapidly; although its nucleus remained mostly Russian for a time, its outlook was international from the start. Whatever the larger problems faced by the new Soviet ballet, the most immediate tangible results of the Sovietization of Russian ballet were the same as for the general population: poverty and isolation. Confusion over the ballet's proper role in the new Soviet state only added to the general disorder in the former Maryinsky.

Even in the turbulence of the postrevolutionary years, *Sleeping Beauty* remained at the heart of the Russian ballet repertory. More to the point, it became Exhibit A in the case to save the ballet when the art form's very existence was questioned. Yet as the state and the ballet joined in a long-term, commensurate partnership, influence flowed in both directions. *Sleeping Beauty* played a central role in the transition from Imperial to Soviet ballet. Yet the competing interests of the state, the public, and the intellectuals (particularly far-left ideologues) would, in turn, shape the ballet as it continued to be performed and produced in the Soviet Union. The first phase of the process, in the 1920s and 1930s, was the most dynamic. The less volatile period that followed allowed for the development of a more fluid and more resilient ideology to defend the nineteenth-century repertory, with *Sleeping Beauty* as its showpiece.

EXTERNAL PRESSURES:

THE BALLET AND THE STATE

From the start, *Sleeping Beauty* occupied a unique place in the history of Russian ballet, summing up the achievements of its century as it hinted at the innovations of the next. A performance of the work on 15 March 1917, the night of Tsar Nikolai II's abdication, epitomized the ballet's liminal state. The hall was overflowing, the audience demanded the "Marseillaise": "One of the artists appeared on the stage to greet members of the Provisional Government, the Soviet of Workers and Soldiers Deputies present in the theater. Someone answered, there was more applause, hurrahs, and the orchestra played the 'Marseillaise' again" (Bezpalov 41). The author, a singer and volunteer commandant of the rechristened "State" Theaters, noted that in the spring season of 1917, "rare was the performance not interwoven with political greetings and rallies" (ibid.).

If republican anthems preceded the performance, the ballet closed, as always, with Tchaikovsky's quotation of "Vive Henri Quatre"—an odd finale for an evening that began full of revolutionary promise. Yet the light-hearted barbs the ballet had once borne at the pens of nineteenth-century "civic" poets became serious questions in the years following the 1917 Revolution. Suddenly, the future of the ballet became more than an idle question; now it was one to be weighed and decided by the workers and peasants who briefly occupied the stalls.[2]

Petrograd arts organizations (including the theaters) had declared their autonomy from state control even before the October Revolution, forming an art workers' union to democratize participation in theater affairs in May 1917 (Swift 29–30). Days after their decisive October Revolution, the Bolsheviks moved quickly to take control of the theaters. The early appropriation of the State Theaters signaled business as usual, with the goal of uninterrupted performances during the transition; nonetheless, the abrupt changes in Russian society in the postrevolutionary years suggests a situation in which everything was, quite literally, up for grabs. By November, responsibility for the theaters was delegated to Anatoly Lunacharsky's State Commissariat for Enlightenment. In 1919, the Maryinsky was among the theaters granted the honorific title "academic." The ambiguous title would prove key to the theater's survival; it also marked a first step along a long path to ideological conformity.

Like many other Russian cultural institutions, the theater benefited from the relatively conservative cultural policies of the Soviet state's two most influential arts ideologues: Anatoly Lunacharsky and Lenin. The latter had expressed the need to assimilate capitalist culture long before the revolution actually occurred (see Frame 154–57). Statements concerning the necessity of building socialist culture from the remnants of capitalist culture became a frequent theme in Lenin's speeches in 1919 and 1920, for example:

> It is impossible to build socialism without using the residue of capitalism. It is necessary to use all of the cultural assets that capitalism created to use against us. This is the difficulty of socialism, that it must build with materials created by other people. (17 January 1919, in Lenin 1980, 149)

> Without the legacy of capitalist culture we cannot build socialism. We have nothing with which to build communism, except what capitalism left us. (18 March 1919, in Lenin 1980, 149)

> Socialism would be impossible if it had not learned to use the technical know-how, the culture, and the apparatus that bourgeois culture, the culture of capitalism, had created. (2 February 1920, in Lenin 1980, 150)

A determination to retain bourgeois culture would not guarantee the preservation of the theaters or other high culture institutions, however. Lunacharsky recalled Lenin's ambivalence concerning such a citadel of rentier culture as Moscow's opera house: "Vladimir Ilyich's attitude towards the Bolshoi Theater was rather nervous. . . . He insisted that its budget be cut and said, 'It is awkward to spend big money on such a luxurious theater . . . when we lack simple schools in the villages'" (quoted in Schwarz 12). If Lenin believed in some generalized need to "save" culture, it was Anatoly Lunacharsky, commissar of enlightenment and inveterate theatergoer, who came to the defense of the theater in general and the ballet specifically.[3] Lunacharsky's statements stress the ballet's potential as a revolutionary art form; like other left intellectuals, he saw little to laud in the ballet of his time. In 1919 Lunacharsky wrote: "Ballet, as a spectacle for the people, possesses colossal strength, but for now that strength is poured into silly melodramas and monotonous pretty *pas*. The ballet doesn't knows its own strength, and doesn't wish to know it. It still trails the chains of recent slavery to a lascivious, perverted public" (1924, 83).

Drama and opera, with classics penned by acknowledged masters of literature and musical composition, needed no justification, though Russia's logocentric intelligentsia viewed the ballet's wordlessness with suspicion. To puritanical Bolsheviks, the ballet's display of physical beauty seemed positively lewd. Lunacharsky addressed these issues repeatedly (and consistently) over the years, as in his 1925 essay that asked "Why Should We Save the Bolshoi Theater?": "The union of dance, beauty, and meaning (which no one opposes) to a plot too conventionally developed by means of mime and stylized choreographic elements, has seemed and seems to many unacceptable. Communist comrades have often expressed the opinion that Russian ballet is a specific creation of the landowning regime, a caprice of the court, and that, as such, bears traits antipathetic to democracy and the proletariat" (1964, 244). Lunacharsky was well aware of the ballet's potential; he wrote reviews of the Diaghilev ballet's European triumphs,[4] yet his remarks acknowledge the myriad difficulties of defending the ballet in the Soviet Union in the 1920s. His essay ultimately justifies saving the Bolshoi Theater for the creation of mass spectacles on appropriate (revolutionary) themes. "The harmony and precision of ballet movements, the complete mastery over one's body, the complete mastery over the moving mass—there is the promise of the enormous role the ballet could play in the organization of such spectacles" (ibid. 251).[5]

Whatever the official pronouncements on the appropriateness of the ballet or the need to maintain it, the liberated masses had their own ideas concerning the suitability of bourgeois art forms. Bogdanov-Berezovsky recalled that "immediately after the Great October Socialist Revolution, the Soviet theater came up against a remarkable fact: the enormous draw of ballet performances among the broadest possible masses, who, aesthetically, were completely unprepared for the reception of ballet" (3). The author quotes Lunacharsky's defense of the workers' "unceasing demand for opera and ballet" (ibid.) in the same period.

Evgeny Dobrenko has written that the state vastly underestimated the complexity of "mass" taste, as well as its dynamism (800)—which could only add to the difficulties faced by those charged with running the former Imperial Theaters. If the masses demonstrated an unexpected (and perhaps unhealthy) interest in the ballet, the new state's cultural workers admitted their bewilderment before the tasks Lenin and Lunacharsky set out for them: utilizing the bourgeois inheritance of the past to create new, appropriately Soviet ballets. In a recollection of the period that smacks of self-criticism, Fyodr Lopukhov recalls the uncertainty and puzzlement felt in the ballet theater regarding these official pronouncements:

> If we hadn't been so backward and unaccustomed to reading theoretical and aesthetic literature, we might have more readily understood what was going on in art, and emerge from the confusion in which we then found ourselves. It would have been enough to study thoroughly the words of V. I. Lenin on prerevolutionary culture and socialist culture. He spoke very clearly on the necessity of cultivating socialist culture, guided by the greatest achievements of all ages and peoples. But we didn't read Lenin then, and having heard about his pronouncements, couldn't always understand how to apply them to the ballet.
>
> We adopted a bit more of what A. V. Lunacharsky said, but we hadn't yet matured to an understanding of the breadth of his ideas either. (Lopukhov 1966, 220)

THE LEFT AND THE CULTURAL REVOLUTION

The greatest danger to the survival of the postrevolutionary Russian ballet was posed not by the Soviet government, whose artistic vision would prove surprisingly conservative, but by the radical advocates of a new proletarian culture, an organization known as Proletkult (a contraction of "proletarian culture"), and other left organizations. Proletkult's goal of creating art for the masses included the expropriation of the State Theaters and the replacement of their repertories with "proletarian" works. The state's decision to place Proletkult under the jurisdiction of Lunacharsky's commissariat in 1920 proved a vital step in sidestepping the threat, though it did not daunt the left organizations, who shared neither Lenin's belief in the necessity of saving bourgeois culture nor Lunacharsky's optimism for its revolutionary transformation.

Even under his control, Proletkult continued to bedevil Lunacharsky. A newspaper essay from 1922 hints at the commissar's frustration with the radical left and its demands: "In the preservation . . . of questionable valuables, the risk is not great. In the destruction . . . of even extremely questionable valuables, the risk is extraordinarily greater. . . . Only naive people could now seriously say that our large opera theaters should change their repertories. . . . To stage new productions is simply beyond us" (*Izvestiya,* 19 February). Naive or not, Proletkult persisted. In a 1923 article, for example, the organization declared the ballet "a thoroughly bourgeois art form, in which only love, or some other simple feeling is expressed through a special language of the legs, which specialize in erotic movements, and where the head and separate parts of the magnificent human body are sacrificed to the dance of the feet" (quoted in Shumilova 51).[6]

In Moscow in 1923, the head of the musical theater section of Glavrepertkom (a section of Lunacharsky's commissariat concerned with repertory questions), reported on the Moscow academic theaters' offerings:

> The ballet repertory imbues the Bolshoi Theater with all the traits of a court theater in tsarist times. There are *paysans* instead of peasants, chocolate-box "heroes," the intolerable fakery of ballet "folklore," the petty-bourgeois sentimentality of sugary romantic intrigues, and the extremely foolish, completely absurd realizations of the librettos. Princes, princesses, kings, and all sorts of devilry. Here is the tradition the academic Bolshoi Theater stubbornly maintains in the seventh year of the proletarian revolution. . . .
>
> In 1919–20 attempts (not lacking in interest) were undertaken to transform this bourgeois ballet into a sort of magnificent mass pantomime spectacle on more or less serious (often revolutionary) themes. But the Bolshoi Theater sidestepped this clearly considered proposal with Olympian indifference—and not one of such librettos found their paths to the stage of the Bolshoi Theater. (in Trabsky 1975, 70)

However shrill or naive, the left raised legitimate concerns. Sheila Fitzpatrick describes the root cause of their frustration with the theater bureaucracy: "The theatrical situation to which the left objected was that the established pre-revolutionary theatres received government subsidies and were free of local taxes, while continuing to perform the same repertoire with the same artists and directors to the same bourgeois public as before 1917" (1971, 239).

The years of Cultural Revolution (1928–31) during the first five-year plan (1928–32) breathed new life into the left's struggle for supremacy in the arts. The Russian Association of Proletarian Musicians (RAPM), for example, gained power in 1928 and immediately set out to "repress and censor musical trends it deemed bourgeois" (Fitzpatrick 1992, 192): "One of its first goals was control of the opera repertoire, especially the operas presented by the major houses of Moscow and Leningrad. RAPM was eager to remove ideologically unsuitable works (such as Tchaikovsky's *Eugene Onegin* and *Queen of Spades* and Wagner's *Parsifal*) from the classical repertoire and prevent productions of new works by contemporary European composers that 'directly or indirectly reflect the degenerate tendency of contemporary bourgeois culture'" (ibid.). Fortunately, *Eugene Onegin, Queen of Spades,* and *Sleeping Beauty* outlasted the threat from the left, though Glaviskusstvo's repertory index of 1929 must be seen as an official answer to RAPM's desire for a purge.[7] The index ranked works on a scale from "A" (ideologically recommended) to "E" (forbidden).

Sleeping Beauty received a "B," for "ideologically acceptable and permitted without hindrance" (Swift 80, 303).

That same year, the journal *The Life of Art* announced a libretto competition intended to spark the composition of new, Soviet ballets. As Swift points out, the announcement is significant "because it concisely formulated many of the features the government and Party considered desirable in the new Soviet ballet at the time" (85). The announcement reiterated familiar failings: the old ballets' irrelevance, the need for new ballets drawn from contemporary life, and the emphasis on drama rather than divertissement. Tellingly, the contest's authors recommended the very themes that soon proliferated in Soviet literature: civil war and (re)construction, ethnography, urbanism, and industrial themes, as well as "healthy" science fiction (in the style of Jules Verne). Mysticism and abstraction were categorically rejected; mass scenes encouraged, as was use of new movement idioms (acrobatics, gymnastics) and new media (radio, cinema). The announcement also stipulated that the libretto must be planned as a full-evening work—another revealing harbinger of the monumental art to come (86–87). The winning entry premiered in Leningrad in 1930 as *Golden Age*, to Shostakovich's music and choreography by committee. Ironically, the RAPM organ deemed the work "a coarse alloy of nauseating fox-trots and other decadent dances" and noted the ballet's obvious "ideological harm" (Swift 88).

The radical left's attacks on a work designed to meet the very criteria it had devised suggest the disarray in these organizations and their inability to influence events to their satisfaction. Yet the ballet libretto contest effectively predicted the major tendencies of Soviet art (including ballet) for the next decade: themes of war and production, industrialization and urbanization, and that favorite passion of Soviet ballet, orientalism dressed up as ethnography. Rest assured, temporary enthusiasm for new movement styles and new media would soon be condemned to the dustbin of 1920s experimentation.

DIAGHILEV AND THE WEST

In addition to new pressures (from the state and from the left) on the young Soviet ballet, there were also—and for the first time—external pressures. Those responsible for the arts policies in the young Soviet state were well aware of the renown Diaghilev's Ballets Russes enjoyed in the West (including the flashy production of *Sleeping Beauty* Diaghilev mounted in London in 1921). Lunacharsky began reviewing the Diaghilev seasons in Paris while in exile from the Russian empire and published his last account of Diaghilev's work in 1927.

Early Soviet histories continued to herald the triumphs of émigré stars abroad. As late as 1933, the dance researcher and critic Ivan Sollertinsky (1902–44) could characterize the recent history of Russian ballet as split along two lines: the Petipa and the Fokine schools (343–44).[8]

Lunacharsky's final report on the Diaghilev enterprise includes fragments of an interview with Diaghilev (published in *Vechernyaya moskva*, 28 June 1927) that offers a rare snapshot of two Russian ballet traditions drifting steadily away from one another. Lunacharsky boasts of the Soviet ballet's popularity, its schools, and its new stars. Diaghilev, who had long mined the Maryinsky and the St. Petersburg school for talent, turns the conversation to questions of repertory and innovation. Lunacharsky notes the whiff of revolutionary spirit in new productions of *Esmeralda* and *Red Poppy;* Diaghilev wonders if such an approach were not simply tasteless. Diaghilev regarded the lack of composers a serious problem for the Soviet ballet; Lunacharsky asked about *Le Pas d'Acier* by Prokofiev (still in the West), with its "slight reflections of our Revolution" (1958, 343–55). The conversation reveals an unfortunately neat bifurcation of Russian ballet in the 1920s. Petrograd maintained the school, theater, and traditional repertory; Diaghilev could boast the leading dancers, choreographers, and collaborators (visual artists and composers). In short, Diaghilev managed to take everything that was not tied down, and though his strategy revealed long-term weaknesses, innovation remained on his side even as the Soviets actively strove for modernity and relevance.

Anxiety vis-à-vis the West was not limited to the ballet. The earliest documents pertaining to the Soviet theaters reveal considerable concern in the opera as well. In a 1922 letter addressed to the *Review of Theater and Sport,* the head of the Petrograd Academic Theaters (the aptly named I. V. Ekskuzovich) began with a diatribe on the difficulties of keeping Russian singers in Russia: "It's not just us. The Americans have robbed all of Europe, buying up talent for divertissements in which singers alternate with acrobats and trained elephants. In the Grand Opéra, they stage incidental guest performances. In Milan the opera is dying, and in London's Covent Garden the cinematograph is established. The dollar—that is our enemy" (in Trabsky 1975, 287).[9] Scattered amidst complaints of the large quantities of cash the capitalist West was prepared to throw at Russian artists, a second motif emerges in these accounts: "our ballet troupe is the most progressive" (288). A *Review of Theater and Sport* report on an open meeting on the work of the former Maryinsky's ballet troupe denounces the theaters of Paris, London, and America ("where there is no theater at all"). Lunacharsky took the high road in 1925: "In countries outside Russia, ballet doesn't even exist as an independent genre. Only in Russia has the ballet been maintained as a complete full-evening performance" (1925, quoted in 1964, 244).

Diaghilev, poverty, and isolation notwithstanding, Russian theater workers prided themselves on the maintenance of full-length ballets, and this questionable distinction was one they were anxious to maintain. In the same Glavrepertkom report on the repertories of the Moscow theaters (in which the ballet is attacked as a court theater), V. I. Blyum derides the tendency to stage "ballet miniatures": If followed systematically, the same repertory plan that promised a production of Rimsky-Korsakov's *Schéhérazade* (a Diaghilev hit) "would turn the ballet theater into a divertissement theater" (quoted in Trabsky 1975, 70). Instead, the ballet administration, headed by Leonid Leontiev, set for itself the task of "raising the ballet to its appropriate stature in the reinstatement of discipline and the artistic level of the era of balletmaster Petipa" (in Trabsky 1975, 289). The ballet administration felt it had passed its first test, weeks earlier, with the first performance of *Sleeping Beauty.* The performance of a full-length work from the Petipa era perhaps justified the administration's boast that "in our day, only Russia has a real theater, and that wholly thanks to the colossal effort of our self-sacrificing artists, who have fulfilled their obligations despite everything, and including, at times, the most difficult working conditions. For example, a temperature of 2 degrees on the stage" (quoted in Trabsky 1975, 289).

The Maryinsky's response to Diaghilev may be characterized as a series of conservative retreats. The model the Diaghilev ballet proposed—shorter ballets to concert music—was rejected by the ballet bureaucrats of the 1920s, despite the fact that no viable multiact work had been created since Petipa's time. For Soviet ideologues, the length of a ballet still varied directly with its seriousness of purpose. The 1929 libretto competition, for example, marked the preference for full-evening work over "miniatures," much as criticism of Western performance venues (musical halls featuring variety acts and movies) signaled the superiority of the Soviet academic theaters. Confidence in the superiority of the Soviet ballet reverberates in the writings of Lunacharsky and others throughout the 1920s and accompanies self-definitions of Soviet dance that mostly react to Diaghilev's innovations. Lunacharsky's conversation with Diaghilev notwithstanding, the Soviet ballet's dialogue with the Russian dance diaspora soon devolved into a hectoring monologue unheard outside Leningrad or Moscow.

THE BALLET DEBATES

The Leningrad ballet, short on resources, personnel, and leadership, responded passively, if at all, to the new demands of the state, the harangues of the left, and the innovations of Diaghilev. Nonetheless, a lively debate on the future of ballet took shape on the pages of Soviet periodicals. Articles interrogating the future of Soviet ballet dotted journals such as *Rabochij i teatr* (The Worker and the Theater), and *Zhizn' iskusstva* (The Life of Art). The latter journal opened its pages to the discussion in 1928, when Sollertinsky posed the following questions:

> What themes could be used in contemporary ballets?
> Can a contemporary choreographic spectacle be built on the basis of classic dance?
> Can acrobats be used?
> How can ballet pantomime be renewed?
> Would an experimental studio help solve the current problem? (quoted in Swift 81)

Yuri Slonimsky summarizes the main positions in these debates: the radical left was far from unified, its factions finding inspiration for a new ballet as far afield as acrobatics, physical culture demonstrations, machines and work, allegorical revolutionary spectacles, folk dance, and games; the conservatives wished to preserve the ballets as they were; and a center gradually emerged that sought compromise between the two extremes (1966, 15–16).[10] Ironically, those contributing to the conversation largely avoided the practical questions Sollertinsky raised. Nor did the ideas discussed influence the repertory in any perceptible way. Nonetheless, the discussion accurately forecast the main theoretical and ideological concerns of the Soviet ballet for decades to come.

One of the more provocative essays on the dance to emerge in this period was written by Moscow ballet critic Alexander Cherepnin (1876–1927), who contributed "The Dialectic of Ballet" to *The Life of Art* in 1927. Cherepnin viewed the radical left's desire to overthrow the ballet and replace it with newer forms as "vulgar sociology," noting that the alternative movement idioms were just as foreign: that Duncanism, acrobatics, and "plastic-eccentric" movement were as alien to Russian society as the dances of European courts. For Cherepnin, the formation of a new ballet would depend on a new understanding of the art form and a new attitude to it, rather than a shift in its form or thematics. Pantomime, for example, had once been theater for the masses, but it had since become a theatrical idiom for "refined" spectators (I, 6–7). In other words, pantomime was a constant presence even though attitudes toward it had changed.

Neither the old nor the new ballet satisfied Cherepnin entirely: "The old ballet is dying because it is illogical. Its antithesis (pantomime justified by dances), if it is alive at all, will die of its logic." In another aphorism, Cherepnin distinguishes between the academy of classical dance, which he values, and a performance tradition he laments: "Classical dance hasn't aged, it is only old-fashioned. The classical ballet isn't old-fashioned, but it has aged" (I, 7).

In the second installment of his article, Cherepnin identifies two types of classical dance: the figurative and the expressive. Expressive dance conveys an emotional state, whereas representation and virtuosity provide the content of figurative dance. (Though figurative dance does not represent art to Cherepnin, only a kind of artistic production.) Figurative dance is thus "pure" dance, though Cherepnin deems expressive dance more organic. Cherepnin then steps into the quintessential dilemma of Soviet arts criticism in the 1920s: the form-content debate. If classical dance (as the thesis of the author's dialectic) represents form with content, and its antithesis (expressive dancing) content with form, Cherepnin sees their synthesis as "form-content," either as symphonic dance or danced drama (II, 4–5). Although couched in too-neat dichotomies, Cherepnin's essay foregrounds the most important debate of the decades to follow the cultural revolution: the place of abstraction in Soviet dance.

If Cherepnin's dialectical approach showed no marked preference for either symphonic ("pure") dance or danced narrative, theater researcher and critic Alexei Gvozdev (1887–1939), who took up the debate the following year, advocated danced dramas in his "On the Reform of Ballet."[11] Gvozdev believed that only large theatrical forms could attract sufficient viewers (he cites the cinema as evidence of the melodrama's power to attract audiences). The new ballet required new, contemporary plots and must be "a *theater,* not a blank slate for musicians to perform symphonies or for dancers to demonstrate their virtuosity" (II, 5–6).

The symphony moved to the center of the debate in *The Life of Art* when N. Malkov (writing under the pseudonym "Islamei") engaged a Sollertinsky essay that argued that dance had lost its immediacy of expression. Malkov turned Sollertinsky's argument on its head, replacing dance with music, to stress the relation between the two art forms, and using Sollertinsky's own, mostly unanswerable questions to interrogate the vitality of music: "Why should every art form unfailingly forfeit its own language, even though it once spoke a language that we all wish to contemplate and hear from artists of various art forms?" (Malkov 1928, 4). In a comment that reveals the author's view of the hierarchy of genres, Sollertinsky could only respond that the dance remained immeasurably poorer than music (1928, 5).

Sollertinsky returned to these questions in 1929 in "What Kind of Ballet Do We Really Need?": "Is there a necessity for an art that cannot link a pirouette with 'content,' say, from Komsomol or factory life, or an entrechat with the reconstruction of heavy industry?" (1929, 5). Sollertinsky decides that no ballet is needed: "We need . . . a new kind of synthesized performance, which unites in itself the word, singing, music, gesture, and dance" (5). In his call for an essentially Wagnerian synthesis of the arts, Sollertinsky admitted that ballet was a dead genre and says so repeatedly. By 1930, Sollertinsky could trumpet the ballet's demise: "Classical dance has been irrevocably dethroned. Nowadays, who but a few old provincial balletomanes, sighing over imperishable beauty, or two or three boys of the species 'Soviet aesthete' in the archives—who else would take upon himself the backbreaking work of defending the validity of the classics? It's a museum inventory" (1930, 8).

SUMMING UP

It was Sollertinsky, the old ballet's most ardent and prolific detractor, who wrote the first official account of the ballet's Soviet-era transformation in the 1933 *History of Soviet Theater*. As always, when attempting to unravel the meanings encoded in Soviet histories, it helps to know that Sollertinsky's work appeared in 1933 at the beginning of the second five-year plan, one year after the 1932 reform of literature and arts organizations.[12] The Seventeenth Party Congress, famous for its imposition of socialist realism as the new official arts doctrine, would follow in 1934. Sollertinsky's "Russian Musical Theater on the Eve of October and the Opera and Ballet Legacies in the Period of War Communism" appeared in the first volume of a relatively premature history of Soviet theater (it had existed for only sixteen years). Not surprisingly, Sollertinsky has mostly unkind things to say about the old ballet and its legacy. Given the predominance of spectacle (and the absence of ideology or even ideas), Sollertinsky asserts that the ballet merely fulfilled its class function in demonstrating the splendor and magnificence of the regime (as it had since the sixteenth century in Europe) (323–24). Petipa brought new brilliance to the "ornamental-abstract creation[s] of a dying feudalism" (323), according to Sollertinsky. Nonetheless, the choreographer's ballets remain little more than "festive, multiact choreographic divertissements that demonstrate the virtuosity of the dancers and the corps de ballet masses in the surroundings of sumptuous, though often crude and tasteless decors" (324). "Somehow or other," Sollertinsky intones, "Petipa lay his powerful and heavy hand on the whole of the choreographic repertory" (325).

Sollertinsky goes on to indict the ballet for all its usual prerevolutionary sins: the ballet's elite audience cared little for the performances and regarded the theater as a backdrop for gossip and business transactions; the ballet's plots were naive and conveyed in the "hieroglyphics" of pantomime; the choreography bore clear traces of its origins in feudal courts; the ballet school wore the reputation of a grand ducal harem. A product of European courts fetishized in Russia by the last Romanovs, the ballet's dancing masses told lurid tales of class-inappropriate love in revealing costumes. In short, ballet was a frivolous entertainment for the rich (294, 324). Soviet prudery aside, Sollertinsky's most serious indictment of the ballet concerns its lack of gravitas: "At the end of the nineteenth and beginning of the twentieth century, opera and ballet were, to a significant degree, 'canned' genres, of little ideological value, that lived mostly off the repertory of the nineteenth century. Elements of the feudal-court style appear in them sufficiently clearly: to a lesser degree in the opera, and to an incomparably greater degree in the ballet. The visual display of the 'grand spectacle' predominated: the lavish, pageant entertainments in the spirit of Meyerbeer's operas or the massive ballets of Petipa's late period. Neither opera nor ballet bore much ideological or semantic weight: 'problematics' were left to other authorities: the dramatic theater, literature, etc." (294). Sollertinsky reserves special disapproval for Petipa's late works, and *Sleeping Beauty* could easily serve as the exemplar of the author's main criticisms of the pre-Soviet ballet: the thin plot lines and the tendency toward divertissement, the degeneration of male dance, and the ballet's ill-founded relation to its musical accompaniment.

For all the predictability of Sollertinsky's criticisms of the prerevolutionary ballet, his article—both temporally and philosophically—dangles uneasily between the radicalism of the late 1920s left organizations and the cultural orthodoxy of high Stalinism as it reflects the uncertainty and flux of cultural policy of the period.[13] Sollertinsky praises the Diaghilev experiment, for example, asserting that the "bourgeois reconstruction" of the ballet could be carried out more easily in Paris, the capital of the "world rentier bourgeoisie" than in the tradition-bound corridors of the Maryinsky (341), and credits Diaghilev for elevating Russian ballet to the vertiginous heights of Russian literature in the world's cultural marketplaces.[14] In capturing the attentions of the Western bourgeois intelligentsia, Sollertinsky notes that the former aristocratic amusement had become an object of national pride (341–42). All the same, the author consigns the experiment to history: "The Russian ballet abroad gradually lost its former glory and now finds itself in a condition of creative decay. Even such a relatively longstanding and durable organization as the troupe of the late Diaghilev didn't escape this crisis and impasse. It seems that the page of choreography titled 'The Russian Ballet Abroad,' may now be considered written" (344–45).

Sollertinsky's repudiation of Diaghilev's progeny recalls the smug certainty of Russian balletomanes in the 1880s, though his desire to both acknowledge and bring closure to the Diaghilev venture typifies the insularity and chauvinism that gripped the Soviet Union in the 1930s. He assures his reader that a "wide, unblazed trail" was then opening before Soviet choreography—without speculating where that trail might lead (345). In fact, the trail was a meandering path, accommodating the varied and changing needs of the state as it led to an imagined bright future. The "Ukrainian Week" held in Moscow in 1936 provides a particularly pithy example. When state prizes were awarded to Ukranian performances, "The whole Leningrad artistic community . . . was saying that the Ukrainian Theater of Opera and Ballet had got awards not for merit but for political reasons, as part of a campaign to exalt non-Russian artists at the Russians' expense. 'The Ukrainians presented folk songs and dances and they had no high, serious, art,' the respected conductor Samuil Samosud was quoted as saying. 'Now in general they are praising and rewarding ethnics,' said Distinguished Artist Rostovtsev less diplomatically. 'They give medals to Armenians, Georgians, Ukrainians—everyone except Russians'" (Fitzpatrick 1999, 168). Moscow (the state) was the new adjudicator in a contest pitting "high" art, Leningrad tradition against newly fashionable "ethnic" forms. The event illustrates the extent to which art criticism had become an affair of state.[15]

A more troubling note for the fortunes of Soviet ballet sounded at the end of the second five-year plan, in 1937. The first issue of the journal *Teatr* opened with a lengthy editorial statement titled "A Momentous Five Years" (3–8). In the course of defending the liquidation of independent arts groups, defaming Trotsky, quoting Stalin liberally, and asserting repeatedly that the center of world culture has moved to Moscow for good, the article cites successful artistic creations of the Soviet era. The list reads like a greatest hits of socialist realism (certainly, the author's intent) and covers virtually every Soviet artistic endeavor: literature, the theater, cinema, opera, and symphonic and popular music. Art and architecture are chastised, though accomplishments in folklore are lovingly recited: folk music, folk dance, woodcarving, ceramics, Palekh boxes, and more (4–5).

In this exhaustive pantheon of Soviet art, the ballet rates no mention, even though Rostislav Zakharov's much-praised *Fountain of Bakchisarai* had premiered only three years before and was restaged in Moscow in 1936. The omission is ever more surprising given the *Teatr* article's veneration of Pushkin, the stimulus for Zakharov's ballet. Nonetheless, in these years before the ballet became an export item, or a viewing of *Swan Lake* de rigueur for visiting world leaders, the ballet remained something of an embarrassment, an unmentionable on the laundry list of ideologically correct artistic achievements.

REHABILITATING THE BALLET: IMPERIAL
TO ACADEMIC (AND BACK AGAIN)

If the vision of the tsar's entourage watching *Sleeping Beauty* from their boxes in the Maryinsky encapsulates the pomp and coziness of life in the Russian empire, the analogous Soviet-era scene shifts to Moscow's Bolshoi Theater, where, from Stalin's time, innumerable *Swan Lakes* were served up to Soviet leaders and their state guests. The distinctly second place that *Sleeping Beauty*, the Maryinsky Theater, and St. Petersburg played in the years of Soviet rule speak to the suspect past of each. Nonetheless, *Sleeping Beauty* played a key role in the reshaping of ballet in the Soviet Union (both ideologically and in a more literal sense). By 1963, Vera Krasovskaya could speak of *Sleeping Beauty* as the archetype of nineteenth-century choreography (310).

One key to the ballet's survival in the turbulent world of postrevolutionary theater was the title given the Maryinsky in December 1919: the theater became known as an "academic" theater. The designation conferred officially the qualities that Lunacharsky valued in the former Imperial Theaters and their repertories: the theaters were tools of learning and enlightenment, possessing valuable repertories. Thus, as before, they bore the imprimatur of officialdom. In a decidedly antiacademic era of European cultural history (in Russia, the sentiment dates most clearly to 1862, when the group of painters known as the Wanderers broke from the art academy), the young Soviet state cast its cultural lot with the cultural establishment of the ancien régime.

Russian writers still use the term "academic" (*akademichesky*) to describe *Sleeping Beauty* (the correspondingly imprecise English-language term would be "classical"). The early Soviet obsession with enlightenment would pave the way for *Sleeping Beauty*'s canonization during the Soviet period. More to the point, the arts bureaucracy's reliance on an academic justification for the State Theaters would focus specifically on *Sleeping Beauty*. The status the ballet quickly gained in the 1920s reveals much about the allure of the Petipa-Tchaikovsky work in the early years of the Soviet Union, a time when the ballet's glorification of cheerful autocracy should have been anathema.

Of all the ballets in the repertory, the State Theaters' 1924 repertory committee singled out *Sleeping Beauty* as the single work that showed promise: "The proletarian masses imperiously demand depictions of heroic endurance and action on the stage of the State Opera Theaters of the Soviet Republic . . . . The ballet is so saturated with rentier-aristocratic culture, that one cannot find even a grain of even the most superficial revolutionary character. . . . The ballet *Sleeping Beauty* attracted the attention of the directorate as one of a very few ballets, written by a good master-composer, among the hundreds of others that are musically inadmissible in an academic theater" (quoted in Trabsky 1975, 293–95). In order to rescue and defend the ballet, its adherents would necessarily turn to its strengths. If the plot and atmosphere of *Sleeping Beauty* made it one of the least appropriate ballets for the new Soviet viewer, one element of the ballet proved irrefutable: its music. Tchaikovsky was then on a trajectory that would lead to his ascension to the status of national treasure in the Stalin era. The ballet's fortunes (both of *Sleeping Beauty* and the ballet in general) would rise with him.

The academic recognition accorded the former Imperial Theaters in 1919 served as a critical first step in the process of saving the ballet, defending it against the extreme left. Throughout the 1920s, the ballet had mostly floundered, uncertain of its ideological role—and ill equipped in any event to indulge the whims of the state or the left. The Zeitgeist of the Stalinist 1930s—the darkest years in Soviet history—proved vastly more hospitable to the ballet. There is no exact English equivalent for the term *kul'turnost'*,[16] used to characterize a semiofficial campaign launched in the 1930s, though it implies being "cultured" or "civilized" in the broadest sense. This new definition of civilized behavior included such everyday practices as the use of (clean) underwear, bed linen, tablecloths, and curtains as well as attending the theater or reading Stendahl (Kelly and Volkov, 296–98). The inherent contradictions of this retreat to petty bourgeois practices in the worker-peasant state were justified by means of a clever manipulation: "One of the great advantages of the concept of *kul'turnost'* in a postrevolutionary society burdened by hangovers of revolutionary puritanism was that it offered a way of legitimizing what had once been thought of as 'bourgeois' concerns about possessions and status: one treated them as an aspect of *kul'tura*. Becoming cultured had always been a proper and necessary individual goal in Bolshevik terms. In the 1930s the concept was simply expanded to include acquisition of the means and manners of a lifestyle appropriate to the news masters of the Soviet state" (Fitzpatrick 1992, 218). To put it another way, "the brilliance of the *kul'turnost'* ideology lay partly in the fact that it was a fusion of two value systems previously thought incompatible, those of the bourgeoisie and the intelligentsia" (Kelly and Volkov 304). Thus, the doors to the State Theaters could now welcome politically mature, upwardly mobile new Bolsheviks to the same lewd spectacles and class-inappropriate love stories that the bourgeoisie had long enjoyed.

Sheila Fitzpatrick uses Bourdieu's term "misrecognition" to describe this paradigm shift in the perception of Soviet elite categories: "Stalin made his contribution to misrecognition by appropriating the term 'intelligentsia' to describe Soviet elites as a whole, thus implicitly conferring on Communist officials the cultural superiority of academicians and writers. This conflation of the elites of power and culture was not mere sleight of hand, but conveyed something important about the Soviet mindset of the 1930s. It means that the social hierarchy was conceptualized in *cultural* terms" (1999, 105).[17]

In *The Sociology of Taste,* Jukka Gronow describes the "luxury" goods and services that became part of everyday life of the privileged in the Soviet Union during this period. Obviously, Soviet luxury goods comprise a rather artificial category, if not an outright contradiction in terms. The products constructed as luxury goods in the Soviet Union in the 1930s were mostly archaisms even then: "They represented a way of life that was lived by rich people sometime in the middle of the nineteenth-century Europe—or rather a life which the Bolsheviks thought the rich had lived: champagne, caviar, chocolate, cognac, perfume: only lackeys, horse carriages, courtesans and roulette are missing from the catalogue" (52). When Gronow points out that Soviet luxury "was basically home-made and not imported" (52), we see how neatly the ballet fit into the new categories of desired products, or that the shift to the aesthetic of socialist realism in the early 1930s recanonized the established genres of the previous century: "classical music, ballet, and architecture, realistic theater, and didactic painting" (Stites 1992, 65). The ballet's new prominence in the Stalin era substantiated Sollertinsky's 1933 assertion that the ballet had fulfilled a consistent class function (demonstrating the splendor and magnificence of the regime) since the sixteenth century (323–24).

By 1935, when Stalin declared that life had become better, happier, and by 1936, when French fashion magazines appeared on the Soviet market (and the USSR boasted of surpassing France in the production of perfume) (Kelly and Volkov 296), the ballet's aristocratic (French) roots could scarcely have presented serious ideological difficulties to a regime that allowed, if not actually promoted, consumerism and the luxuries of the class it had once ridiculed. The campaign for *kul'turnost'* was relatively short-lived (the war soon focused other priorities), yet it provided the ballet enough breathing space to construct an ideology of its own—preferably, one sufficiently pliant and durable to weather the ideological storms of the future.

SYMPHONISM AND ITS IMPLICATIONS

At the time of Russian ballet historian Vera Krasovskaya's death in 1999, the *New York Times* called her "the dean of Russian ballet historians and a ballet writer who was highly respected in the West" (Dunning 1999). Later in the obituary, the writer allows that only one of Krasovskaya's books had been published in English, and that it received mixed reviews. Krasovskaya's histories of Russian and Western European dance were never translated. On what, then, was the considerable authority Western dance writers accorded Krasovskaya based?

Apart from *Nijinsky* (1979), there is very little: the catalog of the New York Public Library's Dance Collection lists a long essay on Shakespeare adaptations for dance (1991) and essays on Soviet ballet (1966) and on Balanchine's *Apollo* (1968). "Marius Petipa and *The Sleeping Beauty*," the only substantive article from that list to be published in English, appeared in *Dance Perspectives* in 1972 in a translation by Cynthia Read. The article, which dance scholars continue to reference, was one of the first English-language articles by a Russian scholar to convey reliable information on the composition of the Petipa ballet.[18] Moreover, the article lent a kind of scholarly confirmation to something the English-speaking dance world well knew: as Krasovskaya put it, "*The Sleeping Beauty* became the acme of nineteenth-century symphonic ballet" (1972, 20).

More important than the place *Sleeping Beauty* might hold in some imagined pantheon of ballets, Krasovskaya's article opened an English-language window into a set of operations that canonized *Beauty* in Russia and selected the ballet, in beauty contest fashion, to represent Russian nineteenth-century ballet and embody its virtues (or at least, the edifice of values then being constructed for it). The translation of Krasovskaya's article acquainted readers with a new designation for those ballets: they were "symphonic." And whatever symphonic might mean when applied to dance, *Sleeping Beauty* was to function as this scheme's exemplar. The article thus represents a kind of English-language introduction to Soviet constructed knowledge of *Sleeping Beauty* in particular and the nineteenth-century ballet in general.[19] What exactly is "symphonic ballet"? Krasovskaya doesn't say, as though the term needed neither introduction nor explanation, though the weight Krasovskaya places on symphonism suggests that the concept is central to the understanding of the history of dance: "The symphonic ballet of the twentieth century is like a tree with a sturdy trunk and many branches. Its roots stretch into the nineteenth century, to the ballet theatre of Russia and the work of Marius Petipa" (1972, 6).[20]

Composer and musicologist Boris Asafiev's 1922 essay on *Sleeping Beauty* marks the debut of the term "symphonism" in the reams of Soviet-era prose devoted to the work.[21] His essay follows a convoluted appreciation of symphonism in *Tchaikovsky's Instrumental Works*, also from 1922. Yet even before Asafiev deploys the term "symphonism" in the *Sleeping Beauty* essay, the author leaves an important clue to the term's actual meaning in Soviet dance writing: "a great composer at the height of his career, could not have written simple ballet music" (1954, 175).

Ivan Sollertinsky's 1933 history of prerevolutionary Russian ballet provides further clues to the uses of the term in the interwar period. For Sollertinsky, the scene of the Shades in *Bayadère* and the dances of the swans in *Swan Lake* "moved beyond purely decorative [dance] composition into the realm of something approaching dance symphonism" (326, 328), though Sollertinsky maintains that "the symphonic development of the internal musical action, the orchestration, etc.,—didn't interest Petipa" (328). Already the salient features of the doctrine of symphonism are in place. First, symphonism is not "simple," and it may be distinguished from the dance music of an earlier era. Second, dance symphonism bears some relation to the structures of the "symphonic" works it accompanies.

In *Music and Musical Life in Soviet Russia,* Boris Schwarz describes the unprecedented yet undeniable allure of symphonic music for Soviet composers (where nineteenth-century Russian composers displayed a marked preference for program music). By the 1930s, symphonism—or, more precisely, Soviet Symphonism—"acquired a slogan-like significance," according to Schwarz (158–59). Bogdanov-Berezovsky offered a highly revealing interpretation of the term as understood in 1937: "Symphony as a genre is nothing but a sonata for orchestra. . . . Symphonism, on the other hand, is the definition of a creative method, a definite procedure for the development of musical material. . . . Symphonism as a principle, as a means of musical representation and of concrete reality in the highest philosophical categories, is becoming the leading and dominant method of the Soviet composer, independent of the genres and forms he uses" (quoted in Schwarz 159).[22] Now regarded as a method, a procedure, a principle, and a means, it is scarcely surprising that symphonism no longer possessed any strictly musical meaning. Nor should it surprise us that this musical term, slipped from its semantic moorings, would soon function as a floating signifier for the dance. Like a deflating balloon, the more ideological weight was applied to the concept of symphonism, the more formless and malleable the term become.

By 1944, Asafiev could write: "Soviet symphonism is our pride, for only in our great land did symphonic music not lose itself . . . did not squander itself . . . in eccentric experiments. . . . The West lives only in the memory of great symphonists and performs the past monuments of glorious symphonies" (quoted in Schwarz 76). The Soviet preference for large-scale "absolute" musical works thus parallels pride in maintaining the full-length narrative ballet (at a time when large-scale musical and dance forms were mostly jettisoned in the West). "Side by side with the 'absolute' concept of the symphony, Soviet composers were using the large-scale form for ideological or topical purposes," Schwarz writes (ibid.). The practice of adding text to a musical composition became so widespread that Shostakovich grumbled, "add a verse—that's 'content'; no verse, that's 'formalism'" (ibid.).

These articles from the 1920s and 1930s set the tone for most subsequent Soviet scholarship of Tchaikovsky and Petipa, including Krasovskaya's. But by the time of Tchaikovsky's ascension to the semiofficial position of Soviet composer laureate in the World War II years, an additional tenet defined the doctrine of symphonism: Tchaikovsky's inability to compose anything but masterpieces. As Sollertinsky's remarks might suggest, Petipa did not fare as well as his native-born collaborator. Although the choreographer occasionally approached the holy grail of symphonism in his dances, he did so unwittingly, to the minds of Soviet critics, and could not be said to participate in the creation of "symphonic" dances until his fateful artistic meeting with Tchaikovsky.

SOVIET PARLANCE

The obvious conservatism of the balletomane critics reviewing *Sleeping Beauty* in 1890 made it easy for Soviet commentators to turn their predecessors' anti-symphonic argument on its head—to transform the pejorative "symphonicism" into the positive "symphonism" and lambaste reactionaries in the process. When Soviet writers used the term "symphonism" to describe the Russian ballet's late nineteenth-century acquaintance with "symphonic" music, they used the writings of the *Peterburgskaya gazeta* columnist (who admitted his preference for "transparent, light, and gracious" ballet music) and his colleagues to demonstrate the philistinism of the old balletomanes. Yet in accomplishing this lexical handstand, Soviet dance writing soon leached the term of any meaning.

Like the former Imperial Theaters, the (perceived) symphonism of Tchaikovsky's ballet acquired academic status in the 1920s. The musicologist, composer, and music critic Boris Asafiev advanced this view in his appreciations of Tchaikovsky's music. The terms "symphonic" and "symphonism" dot Asafiev's article on *Sleeping Beauty,* which attempts to "come to know the work from a comprehensive point of view, its importance, value, brilliance, significance, and vitality" (1954, 175): "The art of Russian ballet, under the leadership of the genius Petipa at the time of *Sleeping Beauty's* creation, already demanded symphonic music to express choreographic concepts, not just to accompany dances and action with rude rhythmic melodies or, rather, dance formulas with wretched melodic, harmonic, and instrumental dress" (175–76).

Asafiev initiated another trend in his writings on *Sleeping Beauty:* rather than define symphonism, he only condescends to outline its antonyms. Decades later, Yulia Rozanova's *On Symphonism in Tchaikovsky's Ballet* Sleeping Beauty (1965) opens with a similar précis of what symphonism is not: "In Russian ballet before Tchaikovsky, music traditionally played a supportive, purely functional role. Most often, music supplied a specific rhythmic scheme, accompanying and organizing the dance. In it, one found the measure, tempo, and accents corresponding to the rhythm of the dance movements" (3). Denunciations of Tchaikovsky's predecessors follow. The music of Cesare Pugni possesses "low artistic worth" according to Rozanova, who reminds her reader that Musorgsky termed Pugni a "musical Scythian" (3–4).[23]

Asafiev's remarks set the stage for wordy appreciations of Tchaikovsky's considerable achievements in the ballet theater, and "symphonism" becomes Soviet shorthand for them. In the Asafiev quote above, and in scores of other Soviet writings on *Sleeping Beauty* and ballet in general, the term "symphonism" carries no literal or denotative meaning. Instead, it serves as a floating signifier to indicate nothing more than the presence of an absence: the lack of "bad" ballet music. Boris Schwarz reports a similar absurdity in discussions of Soviet music in the 1930s: "the term Soviet Symphonism acquired a sloganlike significance, it became a rallying point and revealed the crisis condition of the Soviet symphony" (159). Six decades after Asafiev, Viktor Vanslov in his definition of symphonic dance in the 1981 Soviet *Ballet Encyclopedia* goes further than any other writer in elucidating the term's actual usage or meaning, though he offers no examples of the vague phenomenon: "Symphonic dance is a term that refers to dance that is similar to symphonic music. Their similarity is expressed in the poetic abstraction of the lyrical-dramatic content, the polyphonic structure, the thematic treatment, and the dynamic composition of the forms" ("Symphonic dance").[24] Much as any precise definition of dance symphonism seemed less important than what the term did *not* imply, the denigration of Tchaikovsky's predecessors points to a more important concern of Soviet dance writers: anxiety over the ballet's lowly position in the aesthetic hierarchy.

ELEVATING TASTE

The Soviet obsession with the "symphonization" of dance speaks volumes about the ballet's perceived status on the eve of the revolution. It likewise reveals the degree of anxiety concerning the inferiority of its music. Still, Tchaikovsky's involvement with the ballet, and with *Sleeping Beauty* in particular, provided the means to elevate the lower genre—once certain interpretive operations were put into place. To Rozanova's mind, the potential for the symphonization of dance lay nascent in the pas d'action, the danced "action scenes" that forward the plot of a narrative ballet. As if reading the composer's mind, Rozanova writes: "Tchaikovsky saw his main goal not in the composition of separate numbers, but in the creation of music against which the deep, full content of the ballet spectacle could unfold, in the enrichment of music to the achievements of operatic and symphonic dramaturgy" (21). As a result, "classical dance stopped being a series of beautiful poses and movements designed to show off the virtuosity of its exponents" (ibid.). To extrapolate, the ballet's appeal would extend beyond the old "diamond row" to the more democratic public of the gallery. Rozanova continues: "in this sense, one could speak of the classical dance of *Sleeping Beauty* as pas d'action" (ibid.).[25] Perhaps Rozanova wishes to endow the ballet's set pieces with the "poetic abstraction of the lyrical-dramatic content" Vanslov hints at. Unfortunately, the exact meanings of both authors are left for us to decide.

Soviet writers on dance were understandably eager to seize upon Tchaikovsky's edifying role in the "elevation" of a problematic genre, though the success of their endeavor is hardly decisive. Unlike others who write of symphonism in Tchaikovsky's ballets, Rozanova gives concrete examples, comparing musical examples from the ballet to snippets of the composer's symphonies. Yet in doing so, she exposes the fundamental weakness of her thesis: the juxtaposi-

tion merely reifies the implicit hierarchy of genres, since the strength of the ballet music can only be judged with reference to "real" symphonic music. According to this model, dance would be measured by—as well as against—its
music. This quandary was hardly unique to Soviet studies of ballet music. Carolyn Abbate sees a similar problem in the discussion of what she terms a "Wagnerian myth," the opera as symphony: "Perhaps most troubling are the asper-
sions that use of the phrase symphonic opera casts upon opera itself. The phrase
passes judgment on the relationship of music to the poem and the drama with
which the music must coexist, belittling both the poetic and the dramatic com-
ponent" (1989, 95).

The argument for the ballet's symphonization possesses striking vitality
nonetheless. As recently as 2000, the introduction to a volume devoted to
choreographer Alexander Gorsky deftly sketched the main points of the symphonism argument:

> The basic accomplishment in the evolution of Russian ballet in the second half of the
> nineteenth century lay in the fact that it elevated itself to the level of figurative
> thought in the forms of abstract dance. From the 1860s to the 1880s, still incapable of
> following literature and visual art—in taking up the path to critical realism to ex-
> press the contemporary in forms of life itself, and to give it social meaning—ballet
> stood apart from the problems of the time. But by the 1890s, in alliance with sym-
> phonic music, ballet found new means to express the manifestations of spiritual life
> common to all mankind. And in doing so, proved as capable of grappling with the
> same problems as other art forms. . . .
>
> It was in St. Petersburg, in the 1890s in ballets to music of P. I. Tchaikovsky with
> choreography of Petipa that expressive dance found support in symphonic music.
> (Surits 2000, 9–10)

In the same way that nineteenth-century "civic" criticism entreated literature
to address some moral, philosophical, or social problem, this view of ballet history assigns the ballet (retroactively) a task: to elevate itself.

THE PROBLEMATIC SYMPHONIST

As Surits' quote demonstrates, Tchaikovsky and his compositions served as
linchpins of the symphonism argument. Yet Tchaikovsky, the sentimental ho-
mosexual, would seem an unlikely choice for symphonist laureate of the Union
of Soviet Socialist Republics in heroic times. Even so, a semiofficial status was
conferred on the composer by 1941. In Stalin's report of 6 November (to mark
the twenty-fourth anniversary of the Great October Socialist Revolution),

Glinka and Tchaikovsky were included among the names of distinguished figures of the Russian nation. According to the editor of Asafiev's collected works, the designation "inspired Asafiev to undertake new research on the work of these great Russian composers" (Protopopov 12).[26] Asafiev's 1943 article "The Great Russian Composer" begins:

> The fifty years that have passed since the death of Tchaikovsky have not diminished the viability of his music. The music, as always, stirs and inspires its performers and audiences. Now, in the years of the majestic feats of the mighty Red Army, fighting under the wise leadership of the leader of nations Stalin, the music of Tchaikovsky is understood by all in the nation as native, precious property, for in it is the spring of heartfelt warmth and the deepest sympathy for people. It therefore sounds just as welcome and is heard with an open heart by everyone, because the talented place that the music of Tchaikovsky still holds in the entire world belongs to him naturally. Tchaikovsky long ago became a composer for all nations. (1954, 17)

Tchaikovsky's music was the centerpiece of Asafiev's prodigious scholarly output, and Asafiev's main work on *Sleeping Beauty* ("*Sleeping Beauty*," from the series "Letters on Russian Opera and Ballet," published in the *Weekly of the Petrograd State Theaters* in 1922) focused almost exclusively on the symphonism of *Sleeping Beauty* and the composer's role in elevating the genre. As described by the editor of Asafiev's collected works, "B. V. Asafiev discusses *Sleeping Beauty* as a symphonically developed musical work that elevates classical ballet to an exceptional artistic height. At the basis of the analysis of Tchaikovsky's brilliant ballet, Asafiev creates his theory of the musical form of the ballet, synthesizing the most important principles of symphonism in the ballet" (Asafiev 1954, 363).

A volume published in 1941, *P. I. Tchaikovsky on the Stage of the Theater of Opera and Ballet Named in Honor of S. M. Kirov (the Former Maryinsky)* commemorates Tchaikovsky's ascension to the pantheon of Soviet art: "Tchaikovsky was the founder and forefather of the musically dramatized and symphonized ballet. After him, the ballet music that was fertilized by his creativity received an intense and rich development. An entire line of important composers turned to the ballet, as to a new and noble arena, perhaps closer even to pure symphonism than the opera, connected to words and songs that lead away from scenic-instrumental construction. . . . The very principle of the symphonization of ballet, led first and creatively justified by Tchaikovsky, strengthened the quality of the main guiding principle of ballet music creation" (Bogdanov-Berezovsky 258–59).

Neither Soviet enthusiasm for elevating the ballet as a genre or exploiting

Tchaikovsky's alleged symphonism would seem peculiar were it not for the fact that Tchaikovsky's reputation as a symphonist outside Russia neatly opposes the Soviet view. Western musicologists have long used the composer's symphonies to argue *against* his genius. Richard Taruskin has painstakingly documented the degree to which Tchaikovsky's oeuvre has been exoticized almost out of the Western canon. Addressing the monumental study of the composer by David Brown, Taruskin writes: "The composer's environment, taste and education notwithstanding, Brown works hard to deduce the essentials of Tchaikovsky's musical style from 'pure folksong,' the unmediated musical mirror of 'the Russian mind.' Tchaikovsky, it is categorically asserted, was 'endowed with a mind of this nature.' His musical style was innate, biologically determined, and there was nothing the poor man could do about it. Brown dramatically posits the existence of an unbridgeable gap between 'Russian instinct' and 'Western method,' the latter as categorically and reductively conceived as the former" (1995b). As Taruskin demonstrates, Western musicology did not welcome Tchaikovsky to its club of proper symphonists:

> Citing Tchaikovsky's often agonized self-criticism—something the composer had in common with most master craftsmen, after all, and particularly with the hyper canonical Brahms—Brown sympathetically observes that "as a symphonist he did himself less than justice, for a composer who could show so much resourcefulness in modifying sonata structure so as to make it more compatible with the type of music nature had decreed he should write was no helpless bungler." And yet: "What we experience in the finest classical expositions is not just a modulation but a process of controlled tonal dynamism. Such a command of tonal growth was utterly beyond Tchaikovsky, and this alone would have denied him the symphonic mastery of a Beethoven."
>
> You won't find "controlled tonal dynamism" or "tonal growth" in any musical dictionary, nor are they defined by Brown. They are ad hoc terms of exclusion. (ibid.)

Brown's pronouncements are gratifying in their predictability: even Beethoven, the touchstone of canonical symphonism is invoked. Yet Brown's view of the composer could not contradict the Soviet one more sharply. It seems appropriate, then, that both Russia and the West rely on "ad hoc terms of exclusion" to attack and defend Tchaikovsky. Russian critics cite Tchaikovsky's symphonism to denigrate his predecessors and elevate the ballet by association. Conversely, Western musicologists have painted with a slighter broader palette to differentiate Tchaikovsky from canonical symphonists and lump him with ballet composers.

CANONIZING BEAUTY

The 1920s: Asafiev and Lopukhov

Boris Asafiev (who wrote often under the pseudonym Igor Glebov) leans heavily on the concept of symphonism in his discussion of Tchaikovsky's music for *Sleeping Beauty*. For Asafiev, the genius of the ballet lay in the "strata of sounds" that "create a unity of impressions" (1954, 176). In another of Asafiev's works from 1922, the writer elaborated on his understanding of symphonism: "Although this stream of sound is perceived in a row of changing sound alliances in time, it is conceived as a stopping point in the condition of sound, or, to force the point, a passage through a sphere of sound, out of place and time" (1922, 7). The passage demonstrates the similarity of Asafiev's argument to those describing Wagner's symphonism: "For Wagner, the symphonic was a continuous spinning-out of never-ceasing thematic webs. For us, the term "symphonic" might also mean periodic phrases, tonal coherence, rhythmic urgency. But for us 'symphonic' has a metaphorical meaning as well: a symphonic work is one that is densely interconnected, that evolves organically to its final moments, that is comprehensible as pure music" (Abbate 1989, 115). Asafiev's notion of symphonism thus resembles a familiar argument from his time: a continuous musical development in a work without set pieces, a quasi-Wagnerian notion of continual action without the stops and starts: "In sum: in defining the given music as symphonic, or more accurately, as being satiated with symphonism, we comprehend it in its entirety, unbroken in the given sphere of sound. In other words, in the composition, the stream of sound that moves in the row of changing (but nonetheless linked) musical conceptions, attract us ceaselessly from center to center, from achievement to achievement—to the limits of completeness. In this way, symphonism suggests itself to us as an unbroken musical . . . understanding, when no single element is perceived or understood by us to be independent among many others" (1922, 7).

Returning to *Beauty*, Asafiev maintains that the ballet's dance formulas are "complicated and deepened" by their transformation in this symphonic development (1954, 177). The meter of the dance formula is subordinated, the dance formula (the suite) is suppressed "in the interests of a higher rhythmic and intonational whole" (ibid.): "A waltz formula, taken as such (as a dance) gives one impression. But if the same formula lies at the heart of the rhythm of the whole work . . . it has quite another effect" (178). To illustrate the point, Asafiev contrasts Aurora's first-act variation, in waltz time, to the more conventional (and recognizable) waltz of the first act (the Garland Dance). In the first example, the variation is "based on music that depends on the waltz formula but doesn't appear as a waltz" (ibid.). The second waltz is "just" a waltz.

Lopukhov's discussion of dance symphonism appeared three years later in a collection of essays titled *Paths of a Balletmaster* (1925), which is divided into three parts. The first, "The Evolution of Choreography," leads to chapters on the dance-symphony and dance symphonism. The second section explores the relation of dance to music, while the third explores character dancing. In his chapter on dance symphonism, Lopukhov begins by noting: "Very often, especially recently, voices are raised that it is necessary to symphonize dance, that this is the natural path to its further development" (54). Lopukhov expresses dismay that none of those who advocate for the symphonization of dance ever bother to explain it (did he have Asafiev in mind?),[27] then praises recent attempts to symphonize dance, "for purely symphonic music is the highest form of musical art, to which dance art has not yet ascended" (ibid.).

Lopukhov's arguments are familiar ones, and not only for the usual admission of inferiority vis-à-vis music. Alongside the usual rebukes of "assorted" dance movements, Lopukhov locates the key to the symphonization of dance in the elaboration of choreographic themes, much as a symphony develops musical themes:

> How can symphonism be expressed in dance, either in a variation, a whole act, a ballet, or a dance-symphony? It can only happen when the choreography of all the dances, whether small variations or an entire ballet—not to mention a dance-symphony—are based on the principles of choreographic-thematic elaboration and not on a chance assortment of dance movements, even if they are performed in rhythm with the music. If the staging of a little variation or a large ballet is derived from the principles of choreographic thematic development, then it will contain the essence of danced symphonism (54–55). . . .
>
> Thus, the staging of dances might be unsymphonic despite the fact that it is performed to symphonic music if it is built on a chaotic distribution of dance movements. . . . The ideal of choreographic creation is the close contact between musical and dance symphonism. (57)

However much Tchaikovsky's music (and *Sleeping Beauty* in particular) confounded ballet fans in the 1890s, Lopukhov's writing demonstrates to what extent the composer's "symphonicist" ballet signaled a paradigm shift in the appreciation and use of music for dance for decades to come. (Certainly the influence of the Diaghilev ballet was felt as well, given the quantity of "concert" music borrowed or commissioned for his company's ballets.) Lopukhov's enthusiasm for symphonizing dance led him to formulas that today seem dogmatic and even primitive (turned-out movement to match major keys; turned-in movement for minor keys, as an example). Nonetheless, Lopukhov well understood the basic differences between nineteenth-century choreography (which treated primarily the melody and rhythmic structures of a score) and a more sophisticated approach to more complex music (responding to less obvious musical structures). As dance-makers in Russia began to look beyond the ballet to rejuvenate the art form, Lopukhov's approach not only presaged a general direction of ballet choreography in the twentieth century, it suggested the possibility of reform from within by looking fixedly at the relation of movement and music.

The Problem with Petipa

Three decades after the first publication of Asafiev's article, Vera Krasovskaya published her influential *Russian Ballet Theater in the Second Half of the Nineteenth Century* (1963). Her writing on *Sleeping Beauty* demonstrates that the discussion of the ballet's alleged symphonism had taken on a life of its own by that time and ventured far from Asafiev's analytic approach. (The appearance of Yulia Rozanova's *On Symphonism in Tchaikovsky's Ballet Sleeping Beauty* two years later made this clear.)[28] By the 1960s, symphonism proved a surprisingly content-free designation, though one that served Krasovskaya's purposes well. In her discussion of *Sleeping Beauty*, she cites parallels between the ballet and the structure of a symphony: four acts, like symphonic movements, that could exist independently but whose value can be fully realized only in terms of its relation to the whole (1963, 298): "Aurora's and Désiré's apotheosis of love was also the apotheosis achieved by Tchaikovsky and Petipa in the symphonic formulation of dance" (1963, 310).

To judge from Sollertinsky's and Lopukhov's appraisals of Petipa's musicality, Petipa scarcely kept up with the composer in the ecstatic pas de deux Krasovskaya describes. Authors writing in the 1920s and 1930s find faults in Petipa's choreography to Tchaikovsky's music. Sollertinsky assured his readers that Petipa responded to Tchaikovsky and Glazunov just as he had to the ballet composers of an earlier time: "In the exquisite score of *Sleeping Beauty*, he took only those things that attracted him from before in Minkus and Pugni: the same metrical-rhythmic canvas. . . . The culmination points and the grandiose expansion in the orchestra, for example, are frequently not accented choreographically in any way, and vice versa" (328). Although always averring his faithfulness to the master choreographer, Lopukhov disparages Petipa's composition on similar grounds.

At various points in her writing, Krasovskaya suggests, as Asafiev had before her, that Petipa aspired to better things choreographically (1954, 175–76); Sollertinsky was never so optimistic. Krasovskaya's 1972 article ends with lavish praise for *Beauty*, suggesting the ballet as a reward for the choreographer's diligence and hard work: "*Sleeping Beauty*, the strongest and most perfect of Petipa's works, sums up the choreographer's long, difficult, persistent search for ballet symphonism" (1972, 50). Yet in the beginning of the same article, she portrays him as a docile servant taking orders: "A practicing musician and a good judge of music, Petipa had studied at the Brussels Conservatory along with the famous violinist Henri Vieuxtemps. Faithful to the traditions of the past, however, he recognized music as playing only a subsidiary role in a balletic spectacle; that is, until orders from his superiors led him to collaborate with great composers" (1972, 6). Already, the picture of Petipa is clouded. Although he was a musician and "good judge" of music, Krasovskaya suggests that Petipa remained reactionary in his use of music—at least until "ordered" to collaborate with "great" (read "symphonic") composers. Like other Soviet writers, Krasovskaya sketches conflicting images of Petipa: part court lackey, part genius choreographer.[29]

Petipa finds himself in double jeopardy in Krasovskaya's account. His "faithfulness to the past" paints him a reactionary; and while it is true that Petipa used "nonsymphonic" music to accompany his dances, so did other choreographers of his day—and later. Yet when Petipa joins forces with Tchaikovsky, and later with Glazunov, he gets no credit either. He merely follows orders, according to Krasovskaya, and the laurels for the invention of dance symphonism are passed to a native son: "[*Sleeping Beauty*] may also be seen to sum up the whole path of the choreographic art in the nineteenth century—as the discoveries made by Lev Ivanov in *Swan Lake* appear as the great 'breakthrough' into the twentieth century" (1972, 50).

Petipa's crime was his nationality. If the ideology of Krasovskaya's writing can be filtered out, the chauvinism that was part of the official Soviet myth proves more difficult to screen.[30] The foreword to *Russian Ballet Theater of the Second Half of the Nineteenth Century* begins: "This book is dedicated to Russian ballet theater of the second half of the nineteenth century—an independent and conclusive stage in the history of national choreography" (3). Although Russian ballet in the nineteenth century was a crossroads of French, Italian, Danish, and Russian traditions and influences, Krasovskaya depicts the century as a long drive to finally seize "Russian" ballet for the Russians. The export of the Diaghilev company to Europe at the end of this historical process (when the superiority of Russian ballet was finally "proved") serves as a justification for such a decidedly nationalist point of view.

The chauvinism of Krasovskaya and other Soviet writers remains in the background for discussions of Petipa, whose accomplishments, nitpicking aside, are mostly appreciated. When the subject is Lev Ivanov, however, a strident Russian nationalism comes to the fore. Krasovskaya views the cosmopolitanism of the Russian ballet in the late nineteenth century chiefly as a hindrance for the locals: "In the hospitable family of the Petersburg ballet, where Frenchmen and Italians, Germans and Swedes, Poles and Hungarians all acclimated themselves, the Russian dancer had the most difficult time of all advancing" (1963, 338). Krasovskaya provides no evidence for her allegations but remains consistent in assigning credit for the discovery of Ivanov's latent genius to his homegrown collaborator: "The lyrical gift of Ivanov was discovered unexpectedly: and only thanks to the music of Tchaikovsky" (ibid.).

Petipa's Quest for Symphonism

Like a mythical hero on a quest for symphonism (if indeed he was questing and not passively taking orders), Petipa first had to come into contact with the "music of high quality" (1972, 16) according to Krasovskaya's account. He used music from Delibes' *La Source* in his 1868 version of *Le Corsaire* and Mendelssohn's incidental music for his 1876 staging of *Midsummer Night's Dream* (where he interpolated music of Minkus amongst the Mendelssohn). "It was as if the choreographer were preparing himself for the meeting with Tchaikovsky and Glazunov," writes Krasovskaya, "when the dance and the music had to fuse into a single body of poetic images" (1972, 14).

Even so, Petipa's path did not lead directly to *Sleeping Beauty* or *Raymonda*. "Six months after *A Midsummer Night's Dream,* Petipa produced *La Bayadère,* a ballet to music of Minkus [!] that nonetheless 'reached the heights of dance symphonism,'" according to Krasovskaya (1972, 18). "Even before in his experience of the symphonization of ballet, Petipa gradually approached the formulation of the task that Tchaikovsky now set out clearly. Combining large dance layers, blending characteristic themes in interaction and struggle, he in many ways intuitively sensed one of the most important artistic problems of the nineteenth-century ballet spectacle. The most convincing of these attempts of this type was the Shades scene of *La Bayadère*" (1963, 297).

Krasovskaya's reliance on the Shades scene in an argument for symphonism reveals the degree to which use of the term had devolved in the Soviet era. The scene amply demonstrates Petipa's genius and mastery of the art form, but the key to the success of the scene lies in simplicity, not in sophistication. Where Asafiev had used the term to describe the subordination and transformation of dance structures into a more unified whole, and Lopukhov aspired to choreographic polyphony, Krasovskaya assigns the term to one of the nineteenth-century ballet's most famously monophonic dance and music sequences.

Minkus develops the Shades theme only slightly, and Petipa responds to Minkus' minimalism with a single movement motif. The first dancer appears in arabesque, then leans back, takes three steps forward, and on the repetition of the movement, another dancer appears to perform the same movement phrase. The phrase repeats thirty-two times, until the entire corps de ballets has entered, one by one.[31] The deserved fascination with this stunningly simple formal structure rests in the limpid beauty of both the musical and dance phrases and in the correspondence between the musical and choreographic phrases. As the corps de ballet enters the stage, one by one, performing identical choreography, the dance and the music lend the desired sense of timeless and infinity to the scene.

The music and choreography of the Shades scene create their effect by accumulation and mass, rather than through the complex layering of dance motifs that Petipa exploited successfully in other ensembles (notably, the "Jardin animée" in *Le Corsaire*). The substance of the music and choreography could be conveyed by one dancer and a pan flute. Nonetheless, Krasovskaya names *Bayadère*, "a ballet that reached the heights of dance symphonism" (1972, 18). If this scene, and other pre-Tchaikovsky stagings anticipate the "symphonic development of a mass choreographic image" (1972, 14), these set pieces scarcely suggest either a subordination of themselves into a greater whole (Asafiev's argument) or the choreographic polyphony Lopukhov sees in the coda of the vision scene in *Sleeping Beauty* or the coda of the Shades scene in *Bayadère*.

Moreover, Krasovskaya remains troubled by the same mismatches of plot to music that bothered Sollertinsky: "Despite the external splendors of the productions of *Sleeping Beauty* and *Raymonda*, both contain innumerable 'blunders' relating to the action of the music. For example, culmination points and grand crescendos in the orchestra are often not accented at all choreographically, and vice versa" (328). Krasovskaya elaborates: "Of course, the dramatic structure of this symphonic ballet is by no means identical with the structure of the symphony. It has its own internal rules, its own principles of development: their selection and realization were an important part of Petipa's experimentation, and Tchaikovsky was aware of this. Nevertheless, the form of *The Sleeping Beauty* is closer to that of a symphony than a drama. While completely subordinated to the development of the plot, the ballet's dramatic structure occasionally displaces the climaxes of the plot, finding its own logical and emotional high points" (1972, 24).

As an example, the "culmination of the plot" in the first act of *Sleeping Beauty* is when Aurora pricks her finger, while the choreographic high point is the Rose Adagio (1972, 24). The culmination of the second act comes when Désiré kisses and wakes Aurora, "however, in the music and the choreography these episodes do not appear central" (1972, 24).

In *Sleeping Beauty* and other works, Petipa typically avoids these obvious correspondences, choosing to adorn grand musical climaxes with the simplest movements, or pantomime. The narrative structure of *Sleeping Beauty* necessitates the approach: the most dramatic moments in the ballet (Aurora's death and awakening, for example) do not lend themselves to choreographic fantasy or grand ballabiles, and the latter (the peasant waltz, for example) are usually accompanied by the least symphonic music in the score (by Asafiev's own definition). On the subject of the nineteenth-century ballet composer's awareness of the special relationship of music to dance, Roland John Wiley wrote:

> Complementing the specialist's sensitivity to the visual was [Tchaikovsky's] awareness that the aural attractions of concert music could be defects in ballet. He attempted to adjust the level of inherent musical interest at any given moment to enhance the choreography, and realized that any competition of eye and ear for the audience's attention risked the weakening or loss of a desired effect. This procedure tends to produce in a ballet an inverse relationship between interest in music and interest in dance, whereby music makes its strongest impact when solo dance is the least commanding, and vice versa. The climatic moments of pure music and pure dance almost never coincide, a fact which should give pause to the analyst who seeks to judge ballet music only for its sounds. (1985, 6)

In their search for formulas, graphable climaxes, and symphonism, both Krasovskaya and Sollertinsky disregard Petipa's skill as a theatrical director, his unerring instinct for stepping back to let his composer have his moment (much as Tchaikovsky deliberately recedes, in Wiley's view). Had Petipa resolved to coincide his climactic moments with those of the plot (the spindle prick, the kiss) a strange ballet would have resulted. The small-scale human gestures on which a dramatic plot must inevitably turn would scarcely support the set pieces that function as Petipa's choreographic climaxes: the fairies' pas de six, the peasants' waltz, Aurora's meeting with her suitors, Désiré's encounter with the vision of Aurora, or their adagio in the final act. Though no Soviet critic would say so, the choreographic culminations of Petipa's ballet, listed above, essentially function as abstract dances within the ballet. If abstraction was a taboo concept in Soviet theater, the argument for symphonism took the ballet on a lower road leading to a similar destination.[32]

Krasovskaya's text ends with a favorite provocation: "[*Sleeping Beauty*] may also be seen to sum up the whole path of the choreographic art in the nineteenth century—as the discoveries made by Lev Ivanov in *Swan Lake* appear as the great 'breakthrough' into the twentieth century" (1972, 50). Thus, despite the relentless claims she has already made for *La Bayadère* ("a ballet that reached the heights of dance symphonism" [18]) and *Sleeping Beauty* ("the acme of nineteenth-century symphonic ballet" [20]), Krasovskaya implies that the branch of nineteenth-century symphonic ballet that will stretch into the twentieth century extends not from Marius Petipa, but from Lev Ivanov.

In *Russian Ballet Theater of the Second Half of the Nineteenth Century,* Krasovskaya's thoughts on *Beauty* are further developed, and Petipa is granted a kind of honorary Russian citizenship for his role in the choreography of *Sleeping Beauty.* Tchaikovsky's national, symphonic music saved Russian ballet from the fate of its Western counterpart (the French *féerie*). Twisting Laroche's famous observation ("the local color is French, but the *style* is Russian" [310]) beyond recognition or plausibility, Krasovskaya continues: "the composer created stage music that is unarguably Russian, deeply national in its style. And that is no surprise: the entire creative path of Tchaikovsky increasingly defined him as a Russian national artist" (311). Apparently, this nascent nationalism motivated even Petipa, according to Krasovskaya: "the entire musical/choreographic structure of *Sleeping Beauty* was deeply Russian" (ibid.).

A feature film released shortly after Krasovskaya's history appeared illustrates the acceptance of this view well beyond a small coterie of dance writers. A French-Russian coproduction, *Third Youth: Marius Petipa in Petersburg* was released by Lenfilm in 1965 (and by Lenfilm Video in 2000). The film opens with a shot of the Maryinsky Theater circa 1965. The camera pans to a kiosk advertising the evening's performance of *Sleeping Beauty.* The voice-over promises to take us to the evening's performance, then the camera cuts to the company dancing a portion of the ballet's finale. The voice-over continues: "and every time the wonderful music composed by Pyotr Ilyich Tchaikovsky is heard, and when the overflowing hall is enraptured by the beauty of the dances, staged by the Frenchman Marius Petipa, who became a great Russian balletmaster, I cannot help but think of one meeting, cannot help but think of the collaboration of two great artists of Russia and France."

In the film, Petipa's first meeting is not with Tchaikovsky but with a character named Minkh. An untalented drunk, who tortures the sensitive Petipa with his beer-garden tunes, Minkh is obviously meant as a composite of Ludwig Minkus and Cesare Pugni (whose music Minkh plays). After marrying a Russian wife, Petipa suddenly wishes to find new artistic devices, to reach new creative solutions; and not only as a dancer, now also as a choreographer. At the moment that Petipa decides he has become too much like Minkh (a hack) and should resign, he meets Tchaikovsky in Vsevolozhsky's office.

The film's Vsevolozhsky character suggests that the two men work together, but both fear a flop: Petipa feels he has reached the end of his creative rope; Tchaikovsky still smarts from the failure of *Swan Lake*. When they promenade together in the snowy Summer Garden, however, magical things began to happen. The movements of the soldiers, children, and young women remind Petipa of choreography. Tchaikovsky urges Petipa to think of all that he sees around him as his choreography to the composer's music. The Waltz of the Snowflakes from *Nutcracker* suddenly materializes in one corner of the park. Then the scene shifts to a more authentically Russian setting, with birch trees, troikas, and folk dancing. All of this (naturally) inspires Petipa. As the composer and choreographer part, Petipa confides that he has prepared himself to stage Tchaikovsky's music all his life.

The meeting the film portrays is historical fiction, though the authors of the film's scenario add another level of fantasy: a series of fades suggest that the meeting stretches on endlessly, in obvious imitation of the marathon, seminal meeting of Konstantin Stanislavsky and Nemirovich-Danchenko, when the two spent seventeen hours in a Moscow restaurant in 1897 discussing the formation of what would become the Moscow Art Theater (Stanislavsky 299). Here again, the attempt is made to elevate the ballet to the higher status of a recognized Russian cultural institution by embroidering its history. Petipa not only becomes a "great Russian choreographer" in the film when he arrives at the conscious decision to make better art; the viewer sees him drawing inspiration directly from ordinary Russian soldiers, children, peasants, coachmen, and birches.

By the 1970s, the Soviet stance on symphonism, Tchaikovsky, and Petipa had altered slightly. In a 1976 volume called *The Truth of Ballet,* a tract promoting "realism" in ballet (essentially a valentine to Yuri Grigorovich's *Spartacus*), Emiliya Shumilova revises the history of ballet symphonism slightly and discovers a new source for its inspiration: "The symphonic reworking of dance forms in the operas of Glinka unquestionably predetermined the appearance of the ballets of P. I. Tchaikovsky, which marked the revolutionary leap in the development of the ballet theater" (41). Soviet writers also began revising earlier criticisms of Petipa and views of his contribution to the history of Russian ballet. Galina Dobrovolskaya wrote: "Asafiev, as most of his contemporaries, regarded Petipa as one who managed to express himself within the confines of the court ballet, as a phenomenon of the past. Today we regard Asafiev's appraisal of Petipa's legacy as a mistake" (1977, 237).

Vanslov would go farther, "correcting" the literal, simplistic readings of the correspondence between music and dance begun by Sollertinsky and Lopukhov and parroted by Krasovskaya. Reading the choreography and score of the vision scene pas de deux, Vanslov writes: "Here the dance in no way serves as the rhythmic double of the melody. . . . The melody and the dance flow freely, coinciding only in supporting metrical points. They unite with the commonality of atmosphere, tempo, meter, the common drifting image, but rhythmically relatively independently, combining according to the principles of counterpoint" (1977, 23). Vanslov concludes: "Choreography and music are related internally. . . . But choreography should not become the slave of music, turning itself into a structural-rhythmic copy of music" (24). In part, this shift reflects the rising fortunes of Soviet ballet. By the 1970s, the ballet had become one of the Soviet Union's most recognizable export items, a light industry in no way inferior to Soviet music, visual arts, or theater. Anxiety over the ballet's place in the hierarchy of Soviet arts was no longer an issue.

Writing in 1933, Sollertinsky accused the prerevolutionary ballet of failing to carry its ideological weight, of not making sense. Over the next decades, the ballet would be harnessed to do just that, and no ballet from the past would prove so vital to the framing of the self-definition of Soviet ballet as *Sleeping Beauty*. The key to the rehabilitation of the ballet lay in the symphonic scores that accompanied individual works, by Tchaikovsky and Glazunov first, then by Prokofiev and other Soviet composers (including Asafiev himself). Despite its feudal court atmosphere and obvious roots in monarchical pageantry, *Sleeping Beauty* possessed the greatest of these scores. (Ironically, it was that ballet's ancien régime atmosphere that attracted the composer to the ballet.) As Tchaikovsky became the Soviet Union's favorite composing son, the ballet could be pulled along on his coattails to enjoy a new prestige as a "serious" art form, like the opera or the symphony. Nearly all the Soviet writing on *Sleeping Beauty* (and nineteenth-century ballet in general) bears out this view. To bestow highest praise on dances was to call them "symphonic"—even though the term was used essentially as a cipher.

Soviet dance writers' obsession with symphonism reveals the extent of the ballet's inferiority complex vis-à-vis other art forms. Whereas prerevolutionary writers questioned the symphonization of the ballet (though most eventually endorsed the trend), Soviet writers accepted the term unquestionably and constructed an enormous creaky monument from it. Symphonism quickly became shorthand for a process by which Tchaikovsky's reputation would be used to elevate the genre from an entertainment genre to a finer art: if the score of *Beauty* could be classed among the greatest works of the nation's most revered composer, then the art form should surely deserve the attentions of the serious Soviet and international public. Yet as Rozanova's analysis of the symphonism of *Sleeping Beauty* demonstrates, the reliance on one art form to justify another proved a dangerous game, particularly as modernism's early titillation with intermingled senses (the synaesthesia of the Diaghilev ballet, for example) gave way to the high modernist quest for purity.

Chapter 4 Red Auroras

(The Soviet Ballet in

Practice)

After the Revolution of 1917 choreographers and composers began
to work for the people. The life of simple people interested them.
The themes of ballets were the Revolution and the people. Peasants
and workers went to the theater and saw ballet for the first time.
—From Soviet language-learning materials designed for Swedish
speakers, circa 1978

In the first three tumultuous years to follow the decisive October 1917
Revolution, *Sleeping Beauty* remained the most frequently performed
full-length ballet in the repertory of the former Maryinsky Theater at
a time when revolution and civil war made conditions in the theaters
miserable.[1] During the 1919–20 season, for example, fuel shortages
left the former Imperial Theaters unheated; dancers performed in
sweaters, and ballerinas caught pneumonia. Power outages prevented
daytime rehearsals. George Balanchine, then a student in the theater
school, dined on the stray cats he caught in the street (Frame 163,
Buckle 13).[2] Even if activists for a revolutionary theater art had succeeded in formulating their plans for a new socially conscious ballet,
there would scarcely have been the means to carry them out.

The conservatism of Soviet arts bureaucrats (and Lenin) guaranteed the survival of *Sleeping Beauty* and the ballet in general in these years, but the ballet of the former Imperial Theaters faced an uncertain future. Whatever support the ballet's new "academic" status lent the art form in the 1920s (or Stalin's embrace of court spectacle would provide in the 1930s), the ballet would nonetheless be forced to modernize. Once the immediate difficulties of the civil war era had been surmounted, the theaters faced the task of developing a revolutionary repertory.

The notes of the Administration of Leningrad Academic Theaters "on the creation of works of revolutionary content" foreshadow much of the future of Soviet ballet. The committee met in 1924 to explore the reworking of three operas (Meyerbeer's *Le Prophète* and *Les Huguenots,* Wagner's *Rienzi*) and one ballet (*Sleeping Beauty*) to "solve the problem of revolutionary opera in the 1924/25 season, before the seventh anniversary of the October Revolution" (Trabsky 1975, 293).[3] The committee singled out the Petipa-Tchaikovsky work as "one of a very few ballets, written by a good master-composer, among the hundreds of others that are musically inadmissible in an academic theater" (295).[4] The committee then commissioned Nikolai Glebovich Vinogradov, head of the Studio of Monumental Theater, to rewrite the librettos of the four promising works. In doing so, the committee established two important precedents for the formation of the ballet repertory in the Soviet era: first, evidence of the general worth of a work would be furnished by its music rather than its dancing; and second, the renovation of the genre would commence with its narrative.

Vinogradov wrote: "*Sleeping Beauty* is a brilliant ballet with wonderful music by Tchaikovsky. Unfortunately, Tchaikovsky's music is so 'romantic' that it is impossible to contemplate a direct transposition to a bracing revolutionary plot that vividly communicates the proletarian revolution. Therefore it was necessary to insert a certain share of romanticism in reworking the story, which is justified by the music and by the general style of ballet art in its present state. To this end, the action of the Prologue has been moved back five hundred years, to the first uprising of the proletariat" (295).

Vinogradov's Prologue features cheerful dances of "freedom, beauty, spring, and labor" around a statue of Revolution raised by rebelling tradesmen. When knights quash the onstage revolution, they capture the uprising's leader, who is chained to the statue. An astrologer, dreaming of a sunny commune on earth, appears to the leader, convincing him to break his chains and lead a universal rebellion. The statue comes to life as Aurora, the scarlet dawn of Universal Revolution. The knights, led by a duke, engage the rebels, and Aurora falls upon one of their swords. The duke takes her away on a boat.

The leader of the uprising searches for the kidnapped Aurora and happens upon the tower of the astrologer, who shows the leader a vision of her. They go together to the Sunny Commune, as the panorama unfurls portrayals of universal labor. The reach the city "in the gold of riches, the silver flames of electrical fire and the red smoke of factories." The leader defeats the duke and his knights and ruptures the coffin containing Aurora with his torch: "in scarlet radiance and the flames of red banners, Aurora rises, the beautiful dawn of Worldwide Revolution" (295–96).

Vinogradov's version of *Beauty* never reached the stage, though the act of rewriting the ballet's libretto, recasting the work's monarchical theme in revolutionary light, signaled the future direction of the Soviet ballet: its obsession with story. This fascination with narrative culminated in the creation of a new, uniquely Soviet dance genre in the 1930s, the "*drambalet*," a conjoining (both linguistic and literal) of "drama" and "ballet." Unfortunately, the tensions evident in the numerous *Sleeping Beauty* productions of the late imperial and early Soviet era augured the failure of the new genre, as they also portended problems associated with subsequent Soviet attempts to build a repertory of full-length narrative ballets long after dance-makers in Europe and North America had mostly abandoned the nineteenth-century format.

Of the four productions of *Sleeping Beauty* (1914, 1921, 1922, and 1952) discussed in this chapter, half premiered within a tumultuous ten-year period that witnessed world war, revolutions, and civil war.[5] The final imperial production in 1914 and the first Soviet production in 1922 function as bookends to these years of unrest: the first marks the end of the Imperial Ballet's viability as Russia entered World War I; the second represents an attempt to reinstate that legacy as Russia's civil war ended and the new administration solidified its power. The 1914 Petersburg and 1921 London productions were primarily decorative reworkings of the original *Beauty;* both featured the designs of a prominent World of Art–era visual artist, whereas Lopukhov's 1922 version of the ballet signaled quite different priorities. The first restaging of *Sleeping Beauty* not supervised by Nikolai Sergeyev (the Maryinsky's former regisseur), this new edition of the ballet indicated the Soviet ballet's future curatorial priorities: Lopukhov's 1922 staging of *Sleeping Beauty* paid lip service to notions of faithfulness to the classical inheritance as it trifled with the ballet's choreography.

And if Soviet-era meddling with Petipa's choreography strikes today's reader as blasphemous, one could also argue that the interventions of Lopukhov (and later, Konstantin Sergeyev), might have saved *Sleeping Beauty* (and other works) from more radical renovations of the sort Vinogradov's Sunny Commune libretto proposed.

Like the rants of the far left, the ballet's libretto competitions and repertory indices focused doggedly on one aspect in the creation of properly Soviet ballets: their themes. (An obsession with narrative likewise distinguished much of the art in the Stalin era.) The disparity between the revolutionary desire for a new ballet with new stories and the determination of balletmasters like Lopukhov to preserve the old ones reveals a fundamental tension in the new Soviet ballet that would mark Soviet ballet production for decades to come. The balletmasters who played an active part in the creation of Soviet ballet were more likely to have spent the 1920s experimenting with new forms than theorizing about them, yet it fell to them to create new ballets and maintain (select) existing ones in the repertory.

The thirty years that passed between the 1922 and 1952 productions of *Sleeping Beauty* witnessed a war over words in the Soviet ballet. Pantomime, the ballet's conventional "language" fell out of favor, even as abstraction, or the "pure" dance that reigned in the West, became ideologically impossible. In short, Soviet choreographers had to balance their own desires to modernize the ballet against the state's desire to tell stories. Konstantin Sergeyev's 1952 production of *Sleeping Beauty* represented an apotheosis of sorts to this shaky truce.

DESIGNER PRODUCTIONS

In the late 1950s, Benois wrote that the charm of the 1890 *Beauty* vanished "after some ten or fifteen years" and described the ballet's decline in visual terms: "the decorations faded, the costumes wore out, and the masterwork fell apart" (1993, I, 606).[6] Commissioned to correct the problem in 1914, Konstantin Korovin settled on a solution that continues to appeal to designers of *Sleeping Beauties:* ignoring the careful historicism of Vsevolozhsky and his scene painters, Korovin moved the ballet into the eighteenth century with his decors, disregarding the shift in time from the first and second acts so central to the conception of the original designers. Reviews of the 1914 production, including Benois', were decidedly mixed. Reviewing Korovin's contribution again in 1922 (for Lopukhov's staging), Benois sniped that Korovin had turned *Sleeping*

Beauty into "one of those tacky, empty féeries that they serve up in London and Paris to undemanding audiences" (33–34).[7]

Lopukhov also found the new designs unsatisfactory: "K. Korovin made a mistake when he made the new decors for the Maryinsky: not understanding the essence of the Petipa's choreographic groupings, he used mixed colors in the costumes, and lessened their effect" (1971, 198).[8] Akim Volynsky complained that Korovin's conception had only one aim: "to dress everything up in faded colors. It was a basic and fatal mistake on the part of the artist" (1923).[9] Contradicting Benois' assertion that the ballet could not be reconstructed, Volynsky opined: "If the costumes of Vsevolozhsky were restored during this evolution of morals we are living through, the artist-dilletante would be in tune with contemporary life to a much greater degree than the professional artist, who, for all his talent, only succeeded in smearing everything vital and fantastic in the ballet with monotone pale colors" (ibid.).

The decision to replace the *Sleeping Beauty*'s original sets (the work of nineteenth-century academic painters) with the designs of a more fashionable easel painter (Korovin was associated with both Russia's "new" theater and the Diaghilev enterprise) reflected the new importance placed on visual design for the ballet in these years. Given that the 1890 *Sleeping Beauty* had shown the way to the Diaghilev "formula" (the heady blend of dancing, music, and design—all ostensibly of high quality—that characterized Ballets Russes productions), the 1914 redesign of the ballet represented a revenge of subalterns. Unfortunately, some felt that the Korovin production also represented a fundamental misunderstanding of the role the visuals played in the original version and how they achieved their effect: "*Sleeping Beauty* lost a significant portion of its charm in the 1914 revival. Thanks to the extremely unsuccessful decors and costumes, the enchanting fairy tale, so poetically realized to the smallest details in the original production, disappeared. The fire that glowed in the fireplace disappeared, like the grotto with the cascade, from which the Lilac Fairy emerged, as did Bocharov's divine panorama. The spider web in Aurora's bedchamber was replaced by a clumsy ivy, which grew on the outside, but not inside the castle (Leshkov, quoted in Bakhrushin 1940, 116–17)."[10]

If Korovin's designs amounted to meddling, Diaghilev's 1921 Ballets Russes production for London represented an apotheosis of the triumph of visual design in the ballet. Veteran Ballets Russes designer Leon Bakst conceived fanciful interiors in the style of the Bibienas as the setting for the ballet,[11] shifting the ballet's final settings, as Korovin had, to the eighteenth century.[12] Benois complained that in each of these attempts to redecorate the ballet, the ballet's original poetry was lost: "Korovin moved the epoch of the first part of the ballet forward by eighty years, which made the court of Florestan XXIV resemble in character the court of Louis XIII. This proved that our excellent artist and the director who had allowed him to take this liberty had failed to appreciate the chief charm of the first production. Bakst tried to correct this mistake in Diaghilev's London production of the *Sleeping Princess* in 1922 [*sic*], but instead of frankly going back to the first version he introduced too much elaboration—as was his habit—and the principal idea was again weakened and obscured. The production certainly gained in grandeur, but, as before, it lost its poetic quality" (1941, 132).

Diaghilev's London *Beauty* was meant to recreate the spirit, not the letter, of the 1890 Petipa production. Although Nikolai Sergeyev was on hand to reproduce the choreography (as he had in St. Petersburg in 1914), liberties were taken with both the choreographic and musical texts in London. Stravinsky reorchestrated some numbers; music from *The Nutcracker* was interpolated for others. Bronislava Nijinska added her own choreography, and commedia dell'arte characters appeared in the finale. Aurora's cavaliers acquired new names; the fairies lost their old ones. In short, the production became a Ballets Russes fantasy on the theme of *Sleeping Beauty.* Even if several of the collaborators in Diaghilev's *Beauty* identified the 1890 production as a turning point in their own appreciation of the ballet, and acknowledged the role the production had played in the genesis of the Ballets Russes (as Benois had), they remained more faithful to the mania for interior decoration that characterized the Ballets Russes than the preservationist mood then seizing the ballet in revolutionary Petrograd (or the Soviets' incipient interest in the ballet's story).

LOPUKHOV'S 1922–23 STAGING

If *Sleeping Beauty* remained the most performed of the full-length ballets in the former Maryinsky's repertory immediately following the 1917 Revolution, we are left to wonder what sort of performances these were. Writing of the ballet in those years, Elizaveta Surits suggests the extent of the problems the ballet faced: "It wasn't just the sets and costumes that were wearing out. Distortions crept into the text[s] as well. Cut-backs in the companies necessitated cutting down the casts for many dances. Something would be left out; something else quickly put in its place" (1979, 267). Volynsky's review of a 1923 performance of *Sleep-*

ing Beauty, starring Taisiya Troyanovskaya as Aurora, suggests the magnitude of the problem: "In the first act of *Sleeping Beauty,* after the protracted and wearisome Prologue, Troyanovskaya doesn't complete whole phrases, or even keep up with the orchestra. The delightful pas de chat in that act were hewn to their barest outlines by the shears of an unacknowledged gardener" (1923).

Fyodr Lopukhov became the artistic director of the Petersburg (then Petrograd) ballet in 1922 and, soon after, initiated the revivals of a number of ballets from the Petipa repertory (*Sleeping Beauty, Raymonda, Harlequinade,* and *Humpbacked Horse* in 1922; *Don Quixote* in 1923). In a statement that presages much of the future direction of the Soviet ballet, the new management announced its priorities for the 1922–23 season:

> The new management has, for the most part, chosen the most vibrant classical creations of Marius Petipa as the basis of the repertory. The management will devote special care to the thorough conservation of the original choreographic text, which, unfortunately, was noticeably soiled in the past decade by various interpolations and revivals from "notations."
>
> The management has as its goal to reject all that is alien and foreign to the ballets of Petipa, which, by the way, was accepted not only by the audience, but also those "connoisseurs of ballet" as the authentic inspiration of Petipa. ("Petrogradskie teatry," 56–57)

In effect, Lopukhov announced the new Soviet ballet's first purge, and one with all the hallmarks of those to come from more famous and powerful Soviet leaders. First of all, the action was partly a cover-up. Lopukhov's own variation for the Lilac Fairy (discussed in chapter 2) represents the earliest known interpolation of "foreign and alien" material to the text of the *Sleeping Beauty.* In fine Stalinist fashion, blame for the contamination of Petipa's texts was shifted from Lopukhov to an émigré (Nikolai Sergeyev). Intellectuals are implicated as well (Surits identifies the "connoisseurs" as Akim Volynsky and another critic, Yu. G. Brodersen, 1990, 258), though the announcement's crowning denunciatory touch must be its indictment of a ballet public caught unawares. (The need for constant vigilance was a constant of early Soviet propaganda, which urged highest alertness concerning counterrevolutionaries and class enemies.) The ballet's new leader promised to guard the text of Petipa vigilantly; though the true import of his statement lay in the carte blanche Lopukhov extended himself in refashioning Petipa—all in the service of pious homage to the master and the classical legacy, of course.

Fine print in the appendix to Lopukhov's 1966 memoir, *Sixty Years in the Ballet,* detail Lopukhov's interpolations in these first "after-Petipa" stagings. Of the 1922 production of *Harlequinade,* for example, the editors note: "Neither the playbills nor the programs speak of F. Lopukhov's authorship in the ballet. . . . But from a series of reviews . . . it is clear that the shifting of a number of mises en scène in the first act, the expansion of the dance of the participants in the 'Serenade' scene and the staging of the mass dance in the finale of the first act belong to Lopukhov" (350). On *Raymonda:* "F. Lopukhov's name is not mentioned in any capacity on the bills nor on the programs. . . . However, from the reviews in the press . . . it is clear that Lopukhov dramatically strengthened a number of scenes, including the finale of the second act, and edited a number of dances. According to Lopukhov, the staging of Raymonda's pizzicato variation in the waltz of the first act belongs to him as well" (350). The appendix includes similar annotations for Lopukhov's stagings of Fokine's *Pavillon d'Armide* and *Don Quixote* (1923), as well as his restaging of *Sleeping Beauty:*

> F. Lopukhov's authorship is not indicated on the affiches.
> From information from the theater and various printed reviews . . . it is clear that Lopukhov, beginning in October 1922, revived the ballet in its original guise, eliminated various interpolations, and restored cuts. In particular, he had already strengthened the direction of the first act by this time.
>
> In the programs of the 31 October 1923 version the following announcement appears: "Original Version". Here it is indicated that the gavotte, the passepied, the rigaudon in the second act, and the sarabande in the finale of the ballet were staged by F. Lopukhov. In addition to these, the Lilac Fairy's variation in the Prologue, Aurora's variation in the second act, the entr'acte in the second scene of the second act (the Vision), and the entrée of the pas de deux for Aurora and the Prince in the last act were staged by him without indication of authorship. (351)[13]

Lopukhov detailed his changes to *Sleeping Beauty* in later writings. Essentially, these follow a pattern that Surits summarizes: "In some cases, when Lopukhov and the ballet masters could not remember all the details, the choreographer composed the missing parts, trying to imitate Petipa's style" (Surits 1990, 258–59). Other writers, including Lopukhov, found more diplomatic phrases for the balletmaster's meddling with Petipa's choreography. Nosilov, in his official history of the Tchaikovsky ballets on the Kirov stage, described Lopukhov's treatment of the Petipa works as "an appropriate beginning to the critical assimilation of the repertory heritage" (318).[14]

Lopukhov certainly shared this generous assessment, and he describes his changes to *Sleeping Beauty* as bringing the ballet back to its original state. "From my deep respect for Tchaikovsky, I carefully studied the score of his music, and allowed myself only to reinstate the cuts to *Sleeping Beauty* and create choreography for them anew" (1972, 82). Lopukhov lists some of these cuts that he has reinstated: the Lilac Fairy's variation in the Prologue, the greater share of the dances in the hunt scene, Aurora's variation in Act II, the violin solo [following the panorama], the dance for the metals and jewels and their pages in Act III, as well as the adagio and sarabande (82). As discussed in chapter 2, Lopukhov asserts that Maria Petipa didn't dance in the Prologue; dances for the hunt scene were cut before the ballet's premiere, as was the violin solo. In other words, Lopukhov's insistence that he remained absolutely faithful to the original is undercut by his own descriptions of his changes. The balletmaster ascribes his role as author to a Renaissance model: "In doing so, I maintained the style and signature of Petipa, trying to make it impossible for anyone to tell the difference between what he staged and what I did. In this situation, I didn't consider myself the author, but the student, following after the work of the master, as was done by students of painters in the Renaissance. I am proud of the fact that I never put my name on the posters or the programs of the performances. . . . It wasn't easy work, but I'm happy that I succeeded" (82).

One detail of Lopukhov's production is mentioned each time the choreographer speaks of the 1922 staging: the moment when Carabosse occupies the throne in the ballet's Prologue. "As Carabosse arrives, all the aristocrats, the king, queen, and their guests leave their luxurious chairs and Carabosse and her suite of rats take their place" (1972, 81). Lopukhov maintains that the scene was part of the original Petipa production of the ballet, and that Nikolai Sergeyev changed the scene in 1914 when the Romanov monarchy seemed ripe for usurpation. Lopukhov remarks that, "here, Petipa, who was considered a courtier, showed his real feelings concerning the social structure of those years. I reinstated the scene in 1923, but later A. Vaganova and K. Sergeyev took it out" (81). The Sergeyev notations indicate no such scene. Lopukhov invented another scene for Carabosse and her suite to accompany the musical entr'acte before Aurora's awakening. Despite the fact that the Lilac Fairy has charged her suite with the task of guarding the sleeping kingdom at the end of Act I, Lopukhov's version found Carabosse spinning on the stage as her suite guarded the entrance to the castle.

As Lopukhov frequently wrote, his idea in staging *Sleeping Beauty* was to return the ballet to Tchaikovsky. Unfortunately, this allegiance to Tchaikovsky, increasingly obligatory by the 1940s, guaranteed little in the way of fidelity to

Petipa.[15] Lopukhov's amendments to Petipa did not go unnoticed in Petrograd. Alexandre Benois, one of the few connoisseurs of the original *Sleeping Beauty* to comment on Lopukhov's restaging, noted the hostile reaction to Lopukhov's new editions of the classics: "more than a few among the artists and the public saw in [Lopukhov's] attempts a kind of blasphemy and demanded an immediate halt to them" (1922, 31). Nonetheless, Benois, a friend and adviser to Lopukhov in this period who opposed the "embalming" of the Petipa repertory, supported the balletmaster's new production, and affirmed that the reconstruction was undertaken with "the greatest attention" (ibid.). Benois did note the incongruity of beautiful music paired with senseless action on the stage (34), the price of Lopukhov's enlivened stagings.

THE PATHS OF A SOVIET BALLETMASTER

Lopukhov's ambitious program of restaging the Petipa legacy was scarcely his only occupation in the 1920s. He choreographed his own ballets—including the experimental *Magnificence of the Universe* (1923)—and wrote a book, *The Paths of a Balletmaster,* published in Berlin in 1925.[16] A fascinating choreographer's discussion of the relation of music to dance, the volume added fuel to the discussion of the symphonization of Russia ballet—a debate that "dominated the work of [Soviet] choreographers from 1925 to 1975" and "was at the center of discussion of the ballet world in the 1920s" according to Lopukhov scholar Galina Dobrovolskaya (1998, 225). Going farther than those who sought to elevate the ballet to the level of the symphony, Lopukhov begins his volume with a daring epigraph: "The art of sound and the complex symphonic music that arose from it is not higher than the art of gesture and the dances that become increasingly complex along their march of conquest—it is only younger" (7).

Imbued with the martial spirit that characterized much writing of the revolutionary period, Lopukhov's provocative statement suggests that the dance must overtake music, though it remains the more venerable of the two arts. Much of Lopukhov's book engages the relation of choreography and music, most provocatively when he discusses the new genre of ballet he calls the "dance-symphony." His definition of the dance-symphony is bombastic and vague, but Lopukhov is clear about one thing: the work should have no plot. Instead, it should develop a concept to be revealed in the individual sections (as the individual sections of *Magnificence of the Universe* treated aspects of the larger theme). The necessity of an idea or concept at the center of a symphonic ballet remained central to Soviet conceptions of dance, even as dances veered in the direction of the plotless. Lopukhov's insistence on a concept reminds us that if bureaucrats wanted stories in ballets, even dance innovators believed in the necessity of an idea.

Lopukhov's discussion of dance and music reads like an instruction manual for young choreographers, though much of the discussion concerns Petipa's "mistakes." Lopukhov writes that Tchaikovsky's score for *Sleeping Beauty* dramatically changed the Russian ballet's musical landscape, though he believed that Tchaikovsky's contribution only pointed up Petipa's inability to respond to a complex score in appropriate choreographic terms. Unfortunately, Lopukhov's discussion of the choreography for *Sleeping Beauty* remains more convincing as a display of Lopukhov's inflexibility and single-mindedness than an indictment of Petipa.

Lopukhov criticizes the Lilac Fairy's entrance, for example, because Petipa did not respond to the key change in Tchaikovsky's music (1925, 82). The beginning of the Garland Dance doesn't suit Lopukhov because Tchaikovsky gives four introductory bars, and Petipa responds with four bars of balancés. Lopukhov concedes that these balancés are also introductory in character, but they continue as Tchaikovsky's melody is introduced, and Lopukhov feels that the introduction Petipa's choreographic theme should correspond to the introduction of Tchaikovsky's melody (86).

Although Lopukhov made a thorough study of the score of *Sleeping Beauty,* his insistence on one-to-one correspondences of choreography to music disavow many of the most successful choreographic devices of Petipa or, indeed, of one of the participants in his own *Magnificence of the Universe:* George Balanchine. Both Petipa and Balanchine achieve dramatic effects in their choreography by avoiding obvious choreographic-musical correspondences. In Petipa's variations, for example, the choreographer often pairs a repeated choreographic phrase to a repeated musical one. Once the pattern has been established in the eye and ear of the viewer—usually after the second repetition—the choreographer shifts to a simpler choreographic phrase, even though the musical phrase repeats a final time. Lopukhov insists upon the illustration of important shifts in the music and the marking of musical climaxes choreographically, though Petipa and Balanchine routinely avoid such obvious correspondences. Where the relation of choreography to music in the works of Petipa and Balanchine resembles a conversation, Lopukhov advocates something closer to a vocal duet in lockstep thirds.

At the end of his discussion, Lopukhov lists a series of basic rules for the proper relations of dance to music. The essential plea is for the unity of musical and choreographic forms, though several of his rules reveal the rigidity which with Lopukhov hopes to achieve that accord: "En dedans and en dehors should be shifted only when the music changes from major to minor, and vice versa" (100). "The choreography should underline a shift in musical tonality" (ibid.).[17] Lopukhov may well have explored the possibilities of symphonizing dance before the idea gained general currency (as it did increasingly in the West). Unlike his Western counterparts, however, Lopukhov's investigations of the correlation between movement and music ended almost as soon as they had begun.

THE MAGNIFICENCE OF THE UNIVERSE

One year after the premiere of his recension of *Sleeping Beauty*, Lopukhov debuted a landmark experiment in the history of Russian and Soviet dance. *Magnificence of the Universe* (*Velichie mirozdaniya*), set to Beethoven's Fourth Symphony, was a ballet in six parts, each grandly titled:

"The Conception of Light"
"The Conception of the Sun"
"Life in Death and Death in Life"
"Thermal Energy"
"The Joy of Existence"
"Perpetual Motion"
"Creation"

The work's genre designation was even more revealing than the names of its parts: Lopukhov described his new ballet as a "dance-symphony" (*tancsimphoniya*). Elizaveta Surits' discussion of the work in *Soviet Choreographers in the 1920s* describes Lopukhov's work as expressing "one of the most important tendencies in the development of twentieth-century ballet: the rapprochement of dance with symphonic music to the point of creating ballets that are movement analogues to symphonic work" (1990, 266–67). Surits provides a detailed description of Lopukhov's strange and pretentious work, which had only one performance. (It followed a performance of *Swan Lake* and the revolutionary speeches that generally accompanied theatrical performances in those days.)

The mostly negative reaction to Lopukhov's innovations revealed the outer limits of early Soviet tolerance for formal experiments in the ballet. In his 1941 article on Tchaikovsky ballets on the Kirov stage, Nosilov provided a retrospective view of Lopukhov's "deviations":

The attention of the artistic direction was focused on the search for forms for a new, Soviet ballet spectacle. In those years such a movement could be seen in a number of theaters and expressed itself in the attempts of directors to assert a new theater on the basis of a purely external, formal renewal of the work, by the introduction of until then unseen production devices—a striving that led to a competition among stagers for contrivances and stunts. This wave of formalist innovation seized Lopukhov as well, who bravely took up with experiments in the creation of a new ballet in the most diverse genres, leading choreography far from the old classics, in the direction of circus acrobatics or in the realm of physical culture dances. . . .

Lopukhov's choreographic failures clearly did not reach their spectators. On the one hand, they revealed the bankruptcy of the methods chosen by the balletmaster for the renewal of ballet art, and on the other (and this sharpened the attention of ballet directors), the complete freedom of expression of Lopukhov's successors in the classics. It became clear that a dance classic is, by itself, an inexhaustible source of choreographic value, which can undergo reworking by any of today's means. (320–22)

Whatever the novelty or innovation of Lopukhov's experiment, or the seriousness of Nosilov's charge of formalism, *Magnificence of the Universe* only flirted with abstraction. Lopukhov's conception of the dance-symphony, with a thought or idea at the center that must be worked out over the course of the event, had clearly moved away from nineteenth-century dance narrative, but it left the ballet to function as something of a tone poem: the dance was meant to evoke specific images and associations supplied to the audience beforehand in tedious program notes (as was the case for *Magnificence*).

Lopukhov's experiment may have been denounced in the 1920s or seem naive today, but its inherent paradox—the flirtation with abstraction as it extrapolated on a concept—revealed a future quandary of Soviet dance. Writing on ballet realism in 1976, Emiliya Shumilova quotes Yuri Slonimsky's 1966 pronouncement on the Lopukhov ballet: "It is very important that the dance in Lopukhov's ballet was not abstract, but following the content of the musical forms of the symphony 'revealed the variety of spiritual movement, underscoring the moments of collective feeling and mood'" (59).

Lopukhov's 1922 production of *Sleeping Beauty* signaled a turn from the "decorative" productions of the ballet in 1914 and 1921, and the choreographer articulated a quite different set of guiding principles for his production: faithfulness to the original choreography (though in word rather than deed) and a determination to heighten the ballet's drama. Lopukhov's *Beauty* preceded Vinogradov's 1924 Sunny Commune libretto, the libretto competition, the theater's repertory index, and it outlived them. More troubling where the textual integrity of Petipa's works was concerned: Lopukhov's avowed faithfulness to

Petipa as he tinkered with the master's choreography would become the standard operating procedure for Soviet balletmasters.

Lopukhov's work on the dance-symphony *Magnificence of the Universe* in the same period is likewise revealing. Lurking behind the revival of the Petipa masterwork was a radical work that investigated the possibility of quasi-abstract dance and the role of narrative in the ballet. Lopukhov's flirtation with abstraction or "formalism," insisting all the while on an overarching concept, points up the fundamental dilemma in modernizing Soviet ballet: the centrality of narrative, whether imposed from above or by the balletmasters themselves, would make the Soviet ballet's notion of modernity much different from those then in circulation in the West. Yet the experiment with abstraction, in the work of Lopukhov and other Soviet and Western choreographers, would not soon be forgotten.

MODERNIZING THE BALLET

> What should you write? Poetry is fine. Novels are even better. But plays are best of all. Plays are easy to understand.
> —Stalin, addressing Soviet writers on 26 October 1932

If the *Beauty*s of 1914 and 1921 revealed a Diaghilev-era interest in decoration, the Soviet obsession with plot in the years following Lopukhov's 1922–23 staging is equally striking. The Sunny Commune libretto of 1924, the libretto competition and the repertory index of 1929, and the proletarian screeds that appeared throughout the 1920s reveal a new, single-minded focus on the new ballet's themes. *Sleeping Beauty* became less literal, less tied to particular times and places in the hands of designers Korovin and Bakst in 1914 and 1921. Vinogradov's Sunny Commune libretto took the opposite approach: it attempted to fix the tale in time and space, to make it more "real" if not exactly believable. Although a few writers such as Cherepnin occasionally wandered into the form-content debate, 1920s speculation on the ballet of the future seldom strayed far from questions of themes and plots. As dance-makers in the West experimented increasingly with form, Soviet dance affirmed its allegiance to content.

Soviet choreographers and dance theorists were left to chart a less adventurous path to the future of dance as creeping state control discouraged, then prohibited, the experiment and innovation that characterized Soviet dance in the 1920s. The modernist virtues then taking hold in the West posed obvious problems: abstraction implied subjectivity, the personal, and minimalism found no favor among the twentieth century's totalitarian regimes with their demonstrated preference for kitsch. Even the modernist notion of propriety, that art forms should not trample the terrain of other forms, was at odds with an ideology enamored with narrative.

The second edition of the *Great Soviet Encyclopedia* (1949–58) dismissed Western bourgeois modernism in a short paragraph ("modernism is characterized by the distortion of reality, its repudiation of the depiction of the typical, its affirmation of reactionary tendencies, its inhumanity, and cosmopolitanism"), but it devoted nearly two pages to the question of formalism in art.[18] Modernism, formalism, and decadence are intimately linked in the minds of Soviet encyclopedists: each arose from the stinking decay of late nineteenth-century imperialism. (The encyclopedia admits that formalism had spread in the early years of Soviet art thanks to a "mistaken conviction in the revolutionary promise [*revolutionnost'*] of its method.") By the 1980s, the Soviet definition of dance modernism had crystalized:

> A term that refers to the aggregate of decadent-formalistic tendencies in the art of the late nineteenth and early twentieth centuries. . . . Modernism is characterized by subjectivism and individualism, formalism, and the disintegration of the artistic image. . . . In dance the traits of modernism revealed themselves as dehumanization and formalism, the rejection of the classical dance, the perversion of the natural movement of the human body, the cult of the ugly and base, the disintegration of the dance form (especially in attempts to create mannered, ugly dances without music). . . . In rejecting realism and the classical tradition, in destroying the system of classical dance, modernism in its purest expression could lead to the disappearance of art, to the birth of anti-art. (Vanslov 1981c)

If the developments of the Soviet theater would not parallel those in Western theater, neither would they diverge from them entirely. The experimentation of the 1920s was gone but not forgotten. By 1941, the year of Tchaikovsky's effective coronation as a national treasure, for example, one writer even evoked the quintessentially modernist notion of purity to suggest the ballet's superiority over the opera: After Tchaikovsky, "an entire line of important composers turned to the ballet, as to a new and noble arena, perhaps closer even to pure symphonism than the opera, with its connection to words and songs that lead away from scenic-instrumental construction. Glazunov, Stravinsky, Ravel, Asafiev, Prokofiev, as well as young Soviet composers, essentially follow the road laid in the ballet music of Tchaikovsky" (Bogdanov-Berezovsky 259–60).[19] Although the bulk of writing on dance symphonism suggests that the

dance might eventually reach the level of the symphony, Bogdanov-Berezovsky's extremely optimistic appraisal hints that the ballet may have already
outdistanced its old lyric theater rival and done so by achieving a degree of abstraction —masquerading here as symphonism.[20] (When Bogdanov-Berezovsky expressed a hope for a higher purpose for dance, in circumventing the
tedium and ordinariness of words, he echoed the hopes held out for dance by
romantics of every era.)[21]

If words and songs tainted the opera's incipient symphonism, in Bogdanov-
Berezovsky's minority view, the alternative to plot was abstraction (not symphonism), and abstraction smacked of Soviet art's two cardinal sins: subjec-
tivism and formalism. For Soviet arts ideologues, the latter spoke to the absence
of spiritual and human values, signaled game-playing on the part of the choreographer and a display of "naked technique" (Vanslov 1981a). Nor could better
music alone elevate the art form; narrative had to stay: "Soviet choreographic
art is alien—in equal measure—to formalism, which undervalues content and
leads art to form alone, as well as to naturalism, which undervalues form and
cheapens the means of expression. The heights of realism are attained in the
unity of a deep humanly meaningful, spiritualized content and an artistically
complete, aesthetically developed sublime form" (Vanslov 1981b).

The 1962 tour of George Balanchine's New York City Ballet to Russia revealed the depth of the East-West divide regarding "content" in the ballet. The
New York City Ballet presented a variety of Balanchine's works to Soviet audiences, ranging from "story" ballets (*La Sonnambula, La Valse*) to Balanchine's
least traditional works (*Agon, Episodes*). The company also showed Balanchine's
most famous symphonic work: *Symphony in C,* to Bizet's first symphony. Despite the fact that symphonism had become the Soviet ballet's favorite buzz-
word by the 1960s, Balanchine's work failed to meet the standards of local critics. "It seems that Balanchine believes that by making the music 'visible,' by
reproducing it in dance form, he creates a choreographic symphony that will
produce, through the dance pattern alone, the same emotional effect as nonprogrammatic music. We think that this is possible only when the moods and
the thoughts embedded in that music have been successfully caught" (Roslavleva 1964, 49). In other words, symphonism was more than a formal game, the
symphonic ballet must also convey moods and thoughts.[22] Roslavleva quotes
Yuri Gerber, a Bolshoi Ballet dancer, who related his reactions to Balanchine's
dances in the theater's newspaper. "Music is not only a musical and rhythmic
pattern translated by the choreographer into dance form. There is much more

in music: it has a definite content, it reflects the composer's understanding of the world, a great variety of thought and feeling. Let us imagine a set of beautiful words strung together. Does this make poetry? No, it does not. What is needed is a thought, an idea, and it is the same in ballet" (quoted in Roslavleva 1964, 49). If the Soviet ballet needed stories (or at very least, a concept or idea), it rejected the ballet's usual way of conveying them. Paradoxically, the pantomime so essential in conveying the story lines of the old ballet would find no place in the new ballet fashioned by the Soviets.

THE PROBLEM WITH PANTOMIME

Many among the last generation of Russian dancers to study pantomime in the ballet in the Imperial Theater School had little opportunity to use it or to develop their skills as mime artists. From 1902, when fledgling choreographer Alexander Gorsky's Stanislavsky-inspired production of *Don Quixote* replaced Petipa's own on the stage of the Maryinsky Theater, Russia's "new" ballet sought to dethrone the "old" Petipa ballet by abolishing its conventions: the usual steps, costumes, decors, music, and gestures. As the artists who participated in the new ballet experiments and triumphs matured, choreographed their own works, or taught younger dancers, they remained mostly opposed to the conventionalized gesture that characterized the ballets of the Petipa era.

Alexandra Danilova expressed her views of the old ballet's pantomime succinctly: "We *hated* it!" (personal interview, 19 October 1993). Danilova's frustration was shared by many among the generation of dancers and choreographers who learned Petipa's mime in the school but made their marks as performers in the works of Gorsky, Fokine, Nijinska, Massine, or Balanchine. In a discussion of Tchaikovsky's aversion to realism in the ballet, Balanchine reveals his own dislike of ballet pantomime:

> I remember when *Swan Lake* was performed at the Maryinsky Theater—no one ever understood anything! The ballet was on all night, and half of it was pantomime: everyone spoke with hands. We dancers naturally understood everything, we were taught to use our hands to say, "From there will come a man now who will" . . . and so on. It's all taken from deaf-mutes, from their vocabulary. Dancers use many of the same signs: for house, and money, and things like that. In ballet school in Petersburg pantomime lessons were called *mimika*. We were taught *mimika* twice a week along with makeup lessons. It's a whole science. In Petersburg, I know, some balletomanes took special courses to understand what was going on onstage. (Volkov 1985, 153–54)

Balanchine repeats the usual canards concerning ballet pantomime: (1) it's impenetrability to all but the initiated and (2) its predominance in the old ballet. Neither of these opinions has much basis in fact. Balanchine recalls an awkward moment when Lev Ivanov was forced to mimic scales to convey the idea of a judge in one of his ballets (113), though more familiar emotions and situations (love, anger, betrothal, or death by hanging) could be understood by all but the dimmest members of the audience.[23] Nor did pantomime predominate on the ballet stages of Balanchine's youth. The choreographer claims the mime took "half the night," a figure that roughly corresponds to the amount of mime in the 1841 *Giselle,* according to Marian Smith (2000, 175), but a high estimate for the late Petipa period. Lopukhov supposed that pantomime comprised 5 percent of Petipa's *Sleeping Beauty* (1972, 84).

By the time their opinions were committed to paper, both choreographers had largely abandoned pantomime, and the direction of their respective exaggerations speaks to their divergent paths. Although he worked in theaters that purported to respect the classical legacy, Lopukhov's low estimate downplayed the quantity of pantomime he had excised from the old ballets. The master of twentieth-century plotless dances, Balanchine had little need to defend his rejection of pantomime; yet his allegation that Petipa's pantomime took "half the night" emphasizes Balanchine's own innovation in abandoning it.[24]

If Balanchine and his fellow Western choreographers were free to pick and choose from the old ballet's devices, to rummage among the dustbins of dance for solutions that pleased them, Soviet choreography faced a more serious task: like socialism itself, Soviet dance was meant to evolve and progress. Curiously, in gilded theaters with ancien régime repertories and boxes for royals it was the old ballet's pantomime that was deemed least appropriate for the imagined new spectator in the Soviet theater. In defending her late husband's role in stripping *Sleeping Beauty* of much of its mime in 1952, for example, ballerina Natalia Dudinskaya resorted to a favorite justification: "Konstantin Mikhailovich [Sergeyev] got rid of the pantomime, of course. The new viewer, who came to the theater after the war, didn't understand it. But everything that was good in Petipa he left" (quoted in Gershenzon 1999).[25]

Sergeyev remodeled *Sleeping Beauty* along lines that dance historian Yuri Slonimsky would soon recommend: casting away the "alien and dying for the sake of the flourishing and the increase of the living, the intransient" in Petipa's ballets (1956, 238). Slonimsky wrote at a time when postwar Petipa stagings were at their peak. A time when, following in Lopukhov footsteps, the greater share of the stagers professed pious obeisance to the Petipa tradition as they merrily modernized offending archaisms.

The irony of Soviet approaches to pantomime and storytelling lay in the paradox that dance ideologues wished to retain the narrative in dance (as choreographers elsewhere in the world were turning away from it) while simultaneously turning away from the ballet's traditional means of telling those stories. The answer to this quandary lay, not surprisingly, in the now-familiar argument for the symphonization of dance. Writing in 1965, Yulia Rozanova identified the pas d'action as the "key" to the symphonization of dance and defines this "most flexible" of dance genres: "The pas d'action genre began to appear in ballets at the end of the eighteenth and beginning of the nineteenth centuries as a result of the unification of the genres of pantomime and classical or character dance. This unification made it possible, on the one hand, to significantly enrich the dance with a concrete plot, and on the other, to strip pantomime of its nondance quality, it's mute gestural 'dialogues' that were not always understandable" (21).

Although her writing betrays a romantic wish to return to the prelapsarian idyll of Russian ballet before Petipa, Rozanova speaks more directly to the antipathy to ballet pantomime in the Soviet Union in the 1960s than to the practice of mime artists at the end of either the eighteenth or the nineteenth centuries. After the usual assertion that mime was incomprehensible to its audiences, Rozanova endorses the conjoining of dancing and pantomime to produce a narrative dance of greater efficacy.

The pas d'action—a scene that blends dance and narrative—became a standard feature of the nineteenth-century ballet, yet it is instructive to see how Tchaikovsky uses the term in *Sleeping Beauty*. In Tchaikovsky's score the ballet's first pas d'action includes the Rose Adagio together with the dances of pages and attendants that follow, Aurora's variation, and coda. The music composed for Désiré's meeting with Aurora in the vision scene of Act II carries the same designation. Petipa used the term more restrictively. In both his scenarios for the ballet, he uses the term only for the Rose Adagio (without the subsequent dances Tchaikovsky included); Petipa calls the Act II adagio "adagio volopteuse" (Wiley 1985, 355–70). To an advocate of Soviet-style symphonism, this slight distinction might indicate the composer's progressive stance and Petipa's characteristic intransigence. Yet Petipa's propensity to voluptuousness suggests a more advanced understanding of the ballet than that of either Tchaikovsky or Rozanova: he affirms the abstract potential of the scene, the needlessness of burdening a "pure" dance sequence with a narrative weight it can scarcely bear.

The key to the argument against pantomime, or better, for a new kind of pas d'action, has its origins in a much older argument for symphonism, one that Asafiev's writings on Tchaikovsky's symphonism encapsulated in 1922 when the critic argued for a continuous (symphonic) development (moving from center to center in his terms) in Tchaikovsky's works. This "symphonic" development would suggest the abolition of set pieces in the ballet as well as an absence of musical structures that derived from the repetitive structures of dance forms. Applied to the "action" and plot of a ballet, this understanding of symphonism implied a complete integration of movement and storytelling and well suited the exposition of the one theme central to nearly all the ballets in the repertory: the selection of a mate and resultant ecstasy (as in the Rose Adagio, for example).

The work of Lopukhov, Asafiev, and others in the 1920s fueled the discussion of the relation to dance and music that would long occupy the Soviet ballet. Although Lopukhov's experiment in this domain (his dance-symphony *The Magnificence of the Universe*) demonstrated the danger of a too formal path, the choreographer's hatred of pantomime, so evident in his writings of the 1970s, reflects the path the Soviet ballet took soon after rejecting Lopukhov's experiment. The choreographer's careful analyses of the relation of dance to music were soon forgotten as attention shifted to a new dance genre in the 1930s, the "*drambalet.*" The *drambalet* sought to tell its tales without recourse to traditional pantomime and set out to do so by shifting the onus of meaning from mimed words to danced phrases. Lopukhov had advocated this arrangement in 1925 in *Paths of a Balletmaster* when he proposed: "the conscious destruction of ballet mime, in which every gesture indicates a separate word, freely derived from the music. The old ballet gestures will be replaced by gestures that strongly correspond to the music and its character and express not just a word, but the sense of a phrase" (102). Writing in 1956, Yuri Slonimsky imagines how, from the individual discoveries of Soviet dancers and balletmasters, "something new could develop: a danced treatment of the entire finale" of *Sleeping Beauty*'s Prologue (208). Slonimsky then describes a rather fanciful reworking of many of *Beauty*'s problems, including that of the pantomime: "How to tell of Aurora's impending death? Is the successful solution to this problem so difficult? . . . Soviet balletmasters, without doubt, will find a means to make the exposition of Aurora's future understandable and dramatic, as it is explained by Lilac and Carabosse. A line of increased resistance could lead to an attempt to create a kind of choreographic duet between Carabosse and Lilac, in which both prophecies could be contained. The experience of Soviet choreography, which in part found its solution in R. Zakharov's dialogue between Maria and Zarema in the third act of *The Fountain of Bakchisarai,* opens the possibilities for searches in this direction" (1956, 209).

The Soviet ballet never realized a higher potential for the dumb-show that Slonimsky, in 1956, hoped would replace the mime in *Sleeping Beauty.* That fact did not prevent others from reimagining history, however. Lopukhov left his last thoughts on *Beauty* in 1972:

> Concerning pantomime, Petipa gave it only to the image of the king. And even that was more a pose, a laconic gesture. . . . What makes *Sleeping Beauty* different from other old ballets is that it has no pure mime, the conventional language of the dumb. The exception would be the two extremely silly "tales" of the Lilac Fairy that destroyed the entire choreographic fabric of the ballet. I know from Shiryaev that Petipa had nothing to do with these "tales," that other people created them, including Maria Petipa herself. These tales were constructed of old-fashioned devices. In *Sleeping Beauty* Petipa turned away from them, finding different, innovative ones that motivated the music of Tchaikovsky, which was also written in an innovative way for a ballet of its time. (85)[26]

By the time of Lopukhov's writing, Sergeyev's version was canonical and the pantomime dialogues of 1890 were written off as old-fashioned ballerina caprices. In all likelihood, Maria Petipa did work out her own mime dialogues. Ballet artists of the nineteenth century knew the rules of this conventionalized language and were fluent in its articulation. In the same way that dancers who originate roles necessarily attend and assist in the composition of their choreography, an artist assimilating a pantomime role would surely arrive at his or her own interpretation. One page earlier in his text, Lopukhov acknowledges this in recalling how that performers of Carabosse's role were free to improvise (84).

Slonimsky wished that the dialogue between the Lilac Fairy and Carabosse could be refashioned along the lines of the famous catfight from the Rostislav Zakharov *drambalet* classic *Fountain of Bakchisarai* (1934). (A 1953 film of the production features Galina Ulanova as Maria, the simple Polish girl murdered by a scheming, orientalized harem Beauty, danced by Maya Plisetskaya.) In his history of the Kirov Ballet of 1941, Nosilov views *Fountain* as an example of the Russian ballet returning to its preromantic era, when "dance was allotted psychological and emotional expression, that vastly raised the artistic value of the ballet" (331–32). Nosilov sees in *Fountain* the ballet's return to dramatic tension, though the emotions expressed in the film seem scarcely different from those of the silent feature films of the 1920s and early 1930s. In *Romeo and Juliet* (1940), the *drambalet's* last gasp, the camera tracks Ulanova's face obsessively, turning the ballet into a series of still images unavailable to the audience in the theater. In doing so, the film reveals the *drambalet's* greatest deficiencies as a dance genre: its occasional indifference to movement and its reliance on a display of conventional emotions—as illegible in the theater as the old ballet's pantomime was alleged to be incomprehensible.

In summarizing the era of the *drambalet,* Viktor Vanslov, wrote: "All too many of these ballets were plays, with much pantomime and little dance. In such productions dance was used mostly as background or was introduced for a ballet or festival scene. The choreographers had no use for abstract ensemble structures" (1998). In other words, dance took second place in this second phase of the Soviet ballet experiment, just as it had in the experimental, post-Petipa period that preceded the Revolution. André Levinson condemned Fokine's choreography, circa 1913, for its relegation of dance to a supporting role: "Our current crisis in classical dance is a disease not new to the ballet; it repeats periodically; its unchanging symptom is the prevalence of pantomime" (1913, 19). In their attempt to replace the pantomime of Petipa's era, the creators of the *drambalet* worked to integrate the mime and the dance, to create a pantomime of phrases, not words, and to eliminate the set pieces that divided dance and drama in the old ballet. The hybrid they created failed to satisfy either the impulse to choreography or to storytelling.

1952: SERGEYEV

World War I and its aftermath gave rise to a revival of classicism across Europe. Diaghilev's 1921 London production of *Sleeping Beauty* represented a kind of apotheosis of a classicizing, retrospectivist series of Ballets Russes' ballets that began with its 1909 restaging of Fokine's *Pavillon d'Armide.* The years following World War II witnessed a similar surge in *Sleeping Beauty* productions: the ballet reopened Covent Garden in 1946, and Leningrad and Moscow productions premiered in 1952. Alexander Bland wrote that the London production marked "the beginning of peacetime, as opposed to the mere ending of the war" (1981, 84). Certainly the same could be said for the two Soviet productions. The Bolshoi's old *Beauty* was reinstated in Moscow in 1944, one year after the company returned from wartime evacuation.[27] In stabler times, a 1948 design competition announced a new Bolshoi production that netted 108 entries (Konstantinova 181). The winning designs (by M. Obolensky) lent the requisite Stalinesque classicism to Asaf Messerer's and Mikhail Gabovich's 1952 production of the ballet. Leningrad, meanwhile, marked the 125th anniversary of Marius Petipa's birth in 1947 with a jubilee performance of *Sleeping Beauty* (the company's leading ballerinas—Marina Semenova, Galina Ulanova, and Natalia Dudinskaya—each appeared as Aurora for one act) and the removal of Petipa's remains to a better Leningrad cemetery. Konstantin Sergeyev's landmark production of the ballet followed five years later.[28]

If Tchaikovsky and symphonism were nearly unassailable by World War II, Petipa was not. A 1941 account of Tchaikovsky's works on the stage of the Kirov Theaters calls *Sleeping Beauty* "a spectacle of divertissement character, primarily" (Nosilov 316). Yuri Slonimsky echoed this view of the Petipa legacy years later: "The Soviet theater received *Sleeping Beauty* in Petipa's redaction from the prerevolutionary past. His staging . . . contains much that is of classical value but lacks creative development" (1956, 237):

> One might think that there are two paths to solving this problem: one, together with Petipa; the other, without him. To indict Petipa in the disharmony of the dance and pantomime, to show that in his staging there is not much of what exists in the score, some masters of the ballet are inclined to unite with Tchaikovsky over the head of Petipa. Such a mistake is fraught with serious consequences. Soviet theater is the enemy of the failure to value the past, the advocate of developing art based on the critical assimilation of the best of the gains of the stage culture of the past. On the one hand, the careful culling and use of everything of even the slightest value in the creative experience of our predecessors is essential; as is a decisive turn away from everything decrepit or dead that was alien or extraneous to the work.
>
> *Sleeping Beauty* demands renewal, needs it. Petipa's legacy in this ballet is not monolithic, but it reflects the single combat of contradictory tendencies. The restager of the ballet on the Soviet stage stands before a most difficult task. He must maximally sharpen the conflict in the choreographic images, overcome external pompous elements of the scenic spectacle, develop the hymn in honor of the joy of living, in hour of the victory of love over black malice and envy, of the sun over darkness, of life over death. (237–38)

In calling for the "maximal sharpening" of the ballet's conflict, Slonimsky advocates the kind of caricature Sergeyev made of the ballet in a 1965 filmed version that featured his wife, Natalia Dudinskaya, as Carabosse on pointe. The camp spectacle of Dudinskaya's glowering evil fairy overshadows fine performances by Alla Sizova, Yuri Solovyov, and Natalia Makarova. The conflict has indeed been heightened in this filmed version, though black malice and envy unwittingly triumph. The need to overcome "pompous elements" advocated by Slonimsky speaks to the ongoing purge of the bourgeois heritage. Indeed, a purge is precisely what Slonimsky recommends. Along with a formulaic call to raise the choreography of *Sleeping Beauty* to the level of Tchaikovsky's music, the historian urges choreographers to prune Petipa as a paradoxical means of preserving him: "The more carefully the masters of Soviet ballet apply themselves to the choreographic values of Petipa's staging, the more bravely they will cast away the alien and dying for the sake of the flourishing and increase of the living, the intransient, the more vividly the ballet with shine with new colorations, the more captivatingly will resound the immortal music of Tchaikovsky" (238).

Slonimsky's statement reveals much that was troubling Soviet dance-makers by the 1950s. As we have seen, the "disharmony" between dance and pantomime was among the most vexing problems in dealing with the classical legacy. Fortunately, symphonism could be invoked to save the situation. Much as civilization overcame obscurantism in Luigi Manzotti's 1881 ballet *Excelsior*, Tchaikovsky's symphonism could be turned loose to do battle with the remaining recalcitrant trappings of the old ballet.

According to Marina Konstantinova, Sergeyev objected to the "cold pompousness, the stasis, the lack of clear plot development, and the old, conventional pantomime" in the Leningrad *Sleeping Beauty* (186).[29] In attempting to "bring [the ballet] closer to the day's demands" and "reveal the internal world" (ibid.) of Aurora and Désiré, and also to focus attention on the plot, Sergeyev's production of *Sleeping Beauty* effectively synthesized the two chief fascinations of the Soviet ballet in the postwar years: the *drambalet* formula (with its implied rejection of pantomime as such) and abstraction (though never "as such"). Konstantinova writes that Sergeyev wished to find dance solutions for the perceived problems in *Beauty* (186–87), yet his staging of the work also manages to isolate the ballet's pure dance sections. The result is a somewhat bipolar account of the choreography, yet one that well represents the Soviet ballet's hobbyhorses in the postwar period.[30]

It comes as no surprise that the ballet's Prologue, with its pageantry, pantomime, and lack of action, underwent the most radical interventions. Like much of the 1952 staging, the Prologue is underpopulated, but the courtiers who still linger at the stage's margins also keep the space free for dancing. Sergeyev's desire to highlight the dancing in the ballet is evident from the moment the fairies enter the stage. Sergeyev uses dance to distinguish between the fairies and the mortals in the ballet: mortals enter walking; fairies enter dancing. Carabosse can no longer dance and expresses herself in pantomime gestures; the Lilac Fairy dances throughout, and her role becomes a secondary role for an accomplished ballerina.

The nondancing characters (Carabosse, the king, the queen, Catalabutte) still gesture in pantomime, but Lilac no longer has need of the art. At crucial dramatic moments in the ballet (when Aurora is carried into the castle to be put to sleep after her spindle prick, for example) Lilac dances giddily to choreography invented for her by Sergeyev. And where she once had official functions (casting spells to put the kingdom to sleep, calling her attendants, shrouding the kingdom in vegetation), she now takes the stage to dance small solos. In Act II, Lilac even dances a short duet with the prince.

The confusion of Sergeyev's approach to the production is best seen in the grand pas (d'ensembles) for the fairies. The central set piece of the Prologue, the grand pas, provided a choreographic respite from the processional and pantomime sections that proceed and follow it in Petipa's staging. It is a divertissement, but the fairies remain a part of the onstage world. In Sergeyev's staging, the grand pas is framed differently. From the moment the fairies enter the stage, they and their choreography describe a world within, but quite separate from, Florestan's banqueting hall. This division becomes obvious as the fairies enter the stage. Lilac's suite forms two lines at either side of the stage, with Lilac in the middle, as the rest of the fairies enter. Cut off from the courtiers and posing in relation to one another, their isolation from the other actors on the stage speaks not only to Sergeyev's desire to distinguish them, but also to deepen the dance content of the ballet.

The Prologue that Petipa and Tchaikovsky designed alternates between the two elements that comprise it—the dance and the pantomime—in a kind of dialogue. Had Sergeyev devised a way to heighten the pantomime (or at least, improve upon its functioning), he might have preserved the equilibrium of the scene. Instead, the mime is noticeably weakened. With their dialogues cut and "lines" taken away, the pantomime artists are frequently left to mark time, pose, and glower as Tchaikovsky's music rolls on beneath them. At the moment when Lilac should refute Carabosse's curse, for example, retelling Aurora's tragedy with a happy ending, Lilac merely bourrées toward Carabosse, forcing the evil fairy to back away. The other good fairies then form a circle of bourrées around Lilac, endorsing her stance. These moments of interaction amongst the fairies provide a hint of the choreographer's grander scheme: the image of the upright and good Lilac pushing the bent crone from center stage and the unity implied in the unison movements and the circle recall the moments of the Prologue's grand pas as it establishes relationships in spatial and kinetic terms. Unfortunately, Sergeyev's veneration of pure dance does not lead him to the more radical (or more satisfying) replacement of the pantomime that these short sequences promise.

Rather than explore the possibilities of pure dance in the Prologue, for example, Sergeyev recycled a clumsy theatrical device to substitute for the dialogue between Carabosse and Lilac. In place of the usual mime monologue to tell of Aurora's growth, beauty, charm, and doom, Carabosse calls up a child dressed as a princess-ballerina from an onstage trap. Carabosse mimes the spindle prick, the child mimes death and is lowered from the stage. This macabre scene was borrowed from Chekrygin's and Messerer's 1936 Moscow production of the ballet. In that version, Lilac responds to Carabosse's prophecy by raising a small boy-prince from below the stage, who wakes the ersatz princess with a kiss (Slonimsky 1956, 209n1). Slonimsky rejected the artlessness of these scenes and proposed a duet danced by the warring fairies (in the style of the Maria-Zarema duet in *Fountain of Bakchisarai*) (ibid.). Although Sergeyev's choreography hints at this *drambalet*-style choreographic scrap in the several bars of Lilac's and Carabosse's interaction, he leaves the dancing in the remainder of the ballet and Prologue mostly as he found it.

Sergeyev retained the bulk of Petipa's choreography for *Sleeping Beauty*, though he often reassigned Petipa's steps and changed the shape and direction of much of the ensemble work. Sergei Vikharev summarized the Soviet balletmaster's amendments: "The tableaux, the placement and direction of the movement onstage, the musical accents, the plastique of the individual roles, the dance combinations were all changed in 1952 by Konstantin Sergeyev. Of course, he did not think up new steps, but it turns out that today's coryphées dance the combinations of the corps de ballet and vice versa" (Vaziev et al. 15).

The most flagrant violations of the choreography and spirit of the ballet came in the adagio of Act II, the vision scene. The libretto of the ballet describes the ineffable nature of the vision of Aurora as she appears to our hero: "Prince Désiré is overwhelmed and entranced. He pursues Aurora, but each time she evades him. . . . He wishes to embrace her, but she slips away" (libretto). This pattern of evasion characterizes the vision scene adagios in many of Petipa's ballets—most famously in the balletmaster's Petersburg recension of *Giselle*. In that ballet, and others that depict the man's inability to seize the image before him, the woman continually eludes his grasp. In the Petipa choreography for the scene, Désiré succeeds in lifting Aurora momentarily, but she escapes his reach each time. Sergeyev's choreography pays token heed to this tradition in

Aurora's avoidance of eye contact with the prince, but for longish sections of the adagio's choreography, Désiré succeeds not only in touching Aurora but in lifting and carrying her about the stage. The choreography more closely resembles a standard Petipa supported adagio than one designed to display the ethereal nature of the ballerina.

Sergeyev reinstated the entr'acte music (following the panorama) in his production but used it to accompany a scene he devised to show Carabosse's minions hovering about the kingdom as she spun at its gates. In a fit of machismo hitherto unknown to Désiré, the prince charges the stage with his sword, clearing it of bats and rats as a scrim rises to reveal the sleeping Aurora.

The latter scene highlights a surprising commonplace of Sergeyev's production: throughout, the choreographer shows little of the veneration for Tchaikovsky that characterize earlier Soviet discussions and appreciations of *Beauty*. Sergeyev's attempt to obliterate the pantomime in the ballet had an unexpected result: a new misalliance of movement to music. Like it or not, the ballet's score comprises two types of music, and the attempt to stage dance to the music for pantomime proved as ill-advised as replacing the ballet's dances with gesture. Marian Smith summarizes the problems associated with this leaching of nineteenth-century ballets in her work on *Giselle:* "The upshot of all of this is that the story of *Giselle,* once so well served by the music tailor-made to bring it to life, and by numerous mime scenes, has been pushed into the background to make more room for dancing. The story still matters, but it is no longer—like so many of opera's stories—rife with details, colorful minor solo characters, and lengthy dramatic scenes enacted without dancing. This streamlining is the price it has paid for survival, perhaps. And in this way, it serves as an emblem of the fate of the vital and famous repertory of which it was originally a part" (167–68).

In a 1959 monograph charting the Soviet-era achievements of the State Academic Leningrad Theater of Opera and Ballet named for M. S. Kirov, Valerian Bogdanov-Berezovsky cast Sergeyev's meddlings as achievements:[31]

Sergeyev broadened—in complete correspondence to the detailed "balletmaster's plan" Petipa gave to the composer and incompletely realized in the first production—those dance parts that in their time were only partly sketched. Désiré's part, which had been a mime role, he created from scratch, giving it two variations. He notably increased the Lilac Fairy's role, one of the most important to the narrative of the ballet. He gave a sharply broken, grotesque image to Carabosse and filled in the féerie and pantomime segments of action with group dance scenes (in the finale of the first act, for example).

All this was done very skillfully, in the spirit of the choreographic source and the organic development inherent in the premise of deepening and broadening of the action. The ballet gained in the substance of its ideas and in significance. The humanistic idea of the authors' conception emerged distinctly as did the folktale that served as its prototype. (261)

Bogdanov-Berezovsky's short description of Konstantin Sergeyev's triumph touches on all the hallmarks of the Soviet ideals of his day: the progressive desire to improve on the defective inheritance from the bourgeois past, Soviet certainty in the propriety of fulfilling the unachieved desires of the creative geniuses of the past, the commitment to "humanism," and the veneration of the folktale—an art of the common people, Perrault, and Vsevolozhsky notwithstanding. Bogdanov-Berezovsky's positive view of Sergeyev's achievements was not shared by all, however. Latter-day balletomane Dmitry Cherkassky, who completed memoirs of his fifty years in the parterre of the Maryinsky in the 1980s, offers a dissenting view, after first reminding his readers of the staying power of a production that had survived more than half a century in the repertory before Sergeyev turned his attentions to it, and mostly intact:

> Petipa couldn't defend his child, and Sergeyev gallantly undertook the editing. Of course, all the necessary pronouncements about the "solicitous attitude" to the preservation of the "most valuable" and faithfulness to the "glorious tradition" were uttered. But by now, even Sergeyev could scarcely explain why the Rose Adagio was "most precious" and the final pas de deux was not, and why the pas de deux could be changed. Or why, despite the destruction of the harmony of the choreographic composition, the pas d'action in the vision scene was the most appropriate place in the ballet for the demonstration of the achievements of contemporary partnering. But then, regarding himself an eminent master, Sergeyev believed that he "met the demands of the present day" and well knew where it followed to take stock of technical achievements the obsolete Petipa could not have foreseen.
>
> There were few who knew the old *Raymonda,* and the numerous alterations to *Swan Lake* on the stage of the Kirov and other theaters had prepared for the possibility of varied outcomes, but *Sleeping Beauty* had come down through the decades untouched. And the ballet's new look—luxurious, gleaming with the hues of tutus and blazing with the crimson of an autumn forest (once again, the wonderful work of S. Virsaladze)—graphically demonstrated at what cost the restorer fulfilled his ambitions. With enviable courage, the head balletmaster placed his composition in a line with the original choreography of Petipa. Perhaps the price paid for the "integrity of the regisseur's concept" was too high?
>
> Of course, the too free approach to the legacy was quickly noted, but it was just another argument in a battle that broke out anew. When they removed Sergeyev from the director's post that time around, no one got around to restoring the original

text of the masterpiece. After all, even in distorting the texts, Sergeyev created solid productions, worthy of an academic stage. And the text—well who would seriously worry about the copyright of a long-dead old man? And who really knew of the existence of this original text or could remember it? Nothing to worry about! All the more so since the "most valuable," as we were assured, was conscientiously preserved. Even the ballet encyclopedia (in an article by A. Sokolov)[32] attests that the Sergeyev version turned out to be "most viable." Does "most viable" mean best? Of course, the thirty-year survival on the stage of Sergeyev's version is first thanks to its merits—an obviously poor ballet could scarcely have survived for such a long time. But we shouldn't forget, that for the first twenty years of adjusting to it, the authority of the head balletmaster of the theater guarded over the new version of the ballet (with a few breaks). Succeeding head balletmasters preferred to stage their own ballets and weren't interested in the classical inheritance. (138–39)

Poel Karp,[33] reassessing the 1952 staging of the ballet after seeing the 1999 version, supplies a needed context for Sergeyev's postwar staging of the ballet: "In the press and in oral Party criticism, attacks raised and grew, unfolding not only against new creations, but also against what seemed to be unassailable classics. In the ballet, the choreographer to be emulated was Rostislav Zakharov (*Fountain of Bakchisarai*), who said of Petipa's *Sleeping Beauty:* 'It is staged in the French manner with a disregard for realism,' and that the ballet to Tchaikovsky's music should be restaged. In this atmosphere, well aware of the value of Petipa's choreography and anxious to save it, Konstantin Sergeyev considered the possibility of a fundamental rethinking of the ballet, that would sacrifice substantial parts of it" (2000).

In an appreciation of Sergeyev written in 2000, Russia's ranking dance critic, Vadim Gaevsky, recalls the excitement generated by Sergeyev's 1952 production, especially the remarkable cast the Kirov could then field. Nonetheless, Gaevsky notes the impossibility of reconciling the ballet to the ideology of the Soviet Union in the postwar period.

The problem Sergeyev took upon himself to solve was practically unworkable. It wasn't possible to join the stylistic norms of the late Petipa period to the stylistic norms of the Soviet ballet. It wasn't possible to connect the notion of a festive ballet as conceived by the Directorate of Imperial Ballet and the minister of court to the conception of a festive ballet held by Leningrad Regional Party Committee or the committee awarding Stalin Prizes in the field of arts and letters. To put it plainly: Sergeyev defended Petipa because Petipa's name was not altogether indisputable then. But Petipa's defender occupied an official post and was an official-thinking person. Concepts such as "variation," "coda," and "grand pas" meant a great deal to him.

But such words as "idea-ness,"[34] "realism,"[35] and *drambalet* meant no less. In the end, Sergeyev's personal predilections (the desire to highlight the leadings dancers at center stage and place the corps de ballet in the background) didn't help matters either. (2000)

Gaevsky concludes his account with a story of meeting Sergeyev at a party to honor Sergeyev's staging of *Le Corsaire* in the Bolshoi Theater in 1992.[36] Pale, emaciated, and with tears in his eyes, Sergeyev begged the dance writer: "Tell everyone, that this is Petipa. We have Petipa here. Promise me you'll say that!" (ibid.). Gaevsky agreed that Sergeyev's *Corsaire* "was" Petipa, though Yuri Grigorovich apparently did not: the production was soon pulled.[37] The scene illustrates the continuing tug-of-war over Petipa's legacy as well as the subjectivity involved in the search for some vestige of the "real" Petipa.

Sergeyev's version of *Beauty* reveals the stresses of competing ideologies and confused cultural policies on the ballet as well as the vitality of a frankly dishonest directorial tradition that Lopukhov initiated in the 1920s. Even though Lopukhov had passed his own choreography off as Petipa's long before he undertook his own version of *Beauty* and other ballets, Lopukhov never hesitated to declare his allegiance to Petipa's legacy and its maintenance.

To a point, the tensions already evident in the young Soviet ballet of the 1920s (preservation vs. experimentation; narrative vs. abstraction) were never resolved. The history of the early Soviet ballet is in part, a history of justifications for an art form that should not have flourished in a revolutionary society. In truth, the society was neither revolutionary nor revolutionized, and the bourgeois cultural "dross" the young Soviet state inherited was quickly burnished to glow with the pseudointellectual patina of a prized cultural legacy. Nonetheless, Konstantin Sergeyev's *Sleeping Beauty* reveals the extent to which the interference of competing ideologies had changed the course of Russian/Soviet ballet (including the Petipa-Tchaikovsky ballet) by 1952. The adulation of Tchaikovsky once employed to "save" the ballet turned to disregard for the composer and his music as the ballet gained prominence.

Symphonism, the ballet's new religion in the Soviet era, lacked a clear theology or even a comprehensive understanding of its deity. The dance that symphonism had once been invoked to defend was routinely sacrificed on the altar of fidelity to musical ideals—until even those were ignored. In effect, Soviet reliance on the music of *Sleeping Beauty* to justify the ballet's choreography had effectively derailed the ballet by the 1950s, both in theory (in the works of the dance historians and ideologues) and in practice (in the hands of the stagers).

Chapter 5 Bringing

Beauty Back

The project had a one-and-a-half-year preparation period and five performances. And in that time it became a source of arguments and intrigues.
They succeeded in calling it the project of the century ("the ballet's Cathedral of Christ the Savior"), a fashionable show, and a publicity monster,
a spectacle for intellectuals and a toy for New Russians.
—Kira Dolinina, "Wake up, Sleeping Beauty!"

If the 1890 production *Sleeping Beauty* was meant to awake, like Aurora, from a long sleep in 1999, the revival seemed more like Giselle
emerging from the grave to some: the production returned to haunt
members of a St. Petersburg ballet public that loved to reminiscence
about 1890 but actually preferred that the past remain there. Like all
reconstructions, the 1890/1999 production of *Sleeping Beauty* occupied a strange half-life: it was neither a truly radical nor a genuinely
conservative gesture. Yet the ghosts that accompanied the production
to the stage demonstrated that the 1890 *Sleeping Beauty* had neither
disappeared nor lain dormant. The array of histories that accompanied the ballet back to the theater revealed that the ballet had been at
the heart of an enormous amount of mythmaking in its one hundred

plus years, a testament to the work's unusual vitality. We have examined the stories that surround *Sleeping Beauty:* the myths that lay at the heart of the ballet, the legends the ballet has generated, and the tales that Soviet dance history spun around it. The 1999 production of *Sleeping Beauty* challenged the master narrative of Leningrad dance history: the story of the Soviet ballet's faithfulness to the classical inheritance from Marius Petipa and the company's diligent efforts, over decades and under a variety of conditions, to preserve that legacy authentically.

The 1999 revival of the 1890 production of *Sleeping Beauty* took place in a theater, a city, and a nation preoccupied with unearthing its past. What remained of the Soviet Union was once again Russia; Leningrad had long since reverted to its original name, St. Petersburg. The theater and ballet company that Soviet power had saddled with a variety of names—both clumsy and odious—were now called "Maryinsky" (though "Kirov" was retained to provide better name recognition for foreign tours). And all this as the bones of the last Romanovs were being exhumed, examined, and finally reburied—tellingly, in a St. Petersburg fortress.

Across the Neva, the Savior of the Blood Church, a hulking late Romanov shrine, was on view after decades of renovation. While in Moscow rebuilt churches sprouted like mushrooms, even on Red Square, the sacral space of a quite secular religion until recently. The architectural monstrosity of the reconstructed Cathedral of Christ the Savior began to dominate the Moscow skyline once again (a swimming pool marked its absence in Soviet times). In St. Petersburg's Moscow train station, Peter the Great stood watch from a vantage a likeness of Lenin had guarded vigilantly for decades.

These cultural-historical returns gave rise to a now-familiar genre of news reporting in the Western media, which greeted them with a mixture of smug triumphalism, visible relief, and a lingering hint of Schadenfreude. Yet in Russia, each of these transformations (including the revival of *Sleeping Beauty*) generated controversy. Western media coverage of these events too often fell into a trap that ensnared the early Bolsheviks: casting the new as unquestionably good and the old as counterrevolutionary. (Both Russian and Western media outlets favored images of bedraggled pensioners to illustrate the absurdity of nostalgia for the Soviet era, for example). Yet in each case, the return of the past in various guises in post-Soviet Russia (however inevitable the process may have seemed to outsiders) revealed a jumble of competing histories and collective memories. Beneath the simple ideological narrative ascribed to the true believers in Soviet communism, for example, lay as well the story of people who had survived decades of cataclysmic events.

In *Mythmaking in the New Russia: Politics and Memory During the Yeltsin Era,* Kathleen E. Smith demonstrates how "different layers of national history" were appealed to in the many instances of cultural return in the Yeltsin years—and the complexities that surrounded many of the unprecedented events of that era (3). Smith's analysis of mythmaking, politics, and memory in the Yeltsin era provides a useful context for the atmosphere that greeted the return of the 1890 *Sleeping Beauty* in the final year of that first post-Soviet decade; the evolving discussion of the ballet's reawakening follows the contours of the other engagements with the past that Smith describes.

The problem of inventing, or reinventing, tradition became a central feature of post-Soviet life, manifest in such questions as which holidays to celebrate (Kathleen Smith 78–101) and the quest for a "national idea" (158–72). "Though partial and often inaccurate," Smith writes, collective memories "bind people together by forming the basis of a perceived shared past" (6).[1] The public debate over the decision to revert to St. Petersburg's historic name provided an early post-Soviet indication of the tenacity of this shared past for many Leningrad/St. Petersburg residents.

> When liberal politicians in the Leningrad city council voted to add a referendum on the city's name to local ballots for the upcoming election for president of the Russian Republic in the spring of 1991, the Communist press and Party organizations lobbied hard to preserve the name that paid homage to the leader of the Russian Revolution. Appealing to popular memories of different layers of national history, the defenders of Leningrad pointed not only to the city's status as the "cradle of the Revolution" but also to Leningrad's association with one of the bitterest battles of World War II. They identified the proposed return to St. Petersburg the age of autocracy and sharp class distinctions. In this instance, anti-communists won, with slightly over half of the two-thirds of eligible voters who participated endorsing St. Petersburg. Nevertheless, their opponents' clever manipulation of historic symbolism had put democratic reformers on the defensive. (Kathleen Smith 3)

In contemporary St. Petersburg, no memories bind as powerfully as those that hearken back to World War II, the years of the Siege of Leningrad (1941–44), and the subsequent proclamation of that city as a "hero city" of the Soviet Union. The personal connection that many Petersburg residents still feel with this darkest period of the city's history was long encouraged by the Soviet state. To give one example, approximately 1.5 million citizens received the order "For the Defense of Leningrad" (*Sankt-Peterburg/Petrograd/Leningrad,* "Za oborny Leningrada"). The debate over the city's name change, from Leningrad back to St. Petersburg, revealed the strength and depth of many city residents' personal connection to Leningrad's postwar heroic era.

The discussions, and resulting controversy, over the replacement of the 1952 *Sleeping Beauty* with a new version plunged the Maryinsky Ballet into the same maelstrom of competing histories evident in the myriad other cultural "returns" taking place in post–Soviet Russia. That the old production dated to the immediate post–World War II era only strengthened the resolve of those opposed to a new *Sleeping Beauty.* As in the case of the city's name change, a past remembered gloriously was intruding on a somewhat inglorious present, yet the appeal of the latter, in both cases, proved surprisingly resilient. The critical group that opposed the 1999 *Sleeping Beauty* was the one that "remembered" the 1952 Konstantin Sergeyev production of the ballet and objected strongly to its replacement by a new production—even if that new production were closer to the 1890 original. In Alon Confino's terms, the 1952 production had become, for some, a "vehicle of memory" they were loath to relinquish (1386).

The return of more tangible and imposing physical presences (churches and ballet productions, for example) proved more complex than mere shifts in signifiers (the name changes that became a common feature of the post-Soviet landscape). Names could return unchanged to designate cities and streets that still existed; the reconstruction of physical objects proved more troublesome and controversial. Smith describes the more problematic resurrection of the past as heritage opposing history in the grand architectural/monumental projects of Moscow Mayor Yuri Luzhkov (including the reconstruction of the Cathedral of Christ the Savior, the construction of a shopping mall beside the Kremlin, and a freakish and imposing monument to Peter the Great).

> Luzhkov's investments in shiny replicas of historical landmarks and his interest in forcing new buildings to include historical motifs show the mayor to be a fan of Moscow's heritage, but not of its history. Luzhkov sought to popularize the Russian past, but most often not by recalling specific events or even clearly defined time periods. He would have Russians embrace a vague folkloric concept of their roots—one that included castles and churches, tsars and soldiers. . . . The appearance of history in tidy and imposing forms was sufficient to represent Russia's past. In short, Luzhkov's ideal Moscow more closely resembled a historical theme park than a museum (126–27).

The clash of heritage and history Smith describes became a central theme in discussions of the *Sleeping Beauty* reconstruction. Debate over the 1999 production of *Sleeping Beauty* demonstrated that many St. Petersburg ballet fans preferred their ballet history in the tidy and imposing form Konstantin Sergeyev delivered *Sleeping Beauty* to them in 1952. And although the Sergeyev production could scarcely be described as a "theme park" version of the ballet (though the 1999 production was frequently ridiculed as a museum inventory), the heritage-history dichotomy furnishes a useful juxtaposition of goals and values for an examination of the debate over the ballet.

Being the first reconstruction of its kind (a full-length, nineteenth-century ballet returned to its original stage and company), the very terms used to describe the production reflected ambiguity: it was often termed the "new/old" *Beauty.* The 30 April 1999 performance was hardly a premiere, since the performance's goal was to show something that had been seen in the same place 109 years earlier. Yet the performance did show something new to its audience, and judging from their response, something surprising. The ballet's new/old quality shared much with the other gestures of cultural revival it accompanied, and each of those generated opposition.

Who opposed the revival? In the case of *Sleeping Beauty,* it was unlikely that the opposition would arise from the group of banner-waving pensioners familiar from news reports. The reputation of Lenin would not suffer in any case, and the last Romanovs would be venerated only indirectly. (Paradoxically, *Sleeping Beauty,* like Tchaikovsky, had gained in popularity in the Soviet period.) The opposition the production elicited among those who considered themselves "professionals" and members of the Petersburg dance community proved the greatest surprise. Or perhaps, given the elaborate ideologies spun around ballet generally in the Soviet Union and around *Sleeping Beauty,* in particular, this was no surprise at all. The ballet had come a long way, after all, since 1890. Nonetheless, the fact that a revival with claims to a greater degree of historical authenticity than its predecessor would trouble so many in the microcosm of Russian dance begs explanation.

In the case of both the name change and the new ballet production, the decision to revert to the past was imposed from above (the city's name change was finalized by popular referendum, at least), and the intrusion of officialdom further clouds the issues in both examples. For those personally involved with the 1952 production of *Sleeping Beauty,* for example, a new, more "authentic" production suggests that the Kirov had not properly maintained its legacy. On the other hand, for those in the city who felt that the Kirov had *not* been faithful to its traditions, the notion of the theater now attempting to right the situation was almost equally troublesome. Pavel Gershenzon put it this way: if the "bad"

Maryinsky were now doing the right thing, what would the "good" public have to talk about? (Vaziev and Vikharev 1999, 18) In other words, for an intelligentsia accustomed to defining itself in opposition to authority and institutions, the notion that either the city government or the Maryinsky Theater would decide to come clean with regard to the past would be, on some level, disorienting.[2] Essentially, the decision to restage *Sleeping Beauty* answered a ubiquitous post-Soviet question: to return to the past or not? Yet beyond that first question lay a more difficult one: how?

THE VIKHAREV PRODUCTION

> The efficacy of dance notation is very much on people's minds these days along with the whole questionable business of dance curatorship; also, the state of Russian art and culture has been a subject of curiosity since the collapse of the Soviet Union. The ballet was once the jewel of that culture, and the jewel of the ballet was *The Sleeping Beauty.* It was only a matter of time before the process of recovery in which the Russians seem currently engaged would bring them to it.
> —Arlene Croce, *New York Review of Books,* 12 August 1999

If the inevitability of a reconstructed *Sleeping Beauty* seemed apparent to dance-watchers in the West, the ballet's fate had also occupied those entrusted with its care. In an interview originally published in Moscow's *Russian Telegraph* in April 1998, Makhar Vaziev, the director of the Maryinsky Ballet, recounts that the question of *Sleeping Beauty* had been in the air for several years (Vaziev and Vikharev). The venerable Sergeyev-Virsaladze production had been missing in action for a time: the sets and costumes had been shipped to Japan to be copied. Vaziev and Vikharev gave their interview to the Moscow newspaper to clear the air: one month earlier, a performance of *Sleeping Beauty* was nearly stormed as rumor spread that a reconstructed *Beauty* would be shown in place of the usual production.

The reconstruction of *Sleeping Beauty* that eventually premiered on the Maryinsky stage on 30 April 1999 owes its existence to a set of documents reproduced from the Harvard Theatre Collection's Sergeyev Collection.[3] Named for Nikolai Sergeyev, the former regisseur of the Imperial Ballet who left St. Petersburg with the documents in 1918, the collection includes choreographic notations for some twenty-four ballets and dances from twenty-eight operas. The dances were recorded in a system named for Vladimir Stepanov (1866–86), who devised a means of notating choreography in a system similar to musical

Prologue, 1999 production. The christening of Princess Aurora.

Act II, 1999 production. The Vision. Svetlana Zakharova as Princess Aurora; Veronika Part as the Lilac Fairy.

Act II, 1999 production. Panorama. Veronika Part as the Lilac Fairy; Viktor Baranov as Prince Désiré.

Act II, 1999 production. Aurora's bedchamber.

Apotheosis, 1999 production. The queen, Princess Aurora, Prince Désiré, and the king stand at center stage. The Lilac Fairy stands in the clouds beneath the central arch. Spears threaten Carabosse, who stands in the clouds to the right.

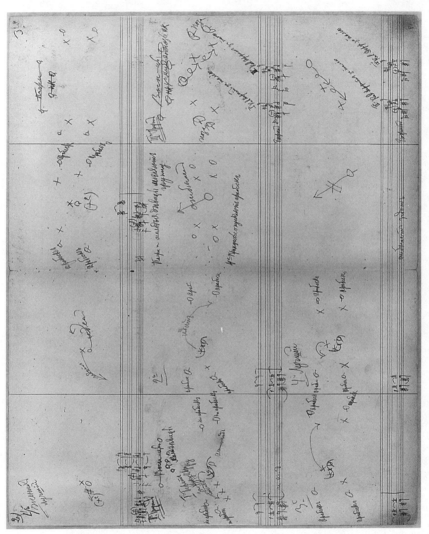

A page of the choreographic notation of *Sleeping Beauty*, detailing a portion of the Rose Adagio.

notation (see Ann Hutchinson Guest 1998). A dancer in the Imperial Theaters, Stepanov spent two years attending lectures in anatomy and anthropology at St. Petersburg University before leaving for Paris in 1891 to continue his studies. (The Directorate of the Imperial Theaters approved Stepanov's request for a leave of absence and granted him a modest stipend.) Stepanov published his book *Alphabet des mouvements du corps humain: Essai d'enrigistrement des mouvements du corps humain au moyen des signes musicaux* the following year. In 1891 and 1893, Imperial Theater commissions studied Stepanov's system, eventually recommending its inclusion in the curriculum of the Theater School. Stepanov became "instructor in the theory and notation of dances" in 1893 and produced a textbook for the system in 1895, the same year he was dispatched to Moscow to teach the system there. He died of tuberculosis the following year, though balletmaster Alexander Gorsky continued to refine Stepanov's system and published his own revisions to Stepanov's text, with exercises for study, in 1899 (Wiley 1976, 103–5).

Stepanov's system adapts a musical stave to support "notes" that represent the placement of (1) the head and torso, (2) the arms, and (3) the legs. Location of the "notes" on the staves indicates placement and direction of the indicated body part relative to a "standard" position. The floor-plan diagrams indicate the positions of the dancers from the audience's perspective. In the more finished Sergeyev manuscripts, each dancer is numbered, with his or her entrances and exits documented throughout each scene. As Roland John Wiley has noted, "the notations vary considerably in degree of detail" (1976, 107). Wiley believed the documents to be "reminders" for dancers already familiar with the choreography rather than completed documents (that could be used to disseminate the ballets, as musical notations are used, for example) (ibid.). Yet some of the notations are more finished than others and were recopied to specially devised paper with staves for the melody line at the top of the page, choreographic notation on staves below, space to indicate the position of dancers on the stage and the direction of their movement, as well as written description of the pantomime. If a contemporary balletmaster intended to reconstruct a nineteenth-century ballet from one of these more complete manuscripts, it would be difficult to imagine what additional information he or she could desire. The notations for *Sleeping Beauty* are not in the "finished" form of some others, but they are relatively complete, even including that rarest of items in the Sergeyev Collection: a variation for the male lead.[4]

Vaziev requested photocopies of the choreographic notations for *Sleeping Beauty* from the Harvard Theatre Collection in July 1997. When they arrived in

St. Petersburg that autumn, Vikharev began to study the Stepanov system, and by the following spring he had restaged the ballet's Prologue and shown this first phase of his reconstruction on the theater's upper rehearsal stage. Vaziev initiated work on the production one year after he requested the Harvard documents. With the possibility of a full reconstruction of the ballet now looming, Pavel Gershenzon, Vaziev's assistant, began combing Russian archives for production materials from the 1890 production. He also identified a costume designer and scene painters capable of bringing the nineteenth-century designs to life.

Work on the revival of the 1890 *Sleeping Beauty* proceeded hesitantly until two 1998 events made the costly, complex project both necessary and somewhat more affordable. The first was a meeting with the Metropolitan Opera to negotiate the ballet's 1999 New York summer season. As usual, when preparing to host a touring company, the Met wanted a novelty, a production new to New York. Although *Sleeping Beauty* was still in its planning stages, the historic production promised good publicity for the season. Ironically, the second event to hasten the production's completion was Russia's financial crisis of August 1998. The 1998 currency devaluation would appear a less hopeful portent for the realization of a production reputed to be the most costly in the history of the Imperial Ballet. Yet the financial crisis probably saved it, or at very least, ensured that the production would be completed as planned, without the usual last-minute skimping that plagues theatrical productions everywhere. Although the currency devaluation priced foreign goods beyond the reach of Russian consumers for a time, labor costs spiraled down dramatically. (In U.S. dollars, the average monthly salary dropped from roughly 200 to 40.) The 1999 production required some 500 costumes and sets for seven scenes; the sharp drop in labor costs made the once-Herculean task suddenly seem more affordable.

As Vikharev noted on many occasions, the Sergeyev notations were but one tool in his balletmaster's arsenal, though their return to Russia set in motion the process of restaging the ballet. Working much like a philologist schooled in textual criticism, Vikharev first attempted to establish common textual material among five versions of the ballet:

1. Natalya Kamkova's version for the Perm Ballet (1968), considered the most faithful to the Lopukhov staging that was performed in Leningrad from 1922 until the Konstantin Sergeyev version replaced it in 1952.
2. Pyotr Gusev's 1978 version for Perm.
3. The Royal Ballet (London) version that derives from the Nikolai Sergeyev

stagings from the notations, first for Diaghilev in 1921, then for the Vic-Wells Ballet at Sadler's Wells in 1939. (The version Sergeyev considered his most authentic was for the International Ballet in 1947, even though, as Alastair Macaulay has pointed out, the production "made the least lasting impression" and was overshadowed by the Covent Garden production of 1946 [1055].)

4. The 1973 Yuri Grigorovich version for the Bolshoi Ballet, in whose staging Lopukhov took an active part.

5. Nikolai Boyarchikov's 1995 staging for the Maly Opera Theater of St. Petersburg (also known as the Musorgsky Theater), based on the choreography of Petipa, Lopukhov, Konstantin Sergeyev, and Pyotr Gusev.

In comparing these five versions with the notations, Vikharev felt he could see "where Petipa ends and where later versions begin" (Vaziev and Vikharev 19). In a later interview, Vikharev summarized his changes to the choreographic text of 1952:

> All the choreography that was changed in later versions has been returned. The composition of the Prologue has been restored completely. Characters that were taken out have been returned, like the entire corteges of the fairies. In Act I the scene with the knitters has been restored, as has the choreography of the dances for Aurora, her maids of honor, the young girls, and the pages with violins. The quantity of dancers in the peasant waltz was returned to the number at the premiere in 1890: now there are forty-eight dancers from the corps de ballet and twenty-four children from the school. In Act II we returned the minuet, the game of blindman's bluff, the farandole, and the staging of Aurora's awakening. In Act III, there are dances for Cinderella and Fortuné, and the dances for the precious stones, all of which had been lost, and changes to the pas de deux for Princess Florine and the Blue Bird, the dances for Tom Thumb and his brothers, for Little Red Riding Hood, and the figures of the final mazurka. (1999)

THE POLITICS OF RECONSTRUCTION

The notion of returning to the original production of *Sleeping Beauty* via choreographic notations, consultations with former dancers, and comparisons of relevant variant productions should not have seemed at all unusual in the former Soviet Union, given the importance placed on the restoration of architectural monuments after World War II and the centrality of architecture as a metaphor in St. Petersburg. Without its neoclassical ensembles, quays, and bridges, or the harmony of its pastel facades, St. Petersburg would be an undistinguished

Baltic seaport. In the former Russian capital, whose architecture remains the most present reminder of past glories, buildings become more than structures and shelters; they are proof of truths long effaced in official information. If the Soviets pointed to the myriad palaces as evidence of the wretched excesses of the aristocratic and rentier classes, they also served as daily reminders of an era more graceful, a life more elegant, and they were for many city residents a source of pride. In the Soviet period, architecture took on quite different and lowlier meanings: in contrast to the grandiose, ornamental, and even superfluous structures that surrounded the ordinary Leningrader, the Soviet citizen's most intimate association with architecture was likely one of shortage, whether he or she lived in a palace divided into communal apartments or a modern, prefabricated high-rise on the seamy edge of the city. St. Petersburg is rightly famous for the quality of its architecture, yet in Leningrad there was never enough of it.

The contrast expressed by Leningrad's architecture, grand but often brought down, made restoration something of a Soviet obsession, most notably of the former imperial palaces that dot the landscape around St. Petersburg. The suburban palaces that were bombed, burned, and looted by retreating Nazis (Peterhof, Tsarskoe Selo, Pavlovsk, and others) still function as narratives of a Soviet view of history and of the Soviet Union's place in it. As Kathleen Smith writes, "for many Soviet citizens, the fate of the former tsarist palaces in the environs of Leningrad symbolized the nation's suffering at the hands of the Germans" (58).

The restored palaces also function as demonstrations of Soviet skill: exhibits in the buildings typically show the visitor how these architectural monuments were painstakingly restored by teams of skilled technicians and artists, from photographs, architectural plans, and charred remains. The displays contrast before and after photographs prominently, and the juxtaposed photographs furnish proof of Soviet victimhood as well as Soviet heroism, the superior humanity of Soviet peoples as well as their resilience. The meticulous (and obviously expensive) restorations carried out by specialists in eighteenth-century textiles or parquetry demonstrate dogged perfectionism and devotion to years of tedious work. They show Soviet respect for the art object to be paramount, even though the art objects preserved only serve as monuments to the Soviet anathema of imperial Russian power.

In short, restoration and reconstruction was nothing new in St. Petersburg; it has long ranked among the city's most important industries.[5] Still, much as place names proved easier to restore than actual places, the reconstitution of physical objects (palaces, or the sets and costumes for a ballet) proved less daunting than the reconstruction of performances and performance traditions. And even though the methods of Vikharev and his colleagues conformed to contemporary norms of resuscitating dance works, the reconstruction of dances remains controversial. Given that the phenomenon generally known as "historical performance" has figured more prominently and far longer in music, it is worth considering discussions of historical performance in music and the implications of that discussion for the reconstruction of dance works.

In his introduction to *Text and Act: Essays on Music and Performance,* Richard Taruskin describes his participation at a 1981 musicological meeting as a personal road to Damascus that significantly altered his thinking about historical performance and authenticity: "What we had been accustomed to regard as historically authentic performances, I began to see, represented neither any determinable historical prototype nor any coherent revival of practices coeval with the repertories they addressed. Rather, they embodied a whole wish list of modern(ist) values, validated in the academy and the marketplace alike by an eclectic, opportunistic reading of historical evidence" (5). Despite the modernist ethos at work in historical performance, Taruskin and others began to understand that the movement's obsession with authenticity reflected romantic as well as modern predilections. Romantic, because, as José Antonio Bowen has shown, "fidelity to the spirit of the composer's intentions came to be understood as 'authenticity'" (quoted in Taruskin 1995a, 9), and romantic notions of musical authenticity (most obviously the notion of *Werktreue,* or fidelity to the musical work in Bowen's terms) ultimately depend on the idea of a text. Taruskin terms this reified text, or *Werk,* "the objectified musical work-thing to which fidelity is owed" (ibid. 10). Romantic-era *Werktreue* ultimately order a stratified, hierarchical society of creators and curators, the former beholden "to no one but the muse," and the latter selfless and sworn to submission (ibid. 11).[6] For Taruskin, this pious submission to the *Werk* results in the contemporary confusion between text and act and a too narrow focus on the *Werk* as a formal construct (whose acolyte-performers seek to render in ever-increasing modernist purity) until the "documentation of a state of knowledge" ultimately replaces performance (ibid. 57).

The arch-romantic idea lurking behind this notion of authenticity venerates the composer and his intentions; the modernist contribution (or fallacy, or sin, according to Taruskin) involves the ultimate identification of the Romantic work-concept "purely and simply with the text" (ibid. 12). Writing on the origins of the *Werktreue* ideal in the first half of the nineteenth century, Lydia

Goehr elaborates on the romantic contribution to the process: "Reconstructing the past was partly motivated by a new sort of academic interest in music history. Bringing music of the past into the present confirmed at least one tenet central to romanticism, that of replacing a traditional, static conception of nature with a dynamic conception of history. . . . Musicians did not look back to the past, as they once had done, to find models for contemporaries to imitate. Instead, they began to see musical masterpieces as transcending temporal and spatial barriers. One level of history was being transcended to reach another" (246). Given that historical musical works have been considered timeless, transcendent, and worth recuperating, since the romantic period, it follows that increasing energy has been devoted to resuscitating them, and that by the present day, "We tend to assume that if we can re-create all the external conditions that obtained in the original performance of a piece we will thus recreate the composer's inner experience of the piece and thus allow him to speak for himself" (Taruskin 1995a, 55).

Certainly, a similar set of intentions and goals was at the heart of the 1999 reconstruction of *Sleeping Beauty* and many other dance works that have recently been resuscitated. Tellingly, the most spectacular events of the recent wave of dance reconstructions have invoked the dance's most romanticized figure: Vatslav Nijinsky. Millicent Hodson and Kenneth Archer's 1987 reconstruction of Nijinsky's *Rite of Spring* received wide publicity and gave rise to a new genre of dance publicity: the sleuthing tale that transformed dance archives into archaeological digs and dance researchers into detectives. At the center of that team's most famous reconstructions (*Rite, Jeux* in 1996, *Till Eulenspiegel* in 1994) was the figure of the dance's most enduring enigma: the mad genius Nijinsky, still the subject of a torrent of speculative pop psychology.

The romantic roots of our modern fascination with historical performance hold special implications for the reconstruction of *Sleeping Beauty* as they reveal another facet of the ballet's unique place between the dance traditions of the nineteenth and twentieth centuries—and the prescience of Vsevolozhsky, Tchaikovsky, and Petipa. As Makhar Vaziev, director of the Maryinsky Ballet put it: "you won't find this much documentation for any other Petipa ballet" (quoted in Scholl 1999). The documents that record the work at the time of its unveiling—still photographs from 1890 (made on the stage and in the studio), light plots, models of sets, and scores of design sketches—tantalize with their implications for future reconstruction. The choreographic notations, a somewhat later and more serious effort to fix the choreography of the Imperial Ballet's repertory in choreographic notations, made it possible to connect the poses in the still photographs with movement. [7]

If *Sleeping Beauty* may be seen as a ballet summing up the achievements of the nineteenth century as it pointed to those of the twentieth, then the ballet's unusual documentation marks a transition from the nineteenth century's relatively casual regard for the choreographic text to a more modernist desire to fix the ballet's choreography. The ballet's visuals were documented immediately, the choreography somewhat later. Still, late romantic and modern impulses coincided as modern principles of preservation served the maintenance of the legacy of a genius choreographer. The archives thus provide the meeting ground for the romantic veneration of the *Werk* and the modern preoccupation with its authentic preservation. And if these turn-of-the-century gestures were motivated by late nineteenth-century Russian hero worship, then the 1999 production speaks to a similar post-Soviet desire to set the pantheon right.

One discomfort of applying Taruskin's critique of historical performance to the ballet is that time's march though the dance is more destructive. Musicologists can afford to be cavalier where questions of text and act are concerned: their texts rarely disappear. Until one generally accepted method of recording the dance text is devised and put into broad use, dance researchers will continue to cling to each extant fragment of the texts they study. And all the more so since those who record dances (whether by video or notation) perform an invaluable but artificial service, concerning themselves necessarily with text more than act. Taruskin criticizes those who lean too heavily on rigid, conventional notions of performing the musical texts in question, yet the absence of established dance texts presupposes an obsession with authenticity when dance works are restored. The more urgent situation in dance helps to explain why in newspaper reviews of dance reconstructions, for example, text pushes act from the page: speculation over the authenticity of the dances often crowds the performers and performance from the reviews.

Hodson and Archer's 1987 reconstruction of Nijinsky's *Rite of Spring,* the production that introduced the fruits of dance reconstruction to a wide audience, occurred some years after Richard Taruskin (and other musicologists) had begun to question the ideology, the tenets, and the circumstances of the phenomenon known as historical performance. Such was not the case in Russia in the late 1990s when the idea to revive the 1890 *Sleeping Beauty* first surfaced. Yet other operations were already in place: Russia's (arch-romantic) cult of the artist and indignation over Soviet slights to that cult demanded expiation.

When asked why he had taken on the reconstruction, Sergei Vikharev replied: "It's not a question of whether the current version suits us or not, but of what is now called *The Sleeping Beauty* at the Maryinsky. Does it have anything to do with Tchaikovsky or Petipa? Should the theater even use their names in its programs?" (Vaziev and Vikharev 15). The 1999 reconstruction elevated Petipa (and finally, Vsevolozhsky) to the height of Tchaikovsky for the first time—Soviet assertions of faithfulness to the choreographer's legacy notwithstanding. Paradoxically, it was a late romantic project—the judicious documentation of Petipa's choreography using Stepanov's system—that made the modern reconstruction possible.

WAR AMONG THE CRITICS

A 1998 ballet school conference (held in honor of the 180th anniversary of Petipa's birth) revealed an unanticipated wellspring of local hostility to the planned 1999 production of *Sleeping Beauty*. In an interview with Vaziev and Vikharev, Gershenzon lists the objections raised by an audience that consisted mostly of local theater professionals: historians, critics, current and former dancers, teachers, and administrators. Some claimed the Sergeyev manuscripts were "not documents," that the notations could not be trusted, and that Sergeyev was a bad person whom the artists did not like (Vaziev and Vikharev 18). It became obvious that reconstructing a ballet would be regarded altogether differently from an attempt to restore an imperial palace, beginning with the primary evidence—the establishment of the text. (Vaziev and Vikharev responded with their lengthy interview—originally published in April 1998—to quell speculation and provide basic information about the project.)

Here, the correct analogy would not be the restoration of a charred royal palace, but the remains of the last Romanovs. Gershenzon noted the similarity of the debate to the one concerning the identification of the unearthed remains of the last Romanovs: once it became clear to Moscow mayor Yuri Luzhkov that the remains of the Romanovs would be buried in the usual place in St. Petersburg, and not in Moscow, he declared the remains fakes and refused to believe any scientific evidence to the contrary. A similar suspension of belief occurred at the ballet symposium where, according to Gershenzon, "People who had never seen the notations and who never wanted to see them were screaming about them" (18–19).

The return of reproductions of a portion of the Sergeyev manuscripts might have been cause for celebration in St. Petersburg. Not only do the notations provide tantalizing clues to the "lost" ballets of the Petipa era (*Talisman, La Vestale,* or *Pharaoh's Daughter,* for example), or Petipa's dances for operas (*Aida, Carmen,* and *Faust,* among many others), the Harvard cache suggests the possibility of "editing" a number of extant works, those either "amputated" in the Soviet era or possessing problematic textual histories generally (*La Bayadère, Esmeralda, Corsaire, Paquita, Raymonda*). Yet to hear the arguments of those opposed to the revival of the 1890 *Sleeping Beauty,* it might have seemed that a particularly intricate conspiracy was put in place at the end of the nineteenth century to misrepresent Petipa's choreography at some point in the future.

Lurking behind the debate over the Sergeyev manuscripts was the resurgent nationalism of late Yeltsin/early Putin eras. The Sergeyev manuscripts left Russian soil in 1918 and hadn't been seen in Russia, or by Soviet or Russian dance historians, since. The debate over their veracity follows the contours of Yeltsin-era controversies regarding the repatriation of the trophy art seized by Soviet troops in Europe during World War II. As early as the 1950s, according to Kathleen Smith, Soviet propagandists had concocted "a heavily dramatized semi-fictional version of how the Dresden artworks had been 'twice saved'": first by the Soviet army, who rescued them from underground storage in Germany, and then by Soviet restorers. The paintings, says Smith, were "likened to wounded soldiers and the [Soviet] restoration workshop to a military hospital" (60).

Smith documents a national Yeltsin-era debate over the trophy art, from embarrassment over the large quantities of art secretly held by the Soviets in 1991 and 1992 (63–66), to the "patriot games" of 1994–97 (66–74). The latter period witnessed a sharp turn in the discussion: as communists and nationalists seized control of the debate, accusing those favoring repatriation of the loot of the usual "servility" to the West as they valorized "the wartime efforts of all citizens, including members of the trophy brigades, curators, and restorers" (70). The Soviet Union had suffered and sacrificed more than the other allies, they contended, even asserting that the United States had "acquired the lion's share of art objects looted from Soviet territory" (70). As Smith demonstrates, different layers of national history could be appealed to in assessing the past—much as Petersburg dance historians could appeal to Nikolai Sergeyev's status as an émigré or Imperial Ballet dancers' alleged dislike of him to refute the value of "his" manuscripts.

A degree of anxiety vis-à-vis the authenticity of the Sergeyev notations and their return from the United States can also be seen in the discussion of the manuscripts in the Russian press. The 20–26 April 1998 edition of the *St. Petersburg Times,* an English-language newspaper, erroneously reported that I

had "found" the "long-lost" Harvard manuscripts in 1997 (Stolyarova). Stolyarova cited the Vaziev and Vikharev interview, originally printed in *Russian
Telegraph* (11 April 1998), in which Vaziev correctly noted that I had seen the
Sleeping Beauty documents at Harvard and "was able to tell [the Maryinsky
administration] what sort of information they actually contain" (Vaziev and
Vikharev 15). Whatever the lure of casting the restoration of a ballet as an archaeological project, complete with spectacular finds, U.S. involvement in
the project was soon deemphasized, much as discussions of the fate of trophy
art soon replaced moral questions with essays on Soviet victimhood and suffering. By the time of the ballet's premiere, a number of Russian dance writers included a formulaic clarification regarding the Sergeyev manuscripts in
their reports on *Beauty*, as did Kira Dolinina: "All Russian ballet historians
knew of the existence of the notations, but none of them had yet seen them"
(1999a).

The latter fact proved especially vexing: the Sergeyev manuscripts had finally
returned, but they were being used without recourse to the expertise of specialists (though the absence of these manuscripts in Russia meant that in practical
terms no local expertise actually existed). As Gershenzon put it, "the frustration
of the ballet community was understandable: there was the Soviet suspicion of
émigrés, and the vexation that an obvious topic for a doctoral dissertation had
fallen into the wrong hands" (Vaziev and Vikharev 18). My own conversation
with a Petersburg dance historian suggested that the substance of Gershenzon's
joke had struck a nerve. It was fine to bring the documents back to Russia and
use them for a production, "but why Vikharev?" the historian asked in raised
tones. Vikharev had not passed through the conservatory or ballet school courses
of study for future balletmasters and choreographers, even though he was already an experienced stager of ballets (including the Konstantin Sergeyev version of *Sleeping Beauty*) whose suitability for the project was noted by several reviewers. He nonetheless lacked proper credentials in the opinion of the city's
academic dance community.[8]

As in 1890, battle lines over *Beauty* were drawn between insiders and outsiders. The insiders were primarily dance professionals who had risen through
the Soviet system. The outsiders represented the "new" people—those who
lacked Soviet credentials but who suggested the possibility of a new meritoc-
racy. The outsider status of both Nikolai Sergeyev (and "his" notations) and
Sergei Vikharev discredited them both in the eyes of the insiders. Worse, the
suggestion that renovation was now necessary (a point that both Vaziev and
Vikharev stressed in their interview) amounted to heresy. It undermined the

carefully cultivated public image of the Soviet ballet as the vigilant guardian of tradition and interrogated the master narrative of the Soviet ballet: its faithfulness to the past and accurate preservation of the precious legacy. Kira Dolinina summarized the schism forming in St. Petersburg:

> The critics split into two camps: the delighted and the vexed. The latter seemed to suffer from an obvious Carabosse complex: someone had forgotten to invite them to the studios and admit them to the mysteries of the staging process. The stagers were prepared for reproaches, and they had already heard them more than once: that Nikolai Sergeyev was an émigré and bad person and that one couldn't trust his manuscripts; that the production undermined the foundation, that it called into question the artistic conclusiveness of the work of Konstantin Sergeyev and thus showed disrespect to the memory of a great man; that serious work with the Harvard manuscripts would require decades and that Vikharev was too young and inexperienced. (1999a)

As work on the ballet progressed, the opposition became more shrill. One dance historian claimed that at the end of the nineteenth century, Flekser (pseudonym of Akim Volynsky) and (André) Levinson had tried to destroy *Sleeping Beauty,* while at the end of the twentieth, (Pavel) Gershenzon and (Vadim) Gaevsky were attempting the same. An obvious anti-Semitic slur, this notion of a "Jewish critics' plot" lingered until, in the spirit of greater inclusion, perhaps, the production began to be discussed as a "Jewish-homosexual conspiracy." The banality of these chauvinisms was underscored months later when Vladimir Putin's presidential campaign smeared rival liberal politician Grigory Javlinsky by asserting that the latter's campaign was supported by Jews, homosexuals, and foreigners.[9] Another writer described the tensions inside the rehearsal halls: "The information that flew from the ballet halls seemed more like war reportage. The coaches were outraged by encroachments on a choreographic text they had known since childhood. Ballerinas announced 'all the same, we're going to dance what we're used to!'" (Galaida). If restorers of artworks and palaces could rest in the assurance that their work would remain mostly as executed, Vikharev had to rely on performing artists to transmit his vision of *Beauty* to audiences. And that problem was made more acute in a theater with a long (and increasingly problematic) tradition of coaching (see Kendall). However romanticized as the careful transmission of choreography from dancer to dancer, generation to generation, the Maryinsky's coaching system is nonetheless at odds with the twentieth-century's ascendance of the theater director. Personal vanities also played a part in generating resistance to Vikharev's experiment:

How can you lace today's ballerina—whose weight has dropped noticeably over the course of a century, while her height has increased by some fifteen centimeters—into a corset, to emphasize bust and hips with the slimmest of waists? The ballerinas protested however they could: some made arrangements with wardrobe, so that their tutus weren't let down "too much," others wanted their costumes made smaller, and still others insisted on substituting the usual synthetics for the natural fabrics. Some began to make scenes onstage. One of the male principals, for example, out-and-out refused to wear the wig à la Louis XIV necessary for Prince Désiré's role ("it didn't look good on him") and talked about leaving the hat somewhere. (Dolinina 1999a)

By the time the new production premiered in April 1999, Gershenzon could describe the war among the critics along "trade unionist" lines, pitting ballet in-siders against supporters of the ballet's reconstruction. "The first group was horrified by everything: the choreography, decors, costumes (and of course, by those who undertook to revive the production). The second group saw in the rehabilitation of 'academicism,' 'historicism,' 'victorianism,'—call it what you will—the Maryinsky's most radically avant-garde gesture of the waning twen-tieth century" (1999).

The most important myth of the Leningrad ballet (which gradually ceded originality, innovation, and a number of its stars and choreographers to Mos-cow in the Soviet period) concerned the Kirov's careful cultivation of its legacy: the curatorship of a style, technique, and repertory—the careful stewardship of the nineteenth-century classical legacy. Obviously, a "scientific" revival that differed in any way from the choreography of the extant version of the ballet would point up lapses in the Soviet curatorship of the precious inheritance. The challenge to this master narrative of the Soviet ballet would also amount to a first significant post-Soviet revision of Russian and Soviet ballet history.

As the previous chapter demonstrates, these lapses in the transference of the sacred legacy were not unknown. In the case of *Sleeping Beauty,* for example, a number of Soviet-era publications discuss the changes made to the ballet before and during the Soviet period. Lopukhov lists his own deviations from Petipa's choreography in his writings in 1966, 1971, and 1972; his editors detail the choreographer's changes to *Beauty* and other Petipa works in the 1920s. Yet Lopukhov's writings (in collaboration with dance historian Yuri Slonimsky) play an important role in the processes of justification and obfuscation of fact and by themselves do much to undo Soviet myths of faithfulness to Petipa and the classical inheritance. Predictably, Lopukhov justifies his changes to the choreography as bringing the dancer closer to the spirit, if not the letter, of Petipa's choreography and congratulates himself for passing off the deception.

Soviet historians, for their part, mostly ignore the shell game Lopukhov, and others, played, eliding the various redactions until the choreographic text is reduced to some generalized notion of the work.

A special issue of the journal *Balet* (formerly *Sovetsky balet*) dedicated to Petipa brought the curious positioning concerning the authenticity of Petipa's choreography into the post-Soviet era. Ex-ballerina Natalia Dudinskaya (the wife of Konstantin Sergeyev) discussed her place in the chain of authority going directly to Petipa, through Agrippina Vaganova:

> Of course, Vaganova had received the roles in their original form from the hands of Petipa himself. . . .
>
> As she always did, Vaganova taught us the original version staged by Petipa, without any simplifications, adaptations, deviations or changes. . . . However, at present, none of the ballerinas dance the original versions as they were taught by Vaganova. All the performers adapt, change, simplify, or slow down the tempo of the variations. This is not right. What is even more dangerous is that teachers permit these changes. (7)

Dudinskaya then notes her late husband's role in "preserving" Petipa's choreography, though by rather unconventional means:

> Here, I would like to add that mention must be made of Sergeyev's decisive role in preserving such masterpieces as *Swan Lake, The Sleeping Beauty,* and *Raymonda.* These ballets in Sergeyev's versions have been presented on the stage of the Maryinsky Theatre for about forty years. Watching Sergeyev's versions, very few can tell what parts were staged by Petipa and what parts were staged by Sergeyev. The dances and fragments by Konstantin Sergeyev have been intrinsically incorporated into the old ballets. Furthermore, in the ballerina-centered Petipa ballets, the male roles, which had very little dancing, became dancing roles thanks to Sergeyev. The fact that new impulse was given to the development of the male classical dance was thus also due to Konstantin Sergeyev. (8)

Dudinskaya's reader is left to assume that Konstantin Sergeyev possessed more authority to change Petipa's choreography than either Vaganova or the ballerinas Dudinskaya criticizes. Once again, Sergeyev's emendations are praised, including his interpolated choreography for leading male dancers (including himself). Dudinskaya's comments suggest that gender also plays a role in the trifling with Petipa's choreography: "In my own teaching I adhere to the same principles to which I adhered while performing on the stage. My students dance exactly what was choreographed, the way I danced, the way that I was taught by Agrippina Vaganova, who learned the originals from Marius Petipa himself. This helps in the preservation of a continuous link between the generations. . . . Our Academy does not have the right to change the choreography of the great masters. Above all, it must preserve the irreplaceable heritage of Marius Petipa" (8). In speaking of the ballet academy, the Vaganova school, Dudinskaya further divides the sexes and their roles in her view of the ballet: the women are priestesses faithful to a tradition they maintain. Yet the men (Lopukhov, Sergeyev), in both curatorship and performance, enjoy the freedom to change the work of other men, and congratulate themselves on their amendments.

A male academician sanctions this unconventional view of the maintenance of the Petipa legacy as the head of a roundtable discussion published at the front of the Petipa issue.

> We must admit that while preserving the greatness of Petipa's ballets, it is impossible to keep a classical masterpiece as a museum exhibit. Some episodes have been lost or forgotten. Some pantomime scenes are out-of-date. There are some parts of the ballet that have been changed at the time that the ballets were restaged in succeeding versions. What can be done about this?
>
> In old works of art, especially in mosaics and murals, there are some lost fragments which have never been restored. To do so would have been considered blasphemy. However, the living theatre is different. A performance changes and develops over time. There cannot be any "blank spots." Therefore, it is the choreographer's job to fill in the blanks. We see this both in *Raymonda* and in *La Bayadère*. Thus, another question arises: What is the best way to overcome the effects of time? Sometimes, within existing masterpieces, there are episodes of a lower choreographic caliber or of a different aesthetic. Nevertheless, all the changes that have been introduced in the Bolshoi Theatre performances were organically rooted in Petipa's choreography. . . . I would like to stress once again that, in the Petipa ballets shown at the Bolshoi Theatre, despite the changes brought to the choreography, there is a unique stylistic unity rooted within an artistic whole. (Vanslov 1993, 3–4)

In Vanslov's writing we see all the hallmarks of Soviet dance ideology at work: the endorsement of a choreographic work's slow evolution, the low regard for pantomime, and, most important, the allegation that Soviet revisions to the ballets somehow conform stylistically to Petipa's originals (the usual distortion of the *Werktreue* concept). Vanslov goes on to note how Vakhtang Chabukiana "enriched" the role of Solor in *Bayadère* (in 1941) and affirms the unquestioned superiority of Gamzatti's choreography in the same ballet, now markedly more difficult than the choreography Petipa devised (4).

A residue of this pragmatic Soviet-era approach to the past could also be seen in the pronouncements of Moscow Mayor Yuri Luzhkov, busily reconstructing his city as *Sleeping Beauty* was reawakening in St. Petersburg. Luzh-kov's pet project, the reconstructed Cathedral of Christ the Savior, included a parking garage, elevators, and modern ventilation. "As the art historian Alexei Komech noted, Luzhkov adopted principles of restoration that valued appear-ance and facade over authenticity and interior. With his pragmatic outlook, the mayor did not see why a historic building should not be altered to meet the needs of modern users. . . . From a religious point of view, of course, it is not the age or appearance of a church but rather the activity that it hosts that mat-ters; but for those who value historical artifacts, authenticity has a value of its own" (Kathleen Smith 125). The controversies surrounding *Sleeping Beauty* and other post-Soviet attempts to return some portion of the historical past ulti-mately revolved around similar arguments: authenticity versus practicality (the need to "modernize" the ballet), a distinction that in Soviet times subsumed even the more basic problem of text versus act.

THE REACTION

Kommersant Daily, the Moscow newspaper read and written by the progressive post-Soviet set, acknowledged the controversy the new/old *Beauty* sparked by offering its readers two radically different assessments of the project (6 May 1999, 10). Tatiana Kuznetsova, the newspaper's dance critic, wrote a long pos-itive review of the production. A sidebar with the comments of Vera Kra-sovskaya, still the doyenne of Russian dance critics, provided a graphic and ideological juxtaposition to Kuznetsova's review.[10] Not surprisingly, given the central role she had played in constructing the Soviet view of *Beauty,* Kra-sovskaya furnished the most peculiar and doctrinaire response to the pre-miere. Her comments appeared under the headline "A Ballet Can't Be Pre-served":

> I saw the old *Sleeping Beauty* in the decors and costumes of Alexander Benois.[11] I be-gan at the ballet school in 1924 and danced in that production in 1925. It was Fyodor Lopukhov's version. I think he revived Petipa's ballet honestly. Now they are trying to do it as it was one hundred years ago. But it can't succeed. The idea is wrong. Petipa wrote—I can't answer for the accuracy of the citation—that ballet changes in the course of its life, like any living organism. I think that a ballet can retain the scent of the past, retain some sort of internal power, but cannot crystallize or preserve itself entirely. The pantomime here is really wretched. I think it wasn't worth working so long and tortuously. You have to work with classics very slowly, calmly, not hurriedly, and not announce to the whole world that we revived Petipa.

The quote Krasovskaya attributes to Petipa is, in fact, the cliché Vikharev anticipated one year earlier:[12] Changes to the choreography of *Beauty* had long been justified by means of convoluted discussions of the "creative path of the Soviet theaters in assimilating their classical legacy" (Vaziev and Vikharev 20). The floating signifiers Krasovskaya and others long relied upon now lacked concrete referents entirely. The Vikharev production struck a blow to the watered-down Hegelianism dear to Soviet arts ideologues and their admiration of slow change based on received wisdom (often false and occasionally falsified). Worse, it reinstated pantomime, the element of the old ballet that Soviet dance writers and dance-makers had long since rejected.

Kuznetsova viewed the premiere differently; she and other critics engaged the Soviet view of *Beauty* in restrained polemics. A week before the premiere of the 1999 production, she admitted, Alexandre Benois' enthusiasm for the original *Beauty* would have been difficult to explain. "But it suddenly became clear that Benois saw a very different production" from the one that Soviet and post-Soviet viewers knew:

> In the years that have passed, *Beauty* was zealously "perfected." Decorations and costumes changed, the Prologue was reworked, "extra" characters were banished from the stage. Three-fourths of the second act was lost, the enlightened Sun King atmosphere was withdrawn, together with the attendant quadrilles. Many variations and whole dances were lost, and the pantomime mercilessly cut. The result of these numerous redactions was a kind of sterile product that offered a monotone and rather exhausting marathon of classical dance: a sequence of variations, ensembles, and pas de deux, linked only by the fraying thread of pantomime that remained essential to the plot. Historians of the ballet suggested that this was the height of ballet symphonism. (1999)

Her colleague Vadim Gaevsky admitted that even among the older generation of critics, the Soviet *Sleeping Beauty*s had become tiresome: "Now it turns out that the aridly academic ballet *Sleeping Beauty* wasn't always that way, but got that way later, in the course of its long life. In the same way that formerly lovely ballerinas grow old, become severe inspectresses, celebrated moralizers, and even hypocrites. . . . It was boring people who dried up the ballet, and boring times" (1999).

Maria Ratanova registered the shock of a younger generation of Russian dance historians upon seeing formerly fixed notions of Petipa and his ballets overturned by the new production:

> It turns out that not only in the West, but also in Petersburg, where almost all the classical repertory was created, no one really knows what Petipa's era was all about and what his ballets were like. . . .

We got out of the habit of thinking about the balletmaster Marius Petipa long ago. And why should we, if the "canonical" versions of his ballet had already been created, if in the 1971 monograph Petipa's status as the creator of the "symphonic ballet" and the forerunner of the contemporary Soviet "dance-symphonists" was already fixed? In a situation of complete inertia of ballet thought and absolute unreadiness to accept any other conception of Petipa's work, the premiere of the original version of *Sleeping Beauty* resounded like thunder on a clear day. All our ideas of the classical ballet spectacle turned out to be turned upside down. (5)

For Ratanova (as for Kuznetsova and Gaevsky) the reconstructed ballet revealed the limitations of the Soviet dance history enterprise and the failure of its central dogma, symphonism: "It would be impossible to exaggerate the significance of this premiere. Before our eyes the principal myths of the Soviet ballet theater collapsed: the myth of the supremacy of continuous dance in the ballet. The idea of the "dance symphony," in its time quite progressive, was transformed into an obtrusive phantom, that led our ballet theater down a blind alley, begat several generations of dancers, and gave them nothing but a classical technique they didn't master" (16).

In other words, the production imploded the carefully constructed ideological facade that had been erected around the ballet in the Soviet era. The critics called into question not only Soviet curatorship of *Beauty* and of the other ballets, but also the dogma of symphonism and the ongoing process of "improving" the works (notably, the desiccation that occurred when nondance elements were eliminated from the spectacle). Krasovskaya's brief remarks contain the unfortunate hallmarks of Soviet dance research—misinformation and disinformation—as they reveal a wholly justified anxiety before an enterprise soon to be exposed.

GENRE TROUBLE AND THE FÉERIE

As in 1890, the visual components of the 1999 production held implications for the genre of the work. Since it was billed as a *ballet-féerie* in 1890, many felt the return of the decors and costumes from that production, rightly or wrongly, signaled the return of a debased, lower genre to the hallowed stage of the Russian/Soviet ballet. First, the sumptuous visuals starkly contrasted the chocolate-box decorative blandness of Soviet versions. Second, the staging of the ballet—its effects and its attention to detail—qualified it once again as the *féerie* the ballet had once been. Not all the critics were pleased. In a text that echoed Krasovskaya's faith in an art form's capacity for self-transformation, Alexei Gosudarev wrote:

In the course of its century, the ballet transformed itself from a *féerie* into a dramatic dance symphony. The choreography grew quantitatively and attained new qualities. In unity with the music, it became the dominant element of the ballet. In this way the most important part of Petipa's legacy was guarded and increased. The striving for prettiness for its own sake in the costumes and decorations gave way to attempts to adequately and completely express the main idea of the ballet scenographically. Now all of that has been effectively wiped away. The *féerie* has returned to the stage, where the main thing is the variety of prettiness. The costumes are one thing, the dances are another, and one craft impedes the other. The logic of the choreography is lost in the production's disparities. . . . The ballet is eclectic in every sense of the word.

Gosudarev echoes the main points of the old view of the ballet and its evolution: the ability to evolve over time (always for the better, apparently) until choreography took its rightful place beside the music and both became "symphonic." Most intriguing is the notion that Petipa was improved in less "pure" redactions (the choreography "grew" and the legacy was "increased"). Moreover, the notion that a "main idea" was developed and expressed in Soviet productions suggests a belief in a kind of latent Lopukhovian abstraction.[13] In short, the reviewer manages to encapsulate all the main fixations and anxieties of the Soviet school of dance history in one short paragraph. (The production inspired Krasovskaya similarly.) Most troubling for the reviewer is the renewed emphasis of the visual, which he regards as the intrusion of an inferior, lower genre.

For others, the eclecticism of the 1890 production represented a virtue. Where Gosudarev saw the subversion of a high-culture genre, Ekaterina Andreeva, a curator at the Russian Museum, saw an evocation of a complex portrait of an age and the ballet's ability to recreate it:

When we think of history and imagine the past, the episodes are separate, especially if we're thinking of countries disconnected by stereotypes of cultural perceptions and the distraction of periods of historical development. These separate episodes rarely come together to make a complete picture. Who would imagine Pyotr Tchaikovsky in the same frame as the French Impressionists—with Edgar Degas, for example? Or Vsevolozhsky with Karl Marx and the leaders of the Paris Commune? Our imagination arranges historical episodes almost like numbers in a ballet—in order, never all at once—relegating the characters to their own realms, like the fairies that sit around Apollo in the apotheosis of *Sleeping Beauty:* each on her own little cloud. . . .

The significance of the revival of *Sleeping Beauty* is not only in the careful historical restoration, but also in the homage to ballet tradition. This revived picture of one hundred years ago reveals a history that is unified and whole, an understanding of

Europe in the last third of the nineteenth century, and the place that Petersburg held on a continent that seemed to have swum away from us, into the past for good.

For Andreeva, the production allows the spectator to see "how inseparably the grandiose (state), the private (human), the archaic (restored), and the contemporary came together" in the first democratic European culture the ballet evokes. Andreeva refers to the 1880s and 1890s, the time of *Beauty*'s genesis, and Russia's vision of Europe—one that extended not much farther than the boulevards of Paris and the Champs Elysées, according to Andreeva. She sees the "happy sailors and waitresses" who populate Petipa's Garland Dance as contemporaries of Guy de Maupassant and Eduard Manet. For Andreeva, the moving tricolor of Vsevolozhsky's costumes in the Garland Dance becomes "the best Russian Folies Bergères number, a monument to the democratic spirit and hedonism, superior in the courage of its form and bright colors (the wonderful colored stockings), to the timid impressionistic attempts of Russian painting at the time. It so happens (and the new production of *Beauty*, with all its Francophilia proves this), that the best ballet of golden Europe (which republican France symbolized in the last half of the nineteenth century) was composed and staged in Russia. Here on the banks of the Neva, the fantastic reverie of Europe perishes and comes to life like Persephone in every performance." Andreeva valued precisely those features of the reconstruction that the Soviet era had rejected. "The restored staging, decor, and costumes, produce one overwhelming impression that builds as the ballet nears the apotheosis: this is how it should be in the real Petersburg ballet, colorful, noisy, and grand as squares in the capital. In these boudoirs of Florestan and parks of Désiré one recognizes the romantic palaces on Palace Quai and the Peterhof repetitions of faraway Versailles. As though fate itself fixes an aesthetic sense to a place, restores the proper respiration of local culture, adjusts the optics of human reception to the classical, and wakens the ear to the noise of time, startling its greatness, diversity, and vitality of artistic experience."

Like Ratanova, Yaroslav Sedov found that the new production had turned the old ballet aesthetics upside down, with visual detail now enveloping those elements that the Soviet ballet had chosen to emphasize:

> It turned out that before us was not just a different ballet, but a spectacle that relates to a significantly different type of ballet theater. In twentieth-century versions, the main thing in *Sleeping Beauty* was classical dance. And the pantomime "conversations" and festive entrées of the supers only set it off.
>
> In the new, reconstructed *Beauty* it's the other way around. It is a *ballet à entrées*.

Act I, 1999 production. The Garland Dance (finale).

Classical dance arises here out of ceremonial ritual. The characters in heavy costumes aren't distinguished from the background of monumental decors that are overloaded with details. Just the opposite, they are literally absorbed in the design—they look like a part of it. Every super is dressed as garishly as the soloists. And even if some details are executed inexactly, the main thing is clear: here is the style of the Imperial Theater. On the one hand, there is the carnival kitsch of a circus performance and illustrations from fashion magazines, just like the ones Petipa collected when he prepared his productions on Spanish-Hungarian-Egyptian themes to Pugni's incendiary cancans. On the other hand, there is the affably grand, carelessly spendthrift kitsch of balls and the entrances of imperial personages. (59–60)

Sedov's recognition of the inherent kitsch of nineteenth-century ballet was enough to topple yet another of the Soviet ballet's best-loved canards, and one inextricably linked to its veneration of symphonism: the myth of the nineteenth-century ballet's good taste.

HISTORICISM/TASTE

Even for many who accepted the return of the *féerie* to *Sleeping Beauty,* Vsevolozhsky's taste proved too heavy an aesthetic burden to bear (the backdrops, less daring, were praised when noticed at all). Arsen Degen attempted a diplomatic justification for the clashing costumes, though with a caution: "The 'rather diverse colors (Benois)' of this festive féerie may disturb the eye, but that was the taste of the time: at court masques no one thought about whether his costume matched his neighbor's. The brilliance of an unbroken carnival is insidious, however. Less striking soloists can be lost in it." Olga Rozanova waxed nostalgic for the classic Soviet production:

The costumes were dazzling, real miracles of decorative art and the tailor's art. Admiring them up close, you couldn't help but be amazed at the graphic quality of the trim, the richness of color, the charm of the smallest details. However seeing them from the auditorium, the delightful details disappear, and the colors, which create unexpected combinations, turn into a varied kaleidoscope. It becomes clear that the talented Vsevolozhsky, in designing the costumes, was concerned about a spectacle as such but didn't take the logic of Petipa's choreographic construction into account. For the ballet theater of the time this was quite natural.

Virsaladze's design, in all its monumentality, was more restrained in its colors. But how noble and subtly beautiful is the appearance of his *Beauty.* In a word, Virsaladze created a Petersburg spectacle, combining the court style with the matte tones of white nights and the tender fragrance of a flowering lilac. . . .

Act III, 1999 production. The wedding. Procession of fairy-tale characters. The Lilac Fairy, Fée Canari, and Carabosse are visible, from left to right, as they are borne across the stage.

The new revival, it goes without saying, will take its place in the annals of ballet history and will have success with today's "New Russian" public.

The term "New Russian" has been used variously since the collapse of the Soviet Union to describe a post-Soviet nouveaux riches and their arriviste taste. The term's appearance in a discussion of the 1999 *Beauty* is somewhat ironic since the costumes for *Sleeping Beauty* were designed not by Gianni Versace or some other paragon of New Russian style, but by Ivan Vsevolozhsky, a nineteenth-century Petersburg aesthete. Yet the characterization reflected a familiar anxiety of the post-Soviet era: that national cultural institution and treasures were being invaded, occupied, and corrupted by "new" people.

Ironically, the 1890 *Sleeping Beauty* became an idée fixe of dance writers over the course of the twentieth century in large part thanks to the wide reproduction of sketches and photographs of the production. Yet as often as these had been reproduced, their capacity to shock a contemporary audience had not been anticipated. The souvenir program and promotional materials prepared for the premiere reproduced the photographs in sepia tones, and the gouaches of the academic stage designs displayed a comforting patina of age. Transferred to silks and velvets, however, Vsevolozhsky's colors took the contemporary post-Soviet viewer into an unfamiliar, even shocking world in which the costumes didn't "match." The production, unlike those of the post-Diaghilev dance theater, was not planned to harmonize in the way that blue or brown tones invariably predominated in Simon Virsaladze's classic Soviet productions. Anna Gordeeva summarized the problem: "Of course, the surprises dazzle the eye. Our century has grown unaccustomed to such bright colors; we prefer half-tones. But just try to be indignant: those two young guys there, dressed in bright-yellow with bright red. It's too much! But then you realize that they're the Canary Fairy's pages. And what else should they wear?"

To see Vsevolozhsky, a celebrated nineteenth-century aesthete, disparaged on the grounds of his taste seemed very odd indeed—particularly by audience members whose theatrical tastes had been formed in St. Petersburg in its Leningrad period. Like Krasovskaya's dismissal of the return of pantomime to the ballet, the question of taste begged an explanation, and Gaevsky concluded his long review of the ballet with a corrective: indeed, the ballet interrogated one of the basic assumptions of Soviet-era theater, a generalized notion of good taste. "It's no surprise that the public taste grumbled loudly. We have somehow inculcated ourselves to the monotonous and wretched public taste and have long since grown unaccustomed to diversity and abundance. When we see it, we feel quite confused and, quite obviously, offended. In fact, Vsevolozhsky only carried what Petipa created to its visual limit" (1999).

The most articulate spokesmen on behalf of the visuals were two curators, Arkady Ippolitov of the Hermitage Museum and Ekaterina Andreeva of the Russian Museum. This split among Petersburg writers (chiefly between dance writers and museum curators) reflected an unexpected irony:[14] Though the Maryinsky, like other ballet companies with repertories shaped by one dominant choreographer, runs the danger of becoming a museum, the museum professionals writing about *Beauty* suggested that in the past, the theater had not been a very good one. The most damning rewriting of the master narrative of Soviet curatorship would come, ironically, from curators from the city's two most prestigious museums. Ippolitov termed the new production "genuine happiness." "The sense of authenticity each moment of the performance produced is the very thing that art history strives to do: to uncover the object's authentic feel, cleansed from the layers of the recent past, and to have the opportunity to enter into a dialogue with the author's pure, unclouded idea."[15]

Ippolitov admitted that this "academic" happiness might not appeal to everyone or even be interesting: "We might die of boredom if we saw Hamlet dressed in the authentic garb of the sixteenth century, especially since the image of the Danish prince remains important for us precisely because so many layers of reflection and meditation have been imprinted on him."[16] Yet *Sleeping Beauty's* rather full documentation allowed for a reincarnation of the ballet rather than a mere revival or mummification, according to Ippolitov, while avoiding the usual retrospectivism, or nostalgia: "Today, when Petersburg is attempting to find its real face after the long and expressionless Leningrad period, with its wan, provincial intellectualism, the only appropriate cultural politic might be one of radical conservatism."

Ippolitov viewed the Petipa-Vsevolozhsky *Sleeping Beauty* in the context of the nineteenth-century European phenomenon known as historicism. An exhibition held in Vienna in 1996–97 (*Der Traum von Glück: Historismus in Europa*) represented a recent attempt to come to terms with what one reviewer termed a "phenomenon . . . more easily described than explained": "The term used by historians to describe this new perception of history, 'historicism,' has also come to be used to account for the striking tendency in the visual arts of the period to create works reproducing the styles of the past" (Vaughan 847). For Ippolitov, historicism offered a way out of the cultural impasse in which contemporary Petersburg found itself: "The twentieth century fed off disdain for historicism. It's a century famous for its revolutions and subversions, and the vanguard in all areas of human activity took up the fight against fossilized dogmas. It's for that reason that at the end of the twentieth century, it seems that nothing could be more modern than a return to historicism."

Yet the contradictions of historicism posed fundamental challenges to a master narrative that presupposed the good taste of prerevolutionary St. Petersburg. Writing of the Vienna exhibition, Will Vaughan maintained "the progressive and reactionary tendencies of the period are sometimes seen as mutually contradictory; but in fact they are both part of the same process" (847), much as Ippolitov's "radical conservatism" represented an appropriate cultural politic for Petersburg at the end of the twentieth century. "Those espousing a post-Leningrad aesthetic grumble about gaudiness and cheapness, and appeal instead to the tidy gray-brown 'aristocratic' palette dear to the heart of Soviet-school directors and bureaucrats. Benois said that *Sleeping Beauty* initiated a mandatory balletomania among Russian intellectuals, which eventually led to the Russian ballet's triumphant seasons in Paris. When contemporary critics began attacking the questionable taste of Petipa and Vsevolozhsky, it seems more than strange" (Ippolitov).

In Ippolitov's essay and elsewhere, Benois' name runs through the Petersburg responses to the *Sleeping Beauty* premiere. Kira Dolinina explains why this is the case: "In the 1970s, Western art historians rehabilitated the nineteenth century with its eclecticism, salons, and academies. Soviet art historians seized upon the *moderne* and the World of Art. The artistic taste of several generations of the local intelligentsia formed in a few decades. The World of Art's monopoly on 'good taste' in visual arts destroyed the Russian avant-garde of the 1980s. In the ballet, Benois and his comrades are still indisputable authorities" (1999b). In an intellectual milieu that looked to Benois as an authority, many of the writers certainly knew of Benois' caution concerning the reconstruction of *Beauty*. After declaring the 1890 production a true *Gesamtkunstwerk* in his memoirs, Benois continues: "The decors faded, the costumes wore out, and the masterpiece deteriorated after some ten or fifteen years. And no reconstruction could save it. All the conditions, all the technical devices change, are forgotten; even, it seem, given the most pious observance of traditions" (1993, III, 606). Dolinina took issue with Benois' dire warning: "The great Benois turned out to be wrong: . . . Petipa's revived *Beauty* shown to the audience in the very same Maryinsky Theater . . . is fresh and vivid. . . . Simply put, it is one of the most beautiful productions of recent years in St. Petersburg" (1999b). Kuznetsova concurred: "The reconstructed *Sleeping Beauty* overturned the established notion of the ballet of the past century—and of Petipa's work with it. The notorious '*passéism*' proclaimed by the World of Art artist Benois turned out to be a myth, just like the 'choreographic symphonism' of Soviet researchers" (1999).

In 1890 public reaction to *Sleeping Beauty* pitted traditionalists (the balletomanes) against innovators (Tchaikovsky, Vsevolozhsky) and their supporters; adherents and opponents to the 1999 production could not be categorized as neatly. In the strange, topsy-turvy world of post-Soviet St. Petersburg, the traditionalists clung to a triumphalist post–World War II Soviet version of the ballet, while a more radical faction desired a return to a more distant past. In the end, the 1890 production of *Sleeping Beauty* proved as controversial when revived in 1999 as it had in 1890. (*Sleeping Beauty* is built on a cyclical legend, after all.) A comparison of the two debates is nonetheless instructive. In 1890, critics objected to the ballet's music and its visuals. To the work's detractors, Tchaikovsky's score was needlessly complex and offered the listener (and the dancer) few rewards, while the ballet's visuals led too obviously to the low-genre *féerie*. By 1999, no one questioned Tchaikovsky's score, yet the visuals were attacked once more, and similar anxieties surfaced concerning the ballet's descent into the decorative and trivial, away from the high-mindedness that generations of Soviet ideologues had worked hard to cultivate and inculcate.

The national argument resurfaced in 1999 as well, though the nationalities in question had changed. Russian dance writers were anxious to assert the independence and superiority of the Russian dance tradition in 1890 and to distinguish their tradition from the perceived vulgarity of the contemporary Italian ballet and the French *féerie*. For some, the 1999 production represented a similar encroachment on the Russian ballet's sovereignty (at a time when the Petersburg ballet was once again emerging from a relative period of obscurity). Yet France and Italy no longer played a role in this drama. Even Great Britain, the other guardian of a national *Sleeping Beauty* tradition, did not loom large in the debates. Instead, the locus of anxiety had shifted to the United States, the home of the Sergeyev manuscripts after their travels in Europe and Britain, and where the 1999 production would go shortly after its Petersburg premiere. The notion that Russia's leading ballet theater should petition a U.S. library to receive copies of unknown manuscripts from the theater's former archive amounted to a humiliation. That the production being prepared would travel only weeks after its Petersburg preaudit, to satisfy the omnivorous and unsophisticated tastes of U.S. audiences, could only add injury to the insult.

WORLDLESSNESS

The confusion over the old and new in the 1999 *Sleeping Beauty* was reflected most conspicuously in the sobriquet heard in both Russian and English to describe the ballet, the "new/old" *Sleeping Beauty*. The ballet's failure to belong entirely to either the past or the present establishes it as a milestone of post-Soviet culture, and one that generated responses strikingly similar to those observed by social scientists as they surveyed the post-Soviet landscape. And although it is beyond the aims of this study of the ballet to try to represent these responses scientifically, the responses to the ballet offered by friends, colleagues, and strangers fit a surprisingly fixed pattern.[17]

Conversations with a range of St. Petersburgers in the weeks preceding and following the premiere shared a common peculiar feature: when the subject of the ballet came up—especially if the speaker's opinion of the production were solicited—a long silence followed a glance to the side. The responses that followed varied slightly, but they generally followed the contours of the response offered by the ballerina who had created the role of Aurora days before in an interview she gave for the *New York Times*. Diana Vishneva began saying that the production seemed inappropriate for the company, the city, and the country (personal interview, 2 May 1999). Vishneva's remarks paralleled those offered to a different reporter by a different dancer: "Another ballerina, denying all the complexities relating to the pantomime and the new costumes, nonetheless secretly confessed: 'I don't think there's anything better than our old production. OK, it's not so beautiful, but this splendor is somehow out of place in our time. It's for New Russians'" (Dolinina 1999a). As the conversation with Vishneva continued, it became clear that the dancer harbored no animosity to the new production and freely discussed how much she liked dancing in it. Nonetheless, she preceded positive comments with suitably negative ones, and she prefaced those with the characteristic pause and glance away.

This pattern was already familiar from many other conversations in St. Petersburg in the weeks surrounding the ballet's 1999 premiere, including one with a "Philharmonia lady." Pillars of present-day Russian high culture, these women attend performances in theaters and concert halls all over the city and can be relied upon for an opinion of most any performance, recent or distant memory. When the conversation turned to *Beauty*, the familiar ritualized response was observed. Once again, the first part of the response centered on the inappropriateness of the production for the time and place. Nonetheless, the speaker followed with a positive appraisal of the production.

The question of post-Soviet silence—or reticence, at least—has captured the attention of social scientists, who interpret the phenomenon variously. Nina Naumova views the "speechless culture" in post-Soviet Russia as a reaction to social instability, whereas Ellen Carnaghan locates the roots of inarticulate "don't knows" in contemporary Russian responses as a problem of apathy, disinterest, or lack of information. Serguei Oushakine has termed the phenomenon he studies "post-Soviet aphasia," borrowing Roman Jakobson's phrase to describe "a *state of lacking,* at which the already formed desire to communicate is not yet complemented by the ability to communicate *something*" (2000, 994). Although "aphasia" might seem an excessively pathological description for the responses I heard to the *Sleeping Beauty,* Oushakine's research identifies a very similar, liminal quality in the responses he records: "being caught in-between: between two classes (poor/rich), between two times (past/future), be-tween two systems (Soviet/non-Soviet)" (2000, 995).[18] Furthermore, this transitional, in-between state provides no direction, only negative examples. The responses to *Sleeping Beauty* proved strikingly similar to those Oushakine recorded in their obvious negotiation of past and present and the seeming in-ability to arrive at some conclusion beyond the articulated impasse.

A ballet coach from another St. Petersburg ballet theater offered a more detailed, yet strikingly similar response to the others I have described. After the ritual silence was observed, the coach launched into a curiously dualistic litany: the pantomime should be performed, for example, but could only be executed properly by artists from the past (from the Soviet period). The same was true of most other elements of the production. Chekhovian pauses punctuated our discussion of the Vikharev *Sleeping Beauty* as the speaker struggled to articulate the impossibility of the production. The speaker allowed that the motivations for the production were proper but its realization was now impossible. In other words, the reconstruction could have been realized in the Soviet era (when there were artists who could properly interpret the ballet), but when realization of the reconstruction would almost certainly have been compromised.[19]

Oushakine sees a metaphor for the generalized wordlessness of post-Soviet subjects in the confusion over the Russian national anthem. In 1990, the Supreme Soviet of the Russian Soviet Federation chose composer Mikhail Glinka's "Patriotic Song" as the newly independent nation's anthem. The song's lyrics, praising the Russian emperor, could not be used, however, and the anthem was performed without them. The conversation with the ballet coach and many others in 1999 reflected a similar sense of verbal impotence—the inability to find appropriate words—and the sense of being caught between past and present.[20]

In the end, wordlessness furnishes an appropriate metaphor for the appearance of the 1999 *Sleeping Beauty*. A variety of stories have accompanied the ballet from its first appearance, from the legends of the first production's splendor, to the elaborate, pseudoscholarly myth of dance symphonism scholars later spun around the work. The ballet's stories have likewise posed their own problems. The cheerful tale of monarchical succession was nearly obliterated in the early Soviet era, while the ballet's traditional means of telling its tales (pantomime) was progressively pruned. The 1999 staging of *Beauty*, with its arsenal of archival sources, rewrote the Leningrad/Petersburg ballet's master narrative of faithfulness to an inherited legacy, careful curatorship, and even trustworthiness. Given the doublespeak that had long surrounded *Sleeping Beauty*, it should come as no surprise that the possibility for a discussion of the revived 1890 production and its merits elicited a brief ritual silence followed by a mass of contradictions. Much as reconstruction proved a meeting place for romanticism and modernism, the collision of past and present in the new/old *Sleeping Beauty* engendered a certain speechlessness.

Appendix: Reviews
of the 1890 Production

Peterburgsky listok
3 January 1890

THEATER COURIER: THE NEW BALLET

Today, 3 January, in the Maryinsky Theater, will be the premiere of the new ballet-féerie *Sleeping Beauty,* in three acts with prologue, whose plot is taken from the tales of Perrault. M. Petipa staged the ballet, P. Tchaikovsky wrote the music. Our best artist-decorators, Mr. Bocharov, Mr. Shishkov, Mr. Levogt, Mr. Ivanov, and Mr. Andreev, painted the decors.

We were able to attend the dress rehearsal of the ballet yesterday afternoon and thus can convey its plot, though we will not touch on either the performance or the general impression for now, though we are certain it will be very, very strong and flattering to all those who labored over the entire production of *La belle au bois dormant.*

The main characters are King Florestan XIV (Mr. Kshesinsky), the Queen (Miss Cecchetti), their daughter, Princess Aurora (Miss Brianza), Prince Désiré (Mr. Gerdt), the Lilac Fairy (Miss Petipa), and the evil fairy Carabosse (Mr. Cecchetti). . . .

[A summary of the plot follows.]

Peterburgskaya gazeta

3 January 1890

THEATER ECHO

Sleeping Beauty!! . . .

Ballet-féerie! . . . A new word, used for the first time on our bills. For the record, this word "féerie," a *foreign* word, ideally suits the new ballet, whose plot is taken from the *foreign* tales of Perrault.

Now if the content of the ballet had been drawn from Afanasiev's rich collection of Russian tales, then the ballet wouldn't have the name "féerie," but either "tale" or "magic tale"! . . . The above-named collection includes a nearly identical tale: the "Sleeping Tsarevna." There could be costumes and decors—and all of it Russian! . . . There hasn't been a Russian fairy tale on our stage for a long time, despite the fact that the Russian fairy-tale world provides a vast material for the fantasy of the librettist and the balletmaster alike! . . .

The first performance of *Sleeping Beauty* is set for tonight. We love everything "Russian" and say this solely in view of the fact that if the designated plot was selected, then wouldn't it be better to make a program on the same subject from *Russian,* and not foreign tales!

Syn otechestva

4 January 1890

THEATER, MUSIC & SPECTACLE: THE BALLET *SLEEPING BEAUTY*

Yesterday, January 3, in the Imperial Maryinsky Theater, the ballet-féerie *Sleeping Beauty,* in three acts, with a prologue, was given for the first time. The scenario was borrowed from fairy tales, the music was composed by P. Tchaikovsky, and the dances staged by M. Petipa. Yesterday's performance was a triumph of art, combining music, dance, and painting. Nearly all the ballet's personnel took part in the performance, from the famous dancer Brianza (who danced beautifully yesterday and called forth friendly applause) to the students of the theater school, who added to the effect of the new ballet. The first two acts of the new ballet were not especially rich in dances, but the third was magnificent in the abundance of its fantasy and variety. The music written for the ballet is wonderful and the esteemed composer fulfilled his obligation honorably. There is hardly any need to single out performers since the strength of their legs and their mobility is well known to Petersburg balletomanes, so we will limit ourselves strictly to external matters. The costumes are fabulously luxurious, rich and varied. The decors are painted artfully, and in general, the production of the ballet is worthy of attention. From the first entr'acte, the audience began calling out the author, the balletmaster, and several performers. The theater was filled with a select public.

Peterburgsky listok

4 January 1890

THEATER COURIER: THE NEW BALLET

The first performance of M. Petipa's three-act ballet *Sleeping Beauty* occurred in the Maryinsky Theater last night, January 3. This sensational premiere attracted a mass of the most elegant and select public, overfilling the hall from top to bottom. It has been some time since we can recall such an assembly of both the male and female representatives of the capital's beau monde and high life. The parterre was an ocean of tailcoats, snow white shirtfronts, and dress uniforms. The viewers in the galleries looked like sardines in tins. The hall was maximally lively as a result. Until the curtain rose and during the entr'actes there was a rumble, a roar of conversation. Arguments, censure, praise, delight, reproaches, and haphazard judgments: it all demonstrated the interest aroused by the new ballet.

We will nonetheless return to the premiere and the performance of Mr. Petipa's latest work.

The details of the plot are already familiar to our readers from yesterday's edition of *Peterburgsky listok*. It remains to speak of the dances, the production in general, the mise-en-scène, the music, decors, and costumes, of which some five hundred had to be manufactured altogether! This one circumstance speaks quite eloquently to the amount of money spent on *Sleeping Beauty*, which cost the directorate more than 10,000 rubles. The decors for the new ballet were painted by our best specialist artist-decorators—Messrs. Bocharov, Shishkov, Levogt, Ivanov, and Andreev—who obviously wished to outdo each other in the creativity and artistry of their executions. Our venerable Russian maestro P. I. Tchaikovsky composed the music. The wonderful illustrated pictures of Gustave Doré, appended to the luxurious edition of Perrault's tales (including Bluebeard, The White Cat, Sleeping Beauty, Little Red Riding Hood, The Blue Bird, Cinderella, Tom Thumb, and others), assisted balletmaster Petipa considerably.

The striking and inexhaustible fantasy of the artist who designed the costumes for our ballet is known to everyone. It seems that after such artistically original costumes as he gave us in the ballet *Caprices of a Butterfly* there was nowhere to go! In fact, it turned out that the fantasy and creativity of this wonderful artist has no limits. We were convinced of this last night, looking at hundreds of the most fanciful garments, each more beautiful, more artistic, and skillful than the last.

Now the curtain has gone up. The Prologue. The christening of Princess Aurora (Miss Brianza) is taking place. A large retinue is on the stage: fairies, pages, genies. Even rats appear! The costumes are delightful. Levogt's decors are spectacular. An unoriginal grand pas d'ensemble is performed. The Prologue ends with the usual ballabile. The impressions lead to the following:

"And where is the 'ballet'?"

"In the next scene," they answer.

The second scene: "The Princess' four fiancés." The decors are again luxurious, painted by Messrs. Bocharov and Andreev, and the costumes delightful. They run and jump and suddenly, for no reason at all, permit themselves to break into a "country" waltz. Why a waltz, exactly, and not a trepak? A mystery.

"Well, and where's the 'ballet'?"

"It will be in the next scene," they answer.

Third act: Prince Désiré's hunt (Mr. Gerdt). Again, spectacular decors, and again, sumptuous costumes on the duchesses, baronesses, countesses, hunters, marquises, and peasants. They play *blindman's bluff!* Aurora and nymphs appear; they mostly dance with their hands.

"And where is the 'ballet'?"

"It will be in the next scene," they answer.

Fourth act: a moving panorama and the castle of the Sleeping Beauty. The decors are the height of taste and beauty: Messrs. Bocharov and Ivanov. The costumes are the height of sumptuousness and richness. A mime scene takes place, and nothing else.

"And where is the 'ballet'?"

"It will be in the next scene," they answer.

"Pfuu!" Someone spits.

Fifth scene: the prince's wedding. The esplanade of the castle can be seen. The entry of the king and the newlyweds takes place. And for no apparent reason Bluebeard, Puss in Boots, Donkey Skin, the Blue Bird, the White Cat, the Wolf, Tom Thumb, and others appear. In a word, a mummer's parade on Mars Field, with the one difference: that once again the costumes are delightful, and the decors of Mr. Shishkov are again, wonderful. This time they perform some small, not altogether successful, pas: diamond, gold, silver, sapphire. The character dances for the cats and the blue bird (Miss Nikitina) aren't bad. But that's all there is! The entrée "of the ballet" (?): a Roman, Persian, Indian, American, Turkish, etc, sarabande. The audience gasps only from the luxury and brilliance of . . . the costumes. Suddenly cats, wolves, rats, and birds descend to break into a "coda," that turns out to be . . . a mazurka!!!

"Well, and when will there be a ballet?"

"In another choreographic (?) work of Mr. Petipa . . . " And where *Sleeping Beauty* is concerned, don't even look. . . . It isn't a ballet, but a luxurious staged . . . féerie, one is forced to remind oneself.

But that's just how it is. *Everything* is done for the eye, but for the choreography, there is almost nothing at all. The féerie reminds one of a book in a luxurious binding with empty pages. The music of Mr. Tchaikovsky does not suit the dances at all. It's not even possible to dance to it. In places it is a symphony, and in others unsuccessfully imitates ballet rhythms. There are two or three musical phrases, but the composer repeats them endlessly.

In general, *Sleeping Beauty* will interest those who don't look for choreography in the ballet, but only amusement for the eye in the decors and costumes.

Peterburgskaya gazeta

4 January 1890

THEATER ECHO: *SLEEPING BEAUTY* (NEW BALLET)

A new ballet! . . . An occasion in the ballet anthill! . . . As always, there are many who like it and many who don't! On the one hand: lovely, delightful. And on the other: dissatisfaction and spiteful whispering with crooked smiles on the lips. Ummyeah! The costumes really are good! The sets, very nice. but what's the sense of it? They didn't skimp, but with money you can make any sort of set you want! . . .

There's no plot and no dancing! But first we'll talk about the program and the cast list!

The cast takes first place because it takes up almost half the program. Concerning the plot, it was cut from a little children's tale of Perrault—simple, short, and sweet . . . for children.

There's a fairy godmother (?), a fairy *christening*, rats at the christening, and good and evil fairies, etc.

In short, it's all—a fairy tale! And in a fairy tale everything is possible. Even the illiteracy in the cast list and the mixing of languages—French with the local dialect—is allowed.

It seems to us, that if you take the titles of the personages from Perrault, then you should stick to that system. Or you end up with quite a mess. One name remains French and the other is translated into Russian. For example, the Lilac Fairy (in Russian) and *Prince Fleur des pois* (in French); the Breadcrumb Fairy (Russ.), and *Fée Violante* (Fr.); Cinderella (Russ.), etc.

One could say the same about the names of the dances. One of them is in French *Valse Villageoise* (exactly as if it were impossible to say in Russian "the waltz of the peasants" or "the peasants waltz"), and others are printed in Russian: the Farandole, Sarabande, etc., etc.

Let's say that all of this is just trifles that don't change the essence of the thing. But why this muddle, this bow to the foreign, when all of this is managed very easily in the Russian language? Why, for example, in the program are the Fairy Misses called fairies here and enchantresses there, these fairy godmothers of Princess Aurora (and how beautiful it would have been to call her by the Russian name, "Princess *Dawn*").

The story is short: in the Prologue the enchantresses "Modesty," "Sharpness," "Breadcrumb," and "Lilac" christen the little girl Dawn.[1] Only Lilac, as befits that flower, is surrounded by spirits and scents.[2] The sorceress Hunchback appears in a wheelbarrow with six rats that devour the hair they pull from the master of ceremonies.

"Even though I'm not 'Dawn's' godmother," Hunchback says, "I want to give her something too."

She laughs, and everyone laughs. Hunchback's spell: "Dawn will be happy until she pricks her finger—otherwise she will sleep for a century!"

Lilac says: "You will wake up when some prince kisses you in the forehead!"

And why wouldn't she wake from a kiss? Even in our unenchanting day, any girl would wake after a passionate kiss on the forehead.

The second scene (twenty years later). Dawn has grown up and four fiancés are courting her. They all dance. General delight! Hunchback appears with a distaff. Dawn takes the spindle and dances. During the dance she pricks herself and falls asleep. Everyone falls asleep, except of course the audience in the auditorium!

In the third scene, Prince Desired (Désiré) is hunting. The enchantress Lilac shows him "Sleeping Dawn" in a panorama. It's clear that he falls in love and rushes to her castle to kiss her on the forehead.

The latter he performs with pleasure in the fourth scene. Here everyone wakes from sleep and moves onto the fifth scene, a feast on the occasion of the wedding of Prince Desired with Princess Dawn.

Et que la fête commence!

All sorts of dances: minerals, Puss in Boots, Donkey Skin, ending with a Roman sarabande, a Persian sarabande (?), and Indian sarabande (??), an American sarabande (???), even a Turkish sarabande (????).

Everyone is satisfied, and the public doubly so. Only leaving the hall they ask each other why, on the playbill, the king is called Florestan XIV, and not the twelfth or the thirteenth. In Perrault's original, he's just "the king."

Turning to the dances, which is to say, to the legs of the dancers. I'll admit, these legs are—a most ticklish place! . . .

In the Prologue the first dance is called "the gifts of the enchantresses." Misses Petipa, Johansson, Kulichevskaya, Nedremskaya, and Anderson hand out these gifts. Which of these enchantresses is sweeter—I won't even try to decide. I only know that smiles were given to the public quite generously. Miss Johansson danced excellently, but little, and the others followed, in order of lessening progression. The genies waved large fans prettily and exuded *perfume*. The latter in such a fragrant ballet was simply gilding the lily. And then young girls brought in gifts—the limit, really, in my opinion! . . . It should be the other way around. . . . It's a fairy tale after all! And a boring one in the Prologue.

Scene 2 begins with a dance, impossible to translate into Russian, so it was called "Caguets [*sic*] des tricoteuses." This dance could comfortably be left off the program for its insignificance.

Village waltz. The best number in the ballet. Graceful, picturesque, and assembled with great taste. The audience liked it, and Mr. Petipa was called out.

Grand dance with ballerina Brianza and her maids of honor. The princess surpasses the "steel toes" of her maids, who nonetheless, in the persons of Miss Tistrova, Fedorova 2, Vorobyova, and Gruzdovskaya, didn't lose heart and dance sweetly, despite their funereal tunics. Here the dances were difficult to perform to music that lacked rhythm. After all, it's impossible to dance without a beat. From the point of view of its music, this dance could be called tact-less.[3]

Scene 3. We are at a hunt and envy Prince Désiré, who has duchesses, baronesses, countesses, and marquises in his suite—each in pairs. Plus, eight huntresses—amazons! This is a happy prince! Willy-nilly, in such a mass of charming women, he's left to a game of blind-man's bluff, in other words, catch what you can. After this, the hunt concludes with a general farandole—short but nicely staged. The panorama brings honor to the designer Bocharov.

Scene 5. This is the highlight of the ballet. A wedding takes place here, so they dance a lot. A polonaise called "the procession of fairy tales" opens the scene. "Blue Beard" (Mr. Orlov) is there, and Puss in Boots (Mr. Bekefi), and Donkey Skin (Miss Ogoleit II—please, ma'am, don't be angry with me! I'm not to blame!), and Cinderella (Miss Petipa), and on and on. A whole kaleidoscope of colors, exposing the taste of author of the sketches and the brilliance of his fantasy. The children in the hall were in ecstasies.

After the polonaise a divertissement followed on the program. Four fairies danced: Misses Johansson, Kulichevskaya, Kryuger, and Tistrova. The diamond among them was Miss Johansson, of course, but the other stones were gems as well.

Individual dances: Puss in Boots and the White Cat. This cat duet danced to catlike imitations from the orchestra and was repeated by Miss Anderson and Mr. Bekefi. The latter was a real cat. *The Blue Bird and Florine.* Lovely! Miss Nikitina and Mr. Cecchetti fluttered. The music is very pretty. Their success was full and deserved. *Cinderella and Fortuné.* Miss Petipa and Mr. Kshesinsky II. *Little Red Riding Hood and the Wolf.* Miss Zhukova I and Lukyanov were rewarded with fitting applause.

In all these dances, which conveyed the appropriate shadings, showed that balletmaster Marius Petipa, as before, is at the peak of his calling. All was sweet, graceful and caressed the eye.

Finally, there was the ballerina Miss Brianza! Bravo! Bravo! . . . She overcomes incredible difficulties. . . . We'll come back to her.

The ballet ends with five sarabandes. There are Turks and Americans and Persians and even Romans! . . . Whatever you like, just ask! . . .

A fairy tale! A fairy tale in the full sense of the word! The pantomime finds itself in an unprecedented absence! . . . Don't even look for any sense! All of Perrault's tales are mixed up, thrown into one pile, and the new ballet doesn't produce any one impression as a result. It is a heap of a whole string of wonderful pictures, with marvelous decors, luxurious costumes—a kaleidoscope that blinds the viewers. It is indeed a fairy tale—a fairy tale for children and old men who have returned to a childish state . . . but a ballet, as we understand it? No! It is the complete decline of choreographic art!

Balletmaster Mr. Petipa, as before, remains the best arranger of dances, as always. All of his dances breathe with freshness and honor his enormous taste, in the group dances and in his ability to direct masses—though, unfortunately, there aren't many in the new ballet. The character dances are elegant in proportion to the talents of their sweet performers. The representatives of the classical school were occupied with their special business, dancing with their legs. And those lacking "classicism"—they danced more with the torso and arms, which still comes off very sweetly and gracefully! Mr. Petipa found a becoming place for every man and woman according to his or her merits.

The decors and costumes were a luxury! . . . The panorama is especially good—Mr. Ivanov's best decor.

Concerning Mr. Chaikovsky's music, its orchestration shines, it is always elegant and transparent . . . but . . . but . . . for the ballet it is nonetheless far from suitable. In the audience they called it either a symphony or a melancholy. There are several numbers, especially in the last scene, that caress the ear . . . but in general the music didn't satisfy the balletomanes.

Novosti i birzhevaya gazeta
5 January 1890

THEATER AND MUSIC: A NEW BALLET

The fairy tales of Perrault, in the poeticity of their descriptions, have always suggested a rich and much-loved subject for graphic artists, painters, tableaux vivants, masquerades, and the like. This material enticed our current [theater] directorate as well, which took the external beauty of production as its motto. To be fair, the material fell into good hands and the spectacle turned out brilliantly. Leaving aside the luxury of the costumes, which was taken to the extreme, much taste and artistic talent was spent on the production of the new ballet *Sleeping Beauty,* which was given for the first time on 3 January on the stage of the Maryinsky Theater. Silk, velvet, plush, gold and silver embroideries, wonderful brocades, fur, feathers, and flowers, armor and metallic adornments—it was extravagant and unstinting, with money lavished on the adornment of even third-rate characters. In the Prologue, where the *Christening* (?) of the newborn Princess Aurora takes place, good fairies (together with "genies, bearing fragrances" and "young girls, carrying gifts") endow her with all virtues, according to the program. The court of Aurora's happy parent, King Florestan XIV, is dressed luxuriously in medieval knightly costumes. This style is maintained in the costumes of the fairies and their suites and pages, with slight modifications, demanded by fantastic beings who lend a barely perceptible but highly poetic character to the personages and events of the fairy-tale world. Especially good are the costumes for the Lilac Fairy, and Miss Petipa is strikingly beautiful in them. The costumes of the first act belong to the same epoch. Princess Aurora appears already as a grown girl, who rejects the advances of four prince-suitors: Chéri, Charmant, Fortuné, and Fleur du pois. She prefers to dance and gambol until the spell of the evil fairy Carabosse submerges her in deathly sleep and the good king and all his court are in despair. (Miss Brianza is dressed in a luxuriant red costume, with gold embroideries and gold lace that especially suit her.) The costumes of the following acts move the action a few centuries ahead, and the hunt of Prince Désiré (Act II) takes us directly into the golden age of Louis XIV, with mincing marquises and curled cavaliers. The awakening of the princess and all her sleeping kingdom leads, of course, to the wedding, which takes place in the last act, in the presence of the entire court of the Sun King (he is Florestan XIV, after all) and characters from all the tales of Perrault, from Tom Thumb to Little Red Riding Hood, including Puss in Boots. The rich costumes of the Sarabande are also exceedingly harmonious: Roman, Persian, Indian, American, and Turkish—foreign nations as interpreted by the artists of Louis XIV and depicted in the Court of Versailles' celebrations and carousels.

The last act takes place on an esplanade (to achieve a full-scale identification of the court of King Florestan with the court of the Sun King, most likely) behind which decors recreate a completely accurate large Versailles palace, with terraces, fountains, a carousel square, gronde pièce d'eau [*sic*], and other luxurious devices of King Louis. For the record, these decors demand a depth of stage much deeper than what is available in the Maryinsky Theater, and because of that, the work of the talented professor Shishkov doesn't create the effect it might in greater perspective. Mr. Levogt designed the decors of the Prologue (Florestan's palace), Mr. Andreev and Mr. Bocharov, the first act (the court garden). Compared to their earlier work, these men didn't create anything especially successful. Mr. Ivanov's decors for the interior of the palace of the sleeping princess are not bad at all. Covered with the dust of many years, overgrown with moss, and fossilized in an unwaking sleep, they suddenly transform into a fresh, bright hall, with a cheerfully burning fireplace. This transformation—like the gradual growth of the forest around the enchanted castle and the moving panorama of the scenery in the second act—drew calls for the machinists, Mr. Berger and Mr. Bocharov, who painted a highly typical and skilled landscape of the panorama, depicting wild places alongside which Prince Désiré sails to the enchanted castle in a boat with the Lilac Fairy. But we must admit that from the point of view of scenic effects and the wonders of the machinists' department of our ballet stage, neither the panorama nor the transformations satisfied. The movement of the cut decors between the audience and the motionless standing boat—and before the completely motionlessness foreground—give a very weak illusion. Much less than with the movement of the backdrop, and that device has been used more than once in the ballet (*Humpbacked Horse*), and in the Zoological Garden, with no less, if not greater effect. The growth of the forest outside the palace, created by lifting cut curtains from the traps onto the forestage, gradually and slowly hides the stage from the audiences' eyes like an ordinary curtain, but from the bottom, not the top. The transformation of the sleeping, lifeless palace into the lively one, and the change à vue (?), from the outside of the castle to the hall, takes place over a very long space of time, behind a cloudy tulle curtain, and in complete darkness (!) on the stage.

As you can see, to speak of the new ballet one must speak most of all about its physical staging, which really does predominate. The choreography's role is not great: there are some fourteen dance numbers in the whole ballet. Of those, the ballerina dances three pas d'action. Miss Brianza performed her dances brilliantly in legibility, strength, and grace, though there is neither nothing new or especially beautiful in their composition. This poverty of imagination also characterizes the large group dance in the Prologue, the allegro variations of the six fairies of the Prologue and the pas de quatre of the four fairies of the final act: familiar cabrioles and entrechats, but this time without the elegant artistic devices that always distinguish the talent of our balletmaster. We must admit that the waltz of the first act is more successful, and more picturesque in its groupings. The groupings in the sleeping castle are good, though Doré helped the balletmaster quite a lot. The most interesting numbers—that carry the stamp of the epoch and the knowledge and taste of Mr. Petipa—are the farandole and the variations of the court ladies at the hunt of Prince Désiré (the "huntresses" as they are called in the program) and the divertissement of fairy-tale characters in the last act. Miss Nikitina danced her pas de deux with Mr. Cecchetti wonderfully and was received as the public always receives its graceful favorite. The dance of Puss in Boots (Mr. Bekefi) and the White Cat (Miss Anderson) was performed very nicely and repeated. Miss Zhukova I was delightful in her naive grace as Little Red Riding Hood with the Wolf (Mr. Lukyanov). Miss Petipa was an extremely beautiful Cinderella, dancing an entire little scene with Prince Fortuné (Kshesinsky II) that well characterizes the sense of the tale. The children depicting Petit Poucet and his brothers with the Cannibal were very funny. The final coda and sarabande seem very strange, as they turn into a mazurka, whose appropriateness to Versailles seems debatable. We will pass over the music for the ballet, inspired by P. I. Tchaikovsky, in silence, leaving it to the competent analysis of a music critic.

To summarize the impressions the new ballet produced on the viewer, one must admit that its artistically delicate manner doesn't satisfy. At the beginning of this article, we said that the tales of Perrault, in the strength of the poeticity of their descriptions, offer good material for the externals of the production. But their internal content, the lack of complexity, the simplicity, and childlike naïveté, cannot feed the fantasy essential for the creation of the program of a grand ballet of this type, to which our audience has become accustomed over the course of many decades. We are prepared to sit for four hours in the theater, but under the condition that the ballet be substantive in its artistic essence, mimetic tasks, and the obvious drama of its situations, which gives the ballet the right to stand among other fine arts. If the ballet will be *only a spectacle,* a varied kaleidoscope of costumes and decors, then no production splendor can purchase its emptiness, lack of content, and the tedium that inevitably takes hold of every "adult" by the end—let alone the aesthetically developed specta-tor. At risk of seeming a purist in art, we cannot help but lament the path chosen by the the-ater's directorate in lowering the artistry of our ballet.

N. [Dmitry Korovyakov]

Peterburgsky listok
5 January 1890

THEATER COURIER: ONCE MORE ON THE NEW BALLET

Like it or not, we must speak once again about *Sleeping Beauty,* which is an irritation for our balletomanes, and also for our painters, set designers, costumers, and composers, thanks to participation of the academic set designers and such a maestro as P. I. Tchaikovsky.

The first condition for the ballet to be a *ballet,* and not a féerie with dances, is that: (a) that the dances correspond to at least the basic needs of the choreography and (b) that these dances must necessarily be a *direct consequence* of the ballet's plot.

Without this, a ballet isn't a ballet but something absurd and incomprehensible. We needn't look far for examples. Why have old ballets such as *Esmeralda, Catarina,* and others like them enjoyed such success? Because their dances are directly linked to the action and arise from the content of the ballet. In *Sleeping Beauty* there is nothing of the sort. The line of action doesn't *illustrate* the dances at all. The dances are neither here nor there and in the majority of cases come as an unexpected surprise, like a hair that fell into the soup. Thus the viewer who hasn't read the libretto in advance or who is not familiar with the plot won't understand anything at all, be lost in guesses, and will finally lose interest little by little. His attention will be directed only to the external features of the ballet if the decors and costumes caress his eye.

That is what happened with *Sleeping Beauty.* The awkward and uninteresting composi-tion of the program, with its mass of inserted, unnecessary scenes and appearances, with no direct link to the path of action, and the dances of all sorts of animals for no reason produced a bad impression, turning the balletomanes into a question mark on the one hand, and on the other, upon seeing the luxurious, rich costumes and artistically exquisite decors, an ex-clamation point. But is the purpose of *ballet* only to arouse surprise and delight by its pro-duction alone, and not by its dances? In the newly compiled (indiscriminately borrowed scenes from various tales of Perrault) choreographic (?) work of M. Petipa, the dances are led off to the background, and all the inspiration, creativity (?) and fantasy (?) of the balletmas-ter results in curious and clumsy entrées and the appearances of either fairies, or cats, or birds, or animals. There are no groups, ensembles, or general poses that are ingenious or artistic in their conceptions. Not a single new adagio, variation, striking solo, or pas de deux was devised for the ballerina. Only Miss Nikitina, in fact, was given a pas de deux that corre-sponds roughly to her talent: the variation in the birds' scene with some sort of prince. The dancer performed that pas brilliantly and received a storm of applause. The character dance of the white cat with Puss in Boots was also a success: Miss Anderson and Mr. Bekefi enjoyed a completely justified triumph. But there was little in the sense of choreography, especially for five or six scenes that lasted four hours!

Concerning the music of such a venerable composer like P. I. Tchaikovsky, it proved in the most positive sense that the most talented *opera* maestro may be unsuccessful as a *ballet* composer. In this case, P. Tchaikovsky suffered the same fate as the great French artist-composer of many wonderful operas, Ambroise Thomas, who wrote the music for the ballet *The Storm*. We attended the premiere of *La Tempête* in the Grand Opera in Paris last summer. The ballet suffered a fiasco, thanks primarily to Thomas' music, which turned out to be completely unsuited for dance, although it was very rich with the beauties of a serious symphony. Almost the same occurred a few days ago in the Maryinsky Theater. The difference being that P. Tchaikovsky's music for the ballet wasn't a failure in the end (and it couldn't be, since there was no *ballet*). But like Thomas' music, it didn't suit dances. Our famous composer isn't the guilty party here: nature grants every artist "his" special purpose. Minkus, Pugni, and Delibes couldn't have arranged such an opera as *Eugene Onegin*. And Tchaikovsky couldn't cope with the demands of ballet music. None of this, by the way, prevents the first three or the last from being great musical artists in his own line and genre.

Peterburgskaya gazeta
5 January 1890

THE BALLETOMANE'S GRIEF

If they began giving operettas instead of operas on the opera stage—even by Offenbach, with cancans—then that would be the decline of lyric drama.

If the Alexandrinsky Theater would spend money only on farces and *bouffes* instead of on comedies and dramas, then that would be the decline of dramatic art.

And finally, if on the best European ballet stage, they begin to stage one ballet a year, and that ballet would be oriented exclusively to decors and costumes, without any sort of plot, then that will be the decline of choreographic art.

These thoughts occurred to us concerning the production of *Sleeping Beauty*, a ballet-féerie on the stage of the Maryinsky Theater. In this supposed choreographic work there isn't any sort of plot. It is summed up in a few words: They dance, fall asleep, and dance again. They woke up and once again started dancing. There is no peripeteia, no development of the plot, no interest to seize the spectator, to force him to follow the play's action.

They will say to us "but it's a fairy-tale!" Yes! . . . But what could be more interesting than a fairy tale? Reading one, everyone wonders what will come next, and how will it all end! Just think of the ballets *Humpbacked Horse* and *The Fisher and the Fish*. Not only children, but adults follow the adventures of the tale's fool and are actively interested in his fate.

But in the new ballet *Sleeping Beauty* there isn't any such peripeteia to justify the title féerie. No, no, and once more, no!

Aside from the costumes and the panorama, there's nothing magical at all! And from that perspective the ballet can't satisfy even the most undemanding viewer.

We, people of good traditions, are accustomed to watching a ballet from a completely different point of view. We like either poetry for light-winged ballerinas or drama, where mime artists can demonstrate the power of their mimetic skills. And in *Sleeping Beauty*, where is the poetry? There is brilliance and variety in the costumes. No one would say "How poetic! . . . What plastique! What aesthetics!!"

Neither would anyone say "What a dramatic scene! . . ." Not even the prima ballerina has a single mime scene, and the rest of the artists have nary a trace!!

Ballets with a *plot,* poetry, only vital somehow! . . . Those can be shown on a large stage or a small one! They are possible everywhere! Take away the brilliance of *Sleeping Beauty*'s costumes—would this "beauty" still be possible without the costly means of the stage! . . . No! . . . Without the kaleidoscope of costumes the ballet would be a trifling skeleton and the "beauty" would turn into a fright.

Dances? . . .

The dances in a ballet must necessarily flow from the action. It's the same for the duets, trios, and choruses in the opera. . . . Just as it is impossible to throw a duet out of an opera, without destroying the general plan of action, so in the ballet all the dances must be composed in such a way that they form the soul of the choreographic work.

What do we see in *Sleeping Beauty*? . . . A divertissement, where dance numbers are either poorly linked to one another or attached like rags to a Trishkin caftan.[4]

"A fairy-tale!" they will say. But a tale is a world of poetry! An arena for fantasy, though inexhaustible, but each tale of any people still belongs to a given, specific epoch. Fantasy has no space, but it has time; the epoch is always in the foreground in a tale.

But anyway, that's how it is! . . .

Today I had to speak with simple "viewers," unacquainted with the mysteries of choreography or its nuances.

"Did you see *Sleeping Beauty?*"

"I did . . ."

"Well, and did you like it?"

"Oh! . . . Puss in Boots and Nikitina's bluebird were wonderful!"

And that's all the acclaim! And about the ballet—not a word! . . . Such reviews! . . . There is nothing whole, nothing constructed harmoniously! . . .

I am demanding of this art because enormous sums of money are spent on a ballet production. That's the first thing, and the second: I wish that choreography would perfect itself as an art that develops the aesthetic tastes of the public rather than sliding to the level of the plotless féerie. It's sad! . . .

Beauty should not be called a ballet-féerie, but a diorama and exhibit of costumes and props. But not a *ballet* in the sense that Noverre and other pillars of the art understood the term.

S. Kh. [Sergei Khudekov]

Peterburgskaya gazeta
6 January 1890

THEATER ECHO

Although the luxury of the costumes in *Sleeping Beauty* has been noted by all, some of these costumes nonetheless present great inconveniences. Here is a fact. . . .

Carlotta Brianza was barely in a condition to finish the ballet. . . . In the pas de quatre of the last act, during the turns, the artist scratched her whole right arm above the elbow on

Gerdt's costume, to the point of drawing blood. The straps of the costume, which seem to cover the cuirass, are unthinkable for the cavalier of a ballerina. . . . Mlle. Brianza suffered even more, and more perceptively, when a lock of her luxuriant hair, suddenly torn from her head, fell on these straps. . . .

Then she almost fainted. Attention should be paid to such an inconvenience on M. Gerdt's costume.

Peterburgskaya gazeta
8 January 1890

THEATER ECHO

Yesterday's benefit for the ballerina Miss Brianza in the Maryinsky Theater netted a full house, flowers, and valuable gifts. The ballet-féerie *Sleeping Beauty* was given for the second time. We have already discussed the performance and production. Our remark on the awkwardness of Mr. Gerdt's costume in the last act was brought to attention. This costume, which scratched the arm of the ballerina, was not changed, but the choreography was slightly reworked. In essence, it is an evil irony for the new ballet in general: as if the dance exists for the costume and may be sacrificed to the latter! The appearance of Aurora, Carlotta Brianza, was greeted in benefit style, which is to say loudly and warmly. We are only left to regret that the talented perpetrator of the celebration had no place to show the full brilliance of her choreographic virtues. Italian women love to dance and are accustomed to dancing a great deal. The extremely difficult adagio of the second scene was but an arid trifle for the benefit's star. Miss Nikitina danced the pas de deux with her worthy partner, Mr. Cecchetti, irreproachably. They received stormy applause. Miss Nikitina's successes grow not by the day, but by the hour. It is not difficult to draw the conclusion that the ballerina works very hard on the development of a genial talent.

Miss Brianza was presented a diamond star in a white box, topped by a silver plate with the donors' names. And then a horseshoe brooch with sapphires, and a bracelet with diamonds. We won't inventory the flowers presented.

Peterburgsky listok
8 January 1890

THEATER COURIER

Miss Brianza's benefit. As might have been expected, last night, the seventh of January, the auditorium of the Maryinsky Theater overflowed from top to bottom with the "cream" of the capital's society, despite the fact that a known quantity of Petersburg's beau monde and the most fashionable high life attended a special performance in the palazzo of Mr. Sheremetev the same evening. Thus, there were two magnetic forces pulling at once, each more interesting and alluring than the other. Nonetheless, there were audiences for both enticements. For her benefit performance, the pretty and talented Milanese ballerina was given the second performances of *Sleeping Beauty,* of which we have already spoken in detail. From her first appearance on the stage of one of our summer suburban theaters (a few years ago in the former Livadia), Miss Brianza immediately drew the attentions of the balletomanes. She scored a completely deserved triumph, and then, after being taken into the state ballet troupe, strengthened her right to be considered a ballerina *di primo cartello* with every new appearance. In the course of her first season of service in the Maryinsky Theater she had less success than now, relatively speaking. The talented artist was not sufficiently sure of herself and was a bit heavy, which impeded her airiness and lightness. But Miss Brianza obviously worked a great deal in the following seasons and persisted with brilliant results. In avoiding extra weight, she gained aplomb, strength, and steadiness. With the gradual development of her acting and mime, she finally became a dancing "star" of first magnitude, whose radiance now dazzles and enraptures true connoisseurs of ballet art. With each new role and each new appearance the ballerina vanquished an ever-greater number of balletomanes. The number of admirers of her gifts is now legion.

The best proof of all this was the enthusiastic reception and the ovations, tributes, calls, and applause conferred on her in the course of the last evening.

For the record, the gifts presented her: a star of diamonds, a brooch (a sapphire horse-shoe), and a diamond bracelet. The flowers, baskets, bouquets and material evidence of admiration could not have been more numerous, nonetheless, the ballerina deserved them completely. We are happy for her and mentally applaud those among us who truly appreciate the distinguished, talented Miss Brianza. She and our Russian ballerina Miss Nikitina are, at the moment, true ornaments of the Petersburg ballet troupe, who have no peers anywhere. And if we lag behind other European ballet stages in the sense of "machine" transformations and all sorts of "tricks," then in the sense of representatives of choreographic art, beginning with the ballerinas, soloists, first dancers and ending with the corps de ballet, we are untouchable and beyond even the most condescending comparisons. We say this not out of a sense of "sour-necked" patriotism but *en toute connaissance de cause,* since each year we personally see ballets on all the large European stages and have thus formed this opinion not on the basis of others' words or rumors but based on what we have seen and witnessed ourselves.

Russkie vedemosti

14 January 1890

THE NEW BALLET *SLEEPING BEAUTY*

[A feuilletoniste who wrote under the pseudonym "Bukva" [letter], I. F. Vasilevsky wrote frequently on the ballet. The first half of Vasilevsky's article discusses social dances at the German Club—T.S.]

The ballet is very beautiful where the decors and costumes are concerned. The libretto was composed to Perrault's famous tale ("La belle au bois dormant"). It is a sweet and poetic tale, but has little movement and is too simple. The plot is pale and watery for the stage. The ballet has no intrigue, drama, or action and leads only to special effects and fairy scenes. The dances are distinguished neither by their originality or their character and don't provide the ballerina (Miss Brianza) gratifying material. The public most enjoys and calls for the very graceful, naive, and melodic group dance, the *valse villageoise.* The sarabande in the last act is also fiery and colorful. The music of *Sleeping Beauty* belongs to Mr. Tchaikovsky. It merits attention, of course, and is clever in its way, with many charming, tender, and captivating moments and fragments. But its symphonic gifts don't fully befit the ballet. Dances demand brighter "thicker" music—coarser, even, and more expressive. Subtle and complex orchestral colorations get lost in the ballet. Concerning the decors and costumes, the Maryinsky now takes first place in Europe. Last summer, I saw almost all the main stages in the West. And they are without doubt inferior to ours. You won't see such splendor and brilliance, and nowhere else will the staging expenditures be felt and "speak" as here, where production splendor has become an artistic goal and end. It gives the theatrical work everything that authorial or directorial resourcefulness, ingenuity, and whimsy could desire. The masterfully painted decors for *Sleeping Beauty* are distinguished by some innovations. In the second act the whole scene grows and becomes a dense forest, gradually rising in view of the spectators, from bottom to top. A moving cut decoration (in the vision scene) is used for the first time in the third act and opens onto several wonderful landscapes and forest scenes. The entire change between the fourth and fifth scenes takes place very skillfully *à vue*. The curtain remains raised and the orchestral divertissement continues. Two excellently executed banks of clouds move from the right side of the wings to the left to gradually close the front portion of the stage. It is very dark in the theater. In a few minutes, the clouds disperse and full illumination instantly lights the enormous, new, and extremely striking scene of the sleeping princess' castle. The costumes merit even more praise and avoided routine. For all their fantasy and fairy-tale whimsy, they are very successfully designed and executed irreproachably. The large march, in the polonaise, with all the famous characters of the fairy tales—Bluebeard, Puss in Boots, Goldlilocks, Cinderella, Little Red Riding Hood, Tom Thumb, the Cannibal, and others—is an utterly artistic gallery of excellent impersonations; each figure a most talented drawing for a chromolithographic keepsake. The characters appear as porcelain statues of Wessex or Sevres. The colors of the costumes for the female corps de ballets groupings are also wonderfully selected. Very soft and tender halftones and shades are blended in them, lending a refined and elusive dandyism to the whole scene. It recalls K. Makovsky's and Prof. Jacobi's manner of arranging color in our painting. According to rumor, all the costumes for *Sleeping Beauty* were executed from watercolor sketches of the director of the theater, I. A. Vsevolozhsky.

"Bukva" [I. F. Vasilevsky]

Peterburgskaya gazeta
16 January 1890

THEATER ECHO

The music for *Sleeping Beauty*, written by our famous composer, P. I. Tchaikovsky, is already his second attempt: his first ballet, *Swan Lake,* given in Moscow, suffers from its too monotonous character. The author turned almost a dozen waltzes loose on the *Lake.* That doesn't happen in *Sleeping Beauty,* but here, there's something else. . . .

In recent times, more than in the past, one notices a striving for originality in the composer's work, a desire to say something new. Of course that is, and ought to be, the desired goal of any artist. Unfortunately, this striving is not as evident in the area of musical thought as in the bounds of its external form.

That P. I. Tchaikovsky possesses all the secrets of contemporary orchestral technique has long been apparent, and in this regard, he rightfully occupies a leading position among European composers. All the same, one must admit that the author of *Onegin, Romeo,* and "Winter Dreams" sometimes abuses his mastery and skill in commanding the powers of the orchestra.

The ballet we are discussing could serve as an example. Why, for instance, did the composer need such dense colors and the massive orchestration for the depiction of Aurora's Christening, the first scene, which is superfluous in the ballet—both to the narrative (is there a christening in the tale?) and to the music. Judging from the music, one might guess that it was something about Macbeth and his witches.

Isn't this like weaving a spiderweb with a rope? In ballet one awaits music that is more or less transparent, light, and gracious, that speaks to the fantasy of the plot. Instead, *Sleeping Beauty's* listeners find themselves under an influence that nearly borders on the sensation that follows some sort of "good" act of *The Ring.* Operaticism, and especially symphonicism in the ballet—when they have no dramatic content whatever (in contrast to Mr. Ivanov's *La Vestale,* for example)[5]—too rich and heavy, are armor in costume's place.

Everything is good in its place. That's why the remaining acts, once the composer has descended from the heavens, create a better impression. Examples include the wonderful dances in the second act (the hunt scene) with their variations; the nice dances at the wedding in the last act, where the fairy-tale heroes appear; the waltz in the first act; the farandole; and others.

There are places in the ballet where Tchaikovsky's talent shines in all its splendor: the little solo for the violin, wonderfully rendered by Mr. Auer (accompanied by the harp), and for the cello, excellently performed by Mr. Loganovsky. This last solo is one of the best pages of Tchaikovsky's music for *Sleeping Beauty.*

In other places in the ballet one hears phrases familiar from his other works: the beginning of the march in the last scene has much in common with the march from *Mazeppa.* Some things recall parts of *Onegin,* though many authors repeat their own ideas and there is nothing surprising in their rewriting. Nonetheless, the music of the ballet generally leaves a rather vague impression. Alongside excellent numbers there are pages that would be better suited for something other than a ballet. However, it is possible that ballet music is undergoing a new phase in its development in our day.

It is only unfortunate that such music is linked to such a banal, unpoetic, plotless work as *Sleeping Beauty,* which is a museum of theatrical props, and nothing more!

L

Novoe vremya

22 January 1890

MUSICAL SKETCHES

Sleeping Beauty, a ballet novelty, whose music was written by Mr. Tchaikovsky, is now the most important event in the musical theater. Even among a public indifferent to art, Mr.

Tchaikovsky attained such a level of popularity after *Eugene Onegin* that he forces it to take an interest in all his new stage works.

I will not touch on the choreographic side of the new ballet, which was already discussed in *Novoe vremya* by a specialist. And where plot is concerned, I will only touch on it in passing, allowing myself to disagree with the opinions expressed in the press regarding the ballet's lack of content.

In my opinion, fairy-tale plots are appropriate for the ballet in their fantasy. They suit the choreographic art better than most others, more readily compelling belief in the reality of the phantasmagoria that the ballet presents. For every ballet is not only conventionalized, but also fantastic. Of course, a better plot more readily induces us to believe in the possibility of what is happening before our eyes. I don't mean to suggest in any way that fantastic plots are the only possibility for the ballet. Recent history offers a mass of evidence to the contrary, adding to its annals the enormous success of ballets with plots that are comic, tragic—even the most serious. But these don't exclude the potential of the success of fairy-tale plots. Why chase the tale from the realm of choreography, even if there was no drama in the most recent one? A fairy tale can also have its meaning, sometimes even a highly instructive one.

It would be possible to discuss the relative preference of the French tale over the Russian, but such a remark wouldn't carry much weight. Does it really matter where ballet plots are ladled from? The content is important and not the external form in which they are expressed. Why try to invent justifications? If all these works were taken from some other world, then it would be something worth fighting.

Mr. Tchaikovsky's music for *Sleeping Beauty* also drew the reproaches of several reviewers for the excess of its symphonicity. We have already had to hear these reproaches with regard to a few ballets staged earlier. I am not well acquainted with our earlier ballet literature, nor have I ever had occasion to hear the ballets of Mr. Minkus, who enjoys a great reputation as a master of his craft. But I must confess that the ballets of Pugni, and even the famous *Giselle* of Adam—the music that old devotees especially recommend as models of this type—didn't satisfy me. By force of its own destiny, the ideal of ballet music now has turned to a new leaf, and we must bid the pure dance music of the majority of the old ballets farewell. Meyerbeer, Gounod, Glinka, and many other opera composers gave us more than a few models of excellent ballet music in their operas that have nothing in common with the ballets of the past. The new generation of composers who write music for the ballet should, and have, followed their example, using means to achieve a symphonic genre of music. Of course, the music of one is more successful than that of the other, and one shows talent and the other is boring. But the direction remains unavoidable, and the ballet composers of other countries are joining the movement begun in France (Delibes, Lalo, Salver, Thomas, and others) and in Russia.

Mr. Tchaikovsky is no newcomer to the ballet. Apart from the dance numbers encountered in each of his operas, he wrote *Swan Lake* some fifteen years ago for the Moscow stage (where, by the way, his ballet didn't last and disappeared after a few performances). In that ballet, which is distinguished by its unusual abundance of waltzes, one can already see the composer's attraction to the symphonic genre—alongside all the waltzes. Already one encounters pages of a symphonic character much more often than in the usual ballets of those years. This disposition is understandable, since Mr. Tchaikovsky couldn't refuse the means his art presented him, whatever the prejudices of earlier choreography. This is even more obvious in *Sleeping Beauty*, where the plot itself demanded of him a greater application of the symphonic genre. If there is little dancing in Mr. Tchaikovsky's new ballet—and the inveterate balletomanes are complaining about this—it's not necessarily the fault of the author of the music. If such a treatment of the tales of Perrault as we see in the ballet's program should not relegate the choreographic contribution to a second place entirely, then it should at least allocate supremacy between the two elements (in the old days the symphonic element found itself in full subordination to the choreography).

If we move from the general character and direction of music in *Sleeping Beauty* to consider its ingenious achievements, even only on the basis of ballet composition, then we must admit that it is worthy of the brilliant talent of Mr. Tchaikovsky. Mr. Tchaikovsky is one of our richest melodists, if not the richest. Melodies—and what is more, melodies that are elegant, with clear contours, and understandable to all—are scattered throughout his ballet with a generous hand. If they are a bit monotonous and elegiac, then such is the nature of the talent of a composer inclined to melancholy. And by the way, this inclination makes itself known in *Sleeping Beauty* less than might be expected, judging from the majority of Mr. Tchaikovsky's compositions. All the same, it is felt. The composer even wrote the final apotheosis in a minor key, for example. It's clear he was unsatisfied with the union of two hearts in love. In general all the music of the third act, aside from the separate character numbers, is less cheerful, less varied, than one might expect from the story. It is brilliant music, as is the music of the first acts, thanks to Mr. Tchaikovsky's great mastery of orchestration. In his new work he displays orchestral color with truly dazzling brightness. By its orchestration, *Sleeping Beauty* is one of the most successful of his works. The orchestration lends color and life to even the insignificant and less successful pages of the ballet.

One would have to admit that the Prologue, first act, and almost the whole of second (save perhaps the dances of Aurora with her suite, called from their torpor by the will of the good fairy to show Prince Désiré his intended) are the best sections of the music of *Sleeping Beauty*. Perhaps if the ballet were shorter, the last act would not elicit the famous fatigue that it now invites—in part because of the size of the ballet, and partly from the music. We begin, unwittingly, to note the notorious lack of cheerfulness and animation that would have been particularly appropriate.

Whoever is acquainted with Mr. Tchaikovsky's instrumental works—and who isn't?— will immediately recognize the pen of the same composer in the music of *Sleeping Beauty* and will then be amazed by the freedom with which the composer gives the listener the pages of light dance music. Only foreign ballerinas—who only recognize rhythms marked by a bass drum—could find these rhythms uncomfortable for choreographic purposes. In the music of these light numbers (principally in the variations),[6] however, there is nothing banal. Quite the opposite, the music actually guards against an insufficiency of another type—harmonic refinement—at times using deliberate dissonance. (At least in the variations for Puss in Boots and the White Cat.) But Tchaikovsky's orchestration cannot only smooth over any dissonance, but even lend it a special piquant quality, as happened in the number we cited.

It is scarcely necessary to list the separate numbers of the ballet. There is so much beautiful music in it. The entire Prologue is interesting. The spectacular march is followed by the graceful scene of the entrée of the good fairies and the delightful adagio in which they present their gifts. Mr. Tchaikovsky has given a sizable role to the harp and the piano in his ballet. And here it sounds especially beautiful. The variations danced by the fairies are graceful. The finale, in which the evil fairy appears, is characteristic not so much for its musical content, but once again for the mastery with which the composer arranges the orchestral combinations. The Lilac Fairy's theme is pretty (the latter found a gracious embodiment in the person of Miss Petipa) and the music appears here in its full realization. This theme plays a large role in the ballet and is heard several times, beginning in the prelude, unchanged in harmony and form, but in a new orchestration each time. We note, by the way, that in the conclusion of the first act the Lilac Fairy's theme acquires a wonderful poeticity, thanks to the sustained and characteristic figure of the violins. Here the music conveys the coming spell with unexpected faithfulness and compels us to recall a similar scene ("the magic fire") in Wagner's *Walkürie.*

In the second act, as already mentioned, there are many wonderful pages. We cannot ignore the wonderful music that accompanies the moving panorama (the prince's journey to the enchanted castle). Once again it would be difficult to convey this circumstances in musical sounds better than Mr. Tchaikovsky has done—as in the number that follows, where the high tremolo of the violins so appropriately and so wonderfully portrays the scene of the sleeping kingdom. Here one hears the influence of the enchanted kingdom depicted several times in Glinka's *Ruslan,* but this in no way diminishes the impression. On the whole, Tchaikovsky had great success with the character of the fairy tale. In the last act of the ballet there are several wonderful character dances, and the scenes themselves add to their interest: Little Red Riding Hood dances with the Wolf, Puss in Boots, Tom Thumb, and other personages from Perrault's tales. One is unwillingly drawn into this whole half-forgotten world of fantastic dreams lost in childhood and feels complete sympathy with them.

In its content and the wonders of its staging it seems that *Sleeping Beauty* is destined for great success.

M. Ivanov[7]

Nuvelist

1890, no. 2

SLEEPING BEAUTY, BALLET-FÉERIE IN THREE ACTS WITH PROLOGUE, M. PETIPA, MUSIC OF P. TCHAIKOVSKY

It has been several years already since the theater administration changed the former order of things regarding the composition of music for new ballets. Before, there was a special post in the theater—the "composer"—who was obliged to write music for all the ballets that appeared on the state stages without exception. This position, which even now still seems to exist in Moscow, was occupied by Pugni for the last thirty or forty years and after him, by Minkus. Both are experienced in their craft and undoubtedly talented, especially the latter. But the choreographic routine in which they were supposed to vegetate, the job of inevitably writing one or even two ballets every year, could not help but weigh heavily on their fantasy and on their very attitude to the work. Mr. Minkus, who, together with Delibes, wrote one ballet for the Paris stage (*La Source,* it seems), should have known of the new tendency in ballet music, a tendency that was revealed in France and that took on a serious aspect that even the music for such a wonderful ballet as Adam's *Giselle* doesn't evoke. Mr. Minkus remained faithful to the traditions that have already ruled on the Petersburg stage more than a half century, traditions that accorded music a distinctly second place and demanded nothing of music but light tunes, with rhythms mostly marked by a bass drum. He has several wonderful ballets in which his talent speaks vividly, but there is no doubt that he has nonetheless remained outside the movement evident among the ballet composers of France.

This movement has roots in the ballet music that famous opera composers have included in their operas. If one listens to the music for the dances in *Robert le Diable, Les Huguenots, La Prophète, William Tell,* etc., or the ballet numbers in the operas of our own composers (Glinka, Rubinstein, and others), it would be impossible to remain in the same style of ballet music that even now predominates in Italy—or the lousy models we have in Marenco's music for *Excelsior, Amor,* and *Sieba.* French composers, with Delibes at the head, first demonstrated that even for the ballet one could write music that was accessible to all, suited to the choreographer's goals, and at the same time, such music that any progressive musician could sign on to. In recent years this tendency took up residence here too. Of course there are differences in style and in the details of the music of our latest ballets as compared with French ballets, and these are determined by differences in temperament of the composers of two nations, but the tendency is undoubtedly the same one. This tendency was already evident in *Harlem Tulip* (Prince Trubetskoy's pretty music for the ballet *Pygmalion* couldn't be considered here) and was realized fully in M. Ivanov's *La Vestale.* The latter was even forced to endure a great number of reproaches from the balletomanes for his "boring symphonies," etc. *La Vestale* was the first of our ballets in which the composer completely and consciously tread new ground in ballet music and made extensive use of the symphonic genre. Mr. Drigo's *Talisman,* which followed *La Vestale,* in part in its plot and in part thanks to the nationality of its author, markedly stepped back from this principle, though it already had little in common in character and instrumentation with the old ballets. In *Sleeping Beauty* Mr. Tchaikovsky followed the same path as Mr. Ivanov in *La Vestale* and, like his forerunners, drew the same reproaches from the balletomanes: of symphonicity and the unsuitability of his music for choreographic purposes.

The fact that these reproaches are completely baseless—and typically originate in the dressing rooms of ballerinas with neither good ears nor musical educations—matters little. With the passage of time both the ballerinas and balletomanes will become accustomed to this style that is new to them, but that in essence presents them nothing so terrible. Having grown accustomed to the "manner" of only one composer, they are not quite themselves when they became acquainted with another. Not to mention that now, not one of the educated composers, no matter where the directorate will turn with a commission for a new ballet, couldn't write in any other style than the one *La Vestale* and *Sleeping Beauty* are written in.[8] It has come to the point that all the lamentations of the old balletomanes will be in vain.

Mr. Tchaikovsky has already written a ballet, *Swan Lake,* for the Moscow stage. In that ballet (which didn't last in the repertory) he is far from the tendency that he now employs in *Sleeping Beauty.* There, conversely, he is closer to the past, and *Swan Lake* consists of a whole string of waltzes. Nonetheless, even in his first ballet one notes numbers written in a symphonic style. Not to mention that in his new ballet, where the plot relegated the choreographic contribution to second place, he nonetheless contributed greatly to the mime scenes, where the composer could and should exercise his disposition to the symphonic genre. It doesn't follow that in *Sleeping Beauty* there were too few dances or that in Mr. Tchaikovsky's music for the ballet there weren't light, playful melodies and numbers. Just the opposite: there were as many as one could want. Perhaps compared to the old choreography, *Sleeping Beauty* didn't have many dances, but in our opinion there were plenty. They pushed to the side even the plot, which, apart from choreography, lays claim as well to common sense.

The plot of the ballet is taken from the well-known tales of Perrault. There is, of course, no dramatic intrigue in them, as in all tales of this world. But all the same, one can read tales with pleasure and find sense in them despite the famous aphorism: "where there are wonders, there is little sense." It is this pleasure that Perrault's tales provide. And heroes of his other tales were added: Little Red Riding Hood, Tom Thumb, Peau d'ne, Cinderella—all the characters that thrilled us in childhood, who forced us to tremble for their fates. Here they are in cheerful masquerade at a celebration given in honor of the marriage of the awakened Princess Aurora and Prince Désiré. We won't discuss the realization of the plot. We'll only note that Aurora's dances with the prince during her sleep are introduced in vain. It seems that having danced to satisfaction, the princess just wants to go off and have a rest in the slumbering kingdom.

Mr. Tchaikovsky wrote music for this plot that is by no means difficult in the choreographic sense. It is beautiful and wonderfully orchestrated and only just a little monotonous, which one notices by the end of the ballet, where a little more *entrain* is just what is needed, more cheerfulness than the composer (distinguished by his noticeable tendency to melancholy) could give. Musically, *Sleeping Beauty* is one of our best ballets, as it is among the composer's most successful scores. Not all the numbers of the ballet are of equal merit; there are some weaker ones. Some of Tchaikovsky's ideas are even insignificant, but the whole conceals itself in the greatness of the orchestral colors, employed by the composer with a marvelous richness of imagination. The entire score shines and sparkles with these colors, which give an impression of something magical. The score suits that fairy-tale world that its sounds accompany. The composer put the piano and harp to great use, as well as the English horn. The orchestra for the new ballet is noticeably strengthened in number, which was not done for previous ballets.

Musically, the best of *Sleeping Beauty* must be the Prologue and Act I. There are a few weak numbers in Act II. And the third, though it is orchestrated as brilliantly as the first two, doesn't take on the character of festivity that is undoubtedly necessary here. We already spoke of this. The ballet begins with a short little prelude, part of which is dedicated to the depiction of the evil fairy, and another part to the theme of the good fairy Lilac. The theme is beautiful and repeats several times in the ballet in all its fullness, only changing its orchestration. At the raising of the curtain a march is heard, followed by gracious music of the arrival of the good fairies and the grand scene in which they bring gifts to the newborn princess. The variations the fairies dance are graceful and offer proof of the art with which Mr. Tchaikovsky can lend form to even insignificant ideas. The finale is characteristic, thanks mostly to the instrumentation, and beautifully conveys the image of the evil fairy and her repulsive suite. The theme of the Lilac Fairy, of which we spoke earlier, appears here in full magnificence. In the first act we note the scene with the spinners and the sweet peasant waltz, which always has success when the ballet is shown. The grand adagio that Aurora dances at her entrance is beautiful. But one of the most successful pages of the first act consists of its finish. The entire theme of the Lilac Fairy is repeated, but this time the orchestration is so magical, and the figure of the violins that depicts the imminent, unexpected spell and growth of the enchanted forest so beautiful, that the viewer is decidedly transported into a magical kingdom and wishes to believe in the truth of what he sees before his eyes.

In the second act we note the "blindman's bluff" and the striking dance of the Baronesses. Several variations are very interesting, but the crowning achievement of this act is the music of the moving panorama (the prince's voyage to the enchanted castle) and the scene of the sleeping kingdom. We can assume that M. Tchaikovsky was greatly aided by Glinka's *Ruslan* here. Nonetheless, the scene is musically magnificent. There are some nice character dances in the third act. The polonaise, to the sound of which pass the fantastic characters from Perrault's tales, is pretty. The ending of ballet, where a mazurka is inserted for no reason, is weak.

The music of the ballet drew reproaches from the majority of the Petersburg press, but, as the reader can see, this censure wasn't fair. *Sleeping Beauty* must be considered one of the most successful works of this gifted composer.

Novoe vremya
5 October 1890

THEATER AND MUSIC

The first appearance of Miss Carlotta Brianza, the only Italian ballerina invited for the Maryinsky Theater's current season, occurred last evening in *Sleeping Beauty*. The luxurious mise-en-scène of this ballet-féerie remained in all its brilliance, and the public's interest in the work of Mr. Tchaikovsky and Mr. Petipa has cooled so little that even on a Wednesday, when ballets are attended reluctantly, the Maryinsky Theater was completely full. The explanation for this is simple: for *Sleeping Beauty* they come not only to see the dancers, the costumes, and the decors, but also to hear Tchaikovsky's music (and there were many of the latter). The orchestra, led by the artful hand of the talented conductor Mr. Drigo, does its job wonderfully. The dancers have warmed to the character of Tchaikovsky's music, and now *Sleeping Beauty* is performed excellently. Miss Carlotta Brianza remains the same technically strong and fearless ballerina. She distinguishes herself, as before, in her *petite batterie,* her pointe work, and double turns. Unfortunately, the intelligibility of the latter in last evening's performance was marred to no small degree by her partners. Only Mr. Gerdt and Mr. Cecchetti have mastered the skill of partnering a ballerina in the difficult groupings and risky turns; the others were clumsy and awkward. The balletmaster would have been wise to place such partners at a respectful distance from the prima ballerina. Miss Brianza was met very warmly, as an old friend. She was much applauded and was presented a basket of flowers. A laurel wreath from the parterre was given to Mr. Bekefi, who appeared for the first time in this ballet after a long injury brought on by a sprained foot. The whole ballet repertory now rests on *Sleeping Beauty* until *Nenufar* and *The Smuggler's Marriage* will be ready. They have already begun to rehearse *Nenufar*.

Herman Laroche, excerpt from *P. I. Tchaikovsky as a Dramatic Composer* (reprinted from the *Yearbook of the Imperial Theaters*, 1893–94 season)
St. Petersburg, 1895

Thirteen years had passed [from the composition of *Swan Lake*]. [Tchaikovsky's] talent grew in breadth and depth. His fame spread much more quickly—not proportionally, but in breadth and depth, conquering ever more of Western Europe. Here, it spread ever lower, from the connoisseurs to the level of half-musical dilettantes.

The powerful development of his talent was more than a quantitative increase. The more important and urgent consequence was the slow rebirth that occurred inside the person and by the end of the 1880s gave us a Pyotr Ilyich with his former manner, in many respects, and aware of technique, but more tempered and sure of himself; with many of the former fascinations and hobbyhorses but with a new spirit, a new direction. In this happy, rich period of his work, fate sent him a libretto, as if made to order for him from time immemorial, as if the music were intended for him in that moment when he would feel his wings, when Tchaikovsky would come into his own. *Sleeping Beauty* was given to him on the 7 January 1890.

In fact the selection of the subject didn't please everyone. To explain it as a quibble of professional jealousy or competition is such a cheap ploy that I prefer to keep quiet about that side of things here. Perhaps it really was one of the reasons, but in no way the only one. The critics winced most at the fact that a "children's tale" served as the canvas for the new plot. Of course, one could simply have smiled at that abyss of local ignorance that those two, seemingly insignificant words open up. I will say, all the same, that in that winter I was unusually distressed and decided to write *two* feuilletons to the *Moscow Herald:* one, in defense of the plot, and the other, about the music itself. I wrote the feuilleton in defense of the plot; the feuilleton defending the music remains in me. Although I wouldn't expect the readers of the *Yearbook* to feel any special revulsion to *Sleeping Beauty* or to its plot, I will, all the same, return once again to this subject and cast a general glance at the relation between Perrault's tales to the choreography and the talent of Tchaikovsky.

"What are these children's tales to us? Couldn't they really think of anything more clever for the ballet?" That's what people ask who have *their* ballet, *their* ideal of dramatic truth in pantomime in mind. Given that this happened in 1890, I can, without any unusual courage, state that that ideal was Zucchi. The brave and charming Italian turned all our heads precisely in the last half of the 1880s. She didn't dance like the others, without a smile, but utterly in her own way. And she chose plots that allowed her originality to shine in all its splendor. The sober truth is that contemporary Italy is now crazy about *verismo,* just as we were thirty years ago. Zucchi is *verismo* translated into the language of dance. Therein lies her strength and also, perhaps, her weakness. Tchaikovsky didn't quite fall in love with Zucchi, mostly because her realism was at odds with his relationship to dance . . . counter to all his ballet fondnesses and traditions. In other words, his ideal was classical. He remained, or wished to remain, a ballet classicist to the present day, despite the fact that he had to write music for a ballet-féerie and not for a string of clever classical solos. Zucchi's weakness, I willingly admit, lay in the fact that the contemporary direction of ballet strives for the certainty of verbal speech—an occurrence that parallels what we see in contemporary instrumental music. In ceasing to be an "abstract play of sounds," music-poetry offers an analogy to ballet-poetry. Pyotr Ilyich wasn't far from music-poetry; he was attracted to its climes already in his youth, and in his middle period, and toward the end of his work. He simply couldn't stand realism in the ballet.

In contrast to opera, which is capable of representing contemporary, everyday, middle-class existence, the ballet is destined to carry us to the kingdom of the fantastic and the impossible, the incomprehensible and the inexpressible. The incomprehensible and the inexpressible—in its primordial creative expression—is myth. Before his first attempt to philosophize, before his first creation of art, and at the time of his first, childlike creative attempts, man encounters myth. Or in popular terms, *creates* it. Richard Wagner somehow expressed myth as the only truth spoken by man. He would scarcely have wanted to be understood literally, but in art, myth truly occupies a high place. It is sacred not only in the power of superstitious populations of yore, but also in the depth of the idea invested in it. Folk epics of all times are based on myth. Aeschylus and Sophocles are based on myth. Distant echoes of myth enchant us in Ariosto, Shakespeare, Goethe, Byron, and Pushkin. The fairy tale is nothing but a remote echo of a myth. In its prosaic form it can touch the realm of humor or irony and assume a form that is folkish or literary. The core of it remains a myth. To be offended by the fact that in 1890 the Petersburg ballet allegedly plundered myth is to fail to understand that myth is present in the ballet and in a significant portion of the opera, drama, comedy, and farce from the very beginning of the theater in our capital.

Another reproach: that the myth was taken from its French version, that the program was borrowed from Perrault's tale. To answer that reproach, it seems that only a few words are necessary. A French version was used because at the time they wanted to stage a French ballet. French costume was a given, a theme for variation. The balletmaster was French, and Perrault was more accessible to him than the brothers Grimm. And by the way, I am quite ready to share a Platonic wish that a ballet in which the dancers are almost exclusively Russian would eventually take on a national direction and be nourished and inspired by a Russian folk epic or Russian art-poetry. And if they reply that it is impossible to find an especially suitable subject, either in an epic or in contemporary poetry, or that Russian nature and Russian costume are too dull and poor for the ballet, I would answer that real talent succeeds in overcoming dull and intractable material. But this is all fortune-telling. At the present we have a wonderful canvas for a series of magical pictures that offer the imagination of the director and the machinist the most splendid assignments and don't hinder the balletmaster from carrying out his own, in other words: choreographing wonderful dances. It's absolutely true that the dramatic action in *Sleeping Beauty* is slow and elementally simple. But it's the same in the *Odyssey,* and in Aeschylus' *Prometheus,* and in Boccaccio's *Griselda,* and in Wagner's *Parsifal.* That is what makes the fairy tale a type of myth; the events in them flow quietly and imperturbably.

I praise the abundance of action in some operas of Da Ponte and in most operas of Scribe so sincerely, that my bias for the libretto of *Sleeping Beauty* can't be construed as a tendentious enthusiasm for Richard Wagner or for a biased scorn for the "tawdry effects of grand historical opera in the Parisian manner." As librettos, Wagner's operas are very boring (espe-

cially the last ones). Scribe's operas (not all, of course, but the preponderance of them) are interesting, and for the composer, rewarding. I only wish to motivate the selection of the plot
and justify its reworking by the balletmaster in light of the fact that Tchaikovsky found in
both of these an unexpected and superb occasion to return to himself.

Of Byron's *Don Juan,* it was said that a middle-aged person takes things as they are and
looks at the world with happy eyes, in the same way that a young person, struck by the incongruity of the ideal with reality, brims with tears or threatens curses. You could say something of the same of Tchaikovsky. Of course, *Sleeping Beauty* isn't his *Don Juan.* But it's per-
missible to look at it as a part of a larger whole, like the first link of a chain of creation, a chain
broken by an unexpected catastrophe and therefore preserved for us only as a fragment. Together with *Iolanta* and *Nutcracker, Sleeping Beauty* represents a new step or a new phase in
the artist's development. The waves of universal grief had subsided; a period of furious romanticism was replaced by an enlightened and vigorous realism. I couldn't bring myself to
ascribe the motto "blessed is he who smiles" to this last phase of Tchaikovsky's, but only because the link snapped too early and the real meaning of this turn is that the genuine conclusion of his work is left to fate. In the incomplete form that his career now presents itself to
us, a separate moment takes on a chance, sometimes exaggerated meaning, and the gloomy
pessimism of the "Symphonie Pathétique" seems to us a key to the entire lyricism of
Tchaikovsky. Although it is quite possible that under normal circumstances, the stunning
and original score would be no more than an episode, like a echo of an experience receding
far into the past.

It seems to me that after the horrors of *The Enchantress,* the composer cheered up. We saw
the transition to *The Queen of Spades.* One year earlier we witnessed the blinding, luxuriant
ballet: it was as if the celebrated elegy writer and melancholic threw a sumptuous feast and
invited both his faithful supporters and a mixed crowd simultaneously, the latter accustomed to feeding on music that is generally accessible. Thanks to *Sleeping Beauty,* Tchaikovsky's name became famous in circles than formerly knew only Pugni, Minkus, Herbert,
Schneitzhöffer, and—Adolphe Adam. All these composers—at times capable melodists, at
time virtuosos of counterpoint—regarded the composition of ballet music with a biased
striving for salon lightness, for the rhythmic expressiveness of ballroom dancing. The ballets
of the adroit and learned Pugni were especially full of this affected vulgarity that, in its turn,
had an oppressing effect on the tastes of the balletomanes. It would be a mistake to think that
lovers of ballet watch without listening. I know people who play arrangements of ballets on
their pianos at home, like we play symphonies. If they didn't actually listen, then France
would not have had the ballets of Lalo and Delibes or ballet numbers in the operas of Auber
and Meyerbeer. The fame of the second act of *Life for the Tsar* would not have thundered
here. It's also true that the audience that hears ballet music in *operas* is not the same public (or
not quite the same) that overfills the hall on ballet days. It's true that this special ballet audience listens with less attention, speaks more noisily, and is probably more forgiving of wrong
notes. But they nonetheless have their favorite effects, motives, and their tradition of forms
and instrumentation. The composer of *Swan Lake* already had occasion to do battle with
those habits. The composer of *Sleeping Beauty* overcame them, as if jesting. And in this, his
powerful nature spoke once again. I insist on that word "powerful" with special pleasure as it
reminds me that before, in my inability to see nuances and proportions, I often said "sup-

ple." Petr Ilyich's nature, as we have seen, never *attained* suppleness. Others twist with the cunning of a stylish cat. Tchaikovsky proceeded directly, knocking over obstacles, bearing defeat, celebrating unforeseen triumphs, making mistakes, and making them constantly, though fewer and fewer with each year. And he became a ballet composer not because he was able to cope agreeably with unusual demands placed on him, but because at the depths of his nature lay, incidentally, an ability to compose dances. In *Swan Lake* that ability is only partially visible. In *Sleeping Beauty* and in *Nutcracker* it speaks fully.

The ability to compose dances is not the same as the ability to compose light music. It's not difficult to imagine a ballet score with dance rhythms, but only that. The ideas themselves and the harmonic trim are cumbersome, like Robert Schumann or even something heavier. One such work is Lalo's *Namouna,* which I heard some twelve years ago. But in general one could say that a similar style in ballet represents either a lack of taste or intentional extremism. Nowhere, apparently, is this simple truth so necessary to bear in mind than in Russia, where anything light is marked "*poshlost'.*"[9] If Tchaikovsky feared *poshlost',* if he paid any attention to the whine of affectation, to the virtuous terror of primness, to the contemptuous grimace of the false aristocracy, he would never have written *Sleeping Beauty,* or *Queen of Spades,* or *Iolanta,* or *The Maid of Orleans,* or romances to French texts. I will go even farther: he wouldn't have been Tchaikovsky. I repeat, he would not have lowered himself. He wouldn't have bowed or kowtowed to the public.

He was exactly what was needed to compose music for the ballet. Let's say for a moment, that this ability comprised one-seventh or one-eighth of his entire worth. Obviously, even after *Sleeping Beauty* he would not have become a composer of light music primarily. He wouldn't have become a rival of Strauss or LeCoq. But it is just as certain that he opened a new vein for himself and that the riches from that vein had barely begun to be mined when death overtook him.

I will say once more that in such beloved, and in places such an accessible music, there is no premeditated compromise. From the first bar of the introduction to the apotheosis, it is authentic, *real* Tchaikovsky. I'm not afraid to add that it is sometimes even the routine Tchaikovsky, as, for example, in the phrase in 6/8, the kind of leitmotif that accompanies the appearance of the Lilac Fairy. But how little there is of this manner, of this ballast compared to earlier scores! The composer's fascination with waltz didn't leave him even here. As in *Swan Lake,* the style of his waltzes is closer to Strauss the younger than to Chopin. But the melodic invention strengthened and became more youthful in that period, as the symphonic development became freer, more elegant, and substantive. It's not only the dances that are good, however. The pantomime is good too, but it doesn't seem at any point that the composer was *resting* in those places where he was supposed to write pantomime, that he sought to compensate himself in seriousness and density for the weight of the coercion he experienced in writing the dance numbers. There wasn't any kind of duress. Both poured down on him from above. I will even dare to say that the fact that the famous tremolo on the upper C (an innumerable quantity of bars are supported and accompanied by a potpourri of various motives and fragments of earlier numbers) is beautifully and skillfully done doesn't particularly impress me. We've heard these devices before and the harmonies aren't especially surprising. The very length of the tremolo (presupposing the intent to play upon our century's much-loved perseverance of monotony) would scarcely surprise anyone after Richard Wagner. We've heard if either from gods, dwarves, or giants! On the other hand, if those purely symphonic episodes don't surprise me in ballet music, then the dances at the wedding of Aurora and Désiré simply blind me with their elegant gaiety, their lively coquettishness, their gusts of passion, and their regal magnificence.

In comparison to this horn of plenty, the "character" spots in the score (for example, Carabosse's leitmotif) while wholly successful and expressive, lack that succulence, freshness, and grace of those (to the minds of extreme progressives) "banal" melodies. The music of *Sleeping Beauty* doesn't present that situation we often see in operas, where the recitatives are performed powerfully and beautifully while the numbers sung around them have a general stamp of conventionality and even banality. In the new ballet it is the cantilena that enchants me. The taste of the public and opinion of the specialist are in absolute agreement here. Being in agreement, they meet as well in the exceptions. In that final scene there is a number that even though danced, lacks what is pleasantly termed a "melody." In style it more closely resembles a transitional and connecting part in an opera than a principal lyrical phrase. I have in mind the famous duets for the cats. There's no doubt that in the usual aesthetic terminology, this comic intermezzo belongs to the category of the "character" rather than the "sublime." Nonetheless, it is one of the pearls of *Sleeping Beauty.* In general, sound imitation in musical composition plays no more than a third-rate role. Apart from the fact that its task is extramusical, its realization is rarely accompanied by wonderful music.

In Tchaikovsky's White Cat scene it is striking, first of all, that the sound imitation is achieved by completely artistic means—melodic motives and counterpoint linked to the instrumentation. And second, that this counterpoint, this instrumentation, could excite and satisfy a musical sense without the aid of any additional representation, without the comic effect of cats kissing and brawling on the stage. What is more, this number captivates and amuses with surprising accuracy, the same accuracy with which the composer overhead the intonations of declarations of love from the roof. Like the quintet in *Chereviki,* this ballet number belongs to the category of jokes delivered with unflappable seriousness. If the joke is a success it becomes even more irresistible in contrast to the serious mien. I repeat, in the depths of the many-layered soul of the composer, a ballet genius lurks below, hiding a talent for comic opera. If Tchaikovsky had been fated to live another ten years, he probably would have tried his strengths there too. Although we have seen more than a few surprises from him, that would even have surprised his friends, and his enemies, and among his friends, it seems, even his fanatical followers.

Alexander Alexeevich Pleshcheev, *Our Ballet, 1673–1896,* pp. 304–7

St. Petersburg, 1896

On 3 January 1890 the huge ballet-féerie *Sleeping Beauty* was given for the first time. The plot was taken from the tales of Perrault's "La belle au bois dormant." P. I. Tchaikovsky wrote the music for this féerie.

Of course neither the balletomanes nor the lovers of choreographic art in general rejoiced at the merger of ballet even with such a refined féerie, where the dances function only as an addendum to the spectacular production, which played the main role.

Fortunately, our talented artist M. I. Petipa applied all his efforts and composed such a mass of choreographic masterpieces that the féerie, despite its unprecedented splendor, didn't succeed in consuming the ballet. It would have been unthinkable to demand that the new fruit of Mr. Petipa's fantasy might have authored anything substantive or polished, because the programs of all féeries are aimed principally at external effects and lend nothing to the mimed dramatic scenes or to a performance in which mind and spirit might be invested.

We saw a beautiful divertissement that had no less success than the remarkable decors and the magical metamorphoses. We must thank the directorate when they show generosity to a production of a real, thoughtful ballet, but it is strange to make choreography dependent on brilliance and transformations. To this they reply that the ballet is not lost, is following its own course, and that one form of art cannot undermine another. But the féerie cannot be considered even a relative of art. Meanwhile, the féerie is taking hold of the repertory and squeezing out the ballet, which, after all, is left with only one day per week. To regard the ballet as an art form—and the directorate does just that, since it has a special school for the preparation of dancers—it would be unfair to put it on the same board with the féerie. It rather reminds me of the repertory invasion in the Alexandrinsky Theater, where the operetta was prudently chased out, despite its incredible success.

The designs for the costumes, which recalled the illustrations of Doré, belong to I. A. Vsevolozhsky and revealed much taste and historical knowledge. But the execution of the designs revealed some of their faults, namely, their heaviness and unsuitability for dancing. As an example, in the last scene Miss Brianza caught her marvelous hair on Mr. Gerdt's costume and nearly cried out in pain (as befits a ballet, she expressed this in mime). The problem with Mr. Gerdt's costume was noticed, but rather than change it in the second performance . . . they changed the choreography!

The music of P. I. Tchaikovsky, who possesses of the secrets of contemporary orchestration, is melodic, beautiful, and heard with pleasure. After the first performance, Messrs. Balletomanes maintained that this music, with its "symphonic combinations," was quite unballetic, and that in places, the rhythm was insufficiently distinct, etc. But with each hearing it was liked more and more. Soon all were in ecstasies over the music, and *Sleeping Beauty* attracted an audience that was scarcely "balletic." Perhaps some specific observations directed at the composer had some basis: perhaps the balletmaster was disadvantaged, for example, by the short little *morceau* Mr. Gerdt dances in the last act, for P. I. Tchaikovsky is neither Mr. Minkus nor Mr. Pugni, who have written hundreds of ballets and studied every artist and all the circumstances of the ballet down to the last details. This transition from conventionalized music to independent music cannot but be greeted. The small concessions made by the balletmaster and composer scarcely mattered, though the musical illustration made the choreographic work even more interesting.

Peterburgskaya gazeta
18 February 1908

BALLET

Sleeping Beauty, the classical work of Tchaikovsky and M. I. Petipa was staged for Miss Kshesinskaya's last appearance this season. How times have changed! After the first performance, which was met by a despondently cold response from the audience, the press delivered this appraisal of the inspired work: "the plot is not very poetic, banal, and unworthy of the Petersburg stage; the production is nothing more than a museum of props." There were reproaches of the music, which was "boring," monumental, incomprehensible, and "unfit for the ballet" (!). And now? Now it is the most valuable pearl of the repertory.

Last night *Sleeping Beauty* was given for the 120th time and afforded special interest: the talented Miss Kshesinskaya, one of those rare artists who doesn't hesitate to furnish her performances with the most talented artists, but who, instead, does everything possible to guarantee their participation. And that's why her performances are always so interesting and dazzling. Last evening, for example *Sleeping Beauty* featured a completely new cast: Miss Pavlova II portrayed the Lilac Fairy, Miss Trefilova danced the cat; Mr. Stukolkin was Carabosse, and Mr. Nijinsky appeared as a fiancé for the first time. Almost the entire cast of the jewels pas de quatre was new. Heavy metals and stones vanished, and in place of the former performers, who had arrived for a long stay, appeared Misses Kyatsh [*sic*], Smirnova, Shollar, and of the former group, Polyakova. Of course, a performance with such a quantity of new performers acquired a double interest, and the audience should be grateful to Miss Kshesinskaya not only for the pleasure they receive from her dances, but also for her trouble on behalf of the artistic interests of the audience.

Aurora is one of the greatest roles in the ballerina repertory. The severe classicism of the dances in *Sleeping Beauty* remains a distinctive feature of her choreographic gift. It would be very difficult to imagine a more distinguished, more brilliant performance of the demanding and complex grand pas d'action with the four partners in the second scene. Her pirouettes, pointe work, jetés en tournant, and the other technical particulars were distinct, bold, and virtuosic. Her variation in the "shades of Aurora" (scene 3) was also wonderfully performed and the variation in the last act was simply brilliant. The precision and the execution of classical dance is the ballerina's strength. The classical dances in *Beauty* abound in complex technical details and virtuoso embellishments; it is, as they say, choreographic coloratura. And Miss Kshesinskaya is the most coloratura of our dancers. Last night her success was complete and deserved.

Miss Pavlova II was a charming Lilac Fairy. This role has no dances except for one small and difficult variation, which she performed with the great elegance she is known for. Having aroused the audience's genuine enthusiasm, the variation was repeated. It was nice to see such a refined fairy. . . .

As the White Cat, that insignificant choreographic trifle, Miss Trefilova was very sweet. These little bagatelles well suit her. As always, Miss Vil [*sic*] had a noisy success as Little Red Riding Hood. She creates a colorful genre scene here, full of delightful naïveté and femininity. Miss Sedova met with full approval in "the Blue Bird" with her airy elevation and the span of her jumps. In my opinion, however, the staging of the venerable Petipa ought not have been changed. *Beauty* already has its "canon," whose performance must be maintained. How freely, easily, without any stress, Miss Sedova dances, and what a wonderful classical dancer! And how our directorate—spiteful to some artists and for whom fairness is not a principal virtue—is unable to exploit her strengths! The refined Prince Charmant, Mr. Nijinsky, as well as the other fiancés, met with full approval. Mr. Stukolkin, the colorful Carabosse, renounced exaggerated overacting, for once.

The pas de quatre, as interpreted by Misses Kyaksht, Smirnova, Shollar, and Polyakova looks like a completely new item. The old performances elicited boredom. The new performers injected life into it. "These are stones of a quite different cut and polish," one of the older balletomanes observed. The pas de quatre and Miss Kyaksht's variation were repeated by common demand—something that has not happened with that pas for many, many years. It would be a shame if this cast of female dancers won't dance the next performances of *Sleeping Beauty.*

The theater was overflowing. Most of the numbers were repeated. The public bid Miss Kshesinskaya a fond farewell before her departure for new laurels in Paris. Miss Kshesinskaya was presented with flowers, and the Lilac Fairy, with lilacs.

V[alerian] Svetlov

Birzhevye vedemosti
15 February 1914

THE STAGING OF *SLEEPING BEAUTY*

The revival of Tchaikovsky's ballet *Sleeping Beauty* will be presented for the first time tomorrow in the Maryinsky Theater.

The ballet was supposed to run in the first half of the current season but was held up by the costumes and decors, which weren't ready in time.

Academic K. A. Korovin told us: "I worked on *Sleeping Beauty* with special love, and regret that I must leave for Moscow before the ballet's dress rehearsal. I will try, nonetheless, to return for the premiere. In the decors for *Sleeping Beauty* I tried to convey a 'festival of color' and a sleeping kingdom."

Ballerina T. P. Karsavina, who will dance the lead, says: "Not so long ago *Sleeping Beauty* was often performed in the repertory of the Maryinsky Theater. In its artistic design, *Sleeping Beauty* is one of the best ballets. On the technical side it offers a test for the ballerina. *Sleeping Beauty* teems with exacting classical dances, and will be one of the 'difficult' ballets."

Sleeping Beauty will be performed with new decors and costumes by the academic K. A. Korovin. The complete harmony of the decors and the costumes is wonderful. Nothing else in the production has changed at all. The dances remain as before. Though there is scarcely a need to change the old pattern of classical dances.

D.

Birzhevye vedemosti
18 February 1914

AT THE FOOTLIGHTS: KOROVIN AND VSEVOLOZHSKY

The artist Korovin painted new decors for *Sleeping Beauty* and redressed the artists in new costumes. But I can't in good conscience say that the ballet gained from this in any way. Just the opposite, the result is a sort of vestimentary heaviness and screaming chic that only interferes with the remarkable virtuosity of Marius Petipa's dances. Along the way, all the fairy-tale nuances of the ballet were wiped away and replaced by a gamut of colors that lack the charming allegorical associations of the former production from Vsevolozhsky's sketches. Now one can identify the onstage characters only with the program. Though exquisite individually, the costumes don't collectively give the fantastic effect of harmonious unity.

In the "prologue" of the ballet, which shows the palace of the king, the decors are festooned with the Lilac Fairy's garlands too early, and the costumes' extraordinary range of colors is shown in paired colors of faded hues. Smirnova's silvery wig marred the fire of ardent temperament in her eyes. Egorova, Polyakova, and Vill have disheveled curls that likewise lend a heavy impression. And finally, the king and queen are shown in robes that, though regal and chic, are heavy and massive.

Thus, immediately after the raising of the curtain, the viewer is seized by the feeling that the fairy tale has finally been extracted from the wonderful ballet and sacrificed to all sorts of magnificence, especially in the costumes, which weren't conceived to harmonize to the general construction and don't correspond to it. Korovin is without doubt a talented artist, but without the sensitivity to dance that Vsevolozhsky possessed, and that is necessary for the illustration of a classical work. A fairy tale is light as smoke. But there are no traces of airy beauty in the latest artist's interpretation. Even the Lilac Fairy seems faded and dark in her current outfit, which lacks play and brilliance.

A milky red color, either lighter or darker, dominates the corps de ballet's costumes in the first act of *Sleeping Beauty.* The dancers are outfitted in half-length cabaret skirts with velvet bodices and white sleeves with puffs. The male dancers are in short pants and vests. Broad-brimmed hats with ostrich feather plumes lend the air of *grands seigneurs* to the latter, though in this scene they are peasants who have come to congratulate the king and queen. The artistic simplicity of Vsevolozhsky's costumes better harmonized with the motif of the moment and didn't introduce a nuance of decaying bravado in ringing, extraneous flourishes. A sensitive balletomane and inspired graphic artist, the illustrator limited himself to white shirts, blue stockings, and modest velvet caps that blended together as painterly touches without pretense to a picture of aristocratic manners.

To continue in this vein, we must note that even Karsavina, in a fiery red wig and pink skirt, doesn't give the needed impression, whereas Vsevolozhsky's costume, strewn with gold spangles on a red field, would immediately set the dancer, with her wonderful plastic gifts, apart from the crowd. The ballerina would doubtless have performed the pas d'action with freshness of animation and tone, especially before the four maids of honor in their black outfits, which lent her dances a deep backdrop. And now Lukashevich, Shimanskaya, Prokhovnikovaya, and Romanova wear varied colors that confound the eye. What is more, all these soloists wear dark red wigs (fatal to Korovin's artistic composition!) that aggrieve by their look alone. The other four confidantes of the princess, in white tutus with silk jackets trimmed with large poppies, create a much simpler, unpretentious, and sweet impression. I will only point out in addition that the decors of the first act depict a bosquet, and the columns to the side, seen from the palace, give a too-soft lilac cast that destroys any illusion.

The second act, the hunt scene, is dominated by costumes with ridiculously large trains that interfere with the dancing. It is exactly the same in the next scene of this act, as in subsequent scenes, right up to the end of the ballet. Neither individual figures of the tale nor the collective groups of dancers hold the attention of the audience or elicit sympathetic emotions in anyone. Only the panorama with its effect of a changing landscape against a velvet backdrop of night lifts the sinking mood of the audience a bit. The colors here have an unusual warmth and freshness, and the smoky blue firmament stretches broadly over the brightening horizon. All of this is infused with the poetry of great talent. But what precedes this change of vision scenes, or follows after it, is correspondingly weaker in the merits of its composition and execution relative to the great perfection of the dances and evokes only bewilderment. Thus Egorova in a long pale lilac dress doesn't elicit a happy sense of light in the soul. The Nereids in their white skirts and jackets covered in water lilies of various colors would be fine and completely in their element if it weren't for the repulsive wigs and the whole cloaks of combed hair that weigh down the figures of the dancers.

Further, in the divertissement numbers of the concluding act of the ballet, well-conceived costumes alternate with the most unsuccessful. Polyakova, Lyukom, Goergievskaya, and Bolshakova have pretty headpieces: silver and gold with plumes, sapphire and diamond with gleaming aureoles of precious gems. But the cat (Smirnova) in a gray tunic and matching wig is too dirty from her wanderings on rooftops and chimneys! The fluff on the head that serves as a little hat with ears is playful, especially with eyes that coquettishly exude twilight or semidarkness. Egorova (in the Blue Bird pas de deux) has sleeves with frills that hide the plastic beauty of her arms. Cinderella (Karpova) has been redressed in the style of a German girl with a cap on her head. And then there is one of the wonders of the ballet tale (Red Riding Hood), distorted almost unrecognizably by the current illustrator.

The previous poor girl with a basket in hand, a bouquet of field flowers, and a red cap of cheap cloth really was one of the most wonderful episodes of the ballet in Vill's performance. There was no chic, but the charm of simplicity in every sense. The skirt to the knees with a white apron and the pantomime of trembling in the wind with the terrible wolf, harmonized with the general appearance of the figure—and with all the other details, seemed a naturalistic daub amidst the fantastic elements of the scene. Nowadays, Vill appears on the scene in a tutu and silk shirt with a velvet corset. What is more, she wears a round hat of fiery spangles with a red topknot on her head just like . . . a little devil in hell. It goes without saying that the tale doesn't count for much here, given the strange combination of a simple-folk basket and an outfit trimmed in silk.

Finally, in the final moments of the ballet, Karsavina's brocade tunic and the white feathers on her head were completely lost against the backdrop of a more magnificently dressed corps de ballet.

Such was Korovin's work in a fleeting comparison with the previous costumes from Vsevolozhsky's sketches. The new artist, so gifted outside the ballet, proved relatively inferior to his predecessor as an illustrator of dances in not realizing the play of fantasy and creativity in them. But in the realm of such an art as that of Marius Petipa, a master of line and color of an entirely different cast was especially needed, with tender sensitivity to the mysteries of classical choreography. Every detail is dear here. Individual moments should open on the horizons of impressions of a definite type: to link the artists with ill-suited costumes is to distort the main, plastic theme of the entire work.

A[kim] Volynsky

Birzhevye vedemosti

22 March 1914

THE DANCES IN *SLEEPING BEAUTY*

The dances in *Sleeping Beauty* were choreographed by M. Petipa and revived by N. G. Sergeyev without any changes. The ballet could thus be viewed with the former interest were it not for the oppressive weight of the wigs and costumes that supplant the perfect refinement and taste of the costumes built from Vsevolozhsky's sketches. Unfortunately, the regisseur didn't share responsibilities with Legat and relinquished the scenic presentation to the latter's supervision—especially the numbers that don't allow deviations from the scheme of classical dance worked out over centuries. In recent years a marked disorder has become noticeable in the performance of the corps de ballet that, in the days of M. Petipa and Lev Ivanov, offered only delight: before one's eyes the evolution of a whole being unfolded, one that separated into many parts only for the effect of spontaneity and collectivity. Nowadays many of the dancers among the acting masses break away from the general plan of the production. Only the individual artists of the troupe don't break from the group, hold the line, and thus maintain the poetry of the alignment of the identically oscillating reverberation among them.

These shortcomings in the group dances are especially felt in the scene of the dancing Nereids, matchlessly devised by the balletmaster, with various figures formed at a difficult tempo to a complex musical rhythm. The river nymphs in white tutus run to the front of the stage in two lines and immediately separate into four lines. Then, after a few bars, the Nereids form tight lines, as before, and the front line drops to its knees. The general adagio begins. The lines scatter across the stage without breaking their linearity. In one especially beautiful moment, two diagonal lines change places and the Lilac Fairy, Prince Désiré, and the Sleeping Beauty pas through the middle of them, as if playing blindman's bluff. Finally, in conclusion of the wonderful adagio, a portion of the dancers with garlands in their hands form a circle with a shell in the shape of a shoe in the middle. Aurora places her foot in it and rises into attitude. The remainder of the corps de ballet then divides into two parallel lines.

It is clear that the entire picture was built on the *plastique* of the play of lines, on the combinations of figures according to some specific principle, so that the smallest deviation from the picture described inevitably destroys the poetic effect of the whole act. In fact, this number is now performed on the stage of the Maryinsky Theater rather pallidly, not decisively, without the passionate animation that transforms the mass into a collective unity, even though dancers so noticeably gifted as Leontieva, Lyukom, and Bolshakova take part. They often make successful appearances not only in the corps de ballet, but in important roles alongside the best dancers of the company.

In short, without going to detailed critical evaluations, I will note the character of interpretation of separate sections of *Sleeping Beauty.* The Prologue is performed in a sufficiently lively way. Shollar dances the slow polka elegantly and consistently. Polyakova performs a run on point that is forceful, correct, and smooth, without faltering. Vill performs her variation wonderfully, enlivening it with rays of plastic laughter. Smirnova dances the strong circles with passion. Egorova's waltz of soft figures *en dedans* and the rhythmic plastique of the hands shimmer with the nobility of the quiet moment of the mood. Lyukom performs an essentially elementary exercise with a beautiful radiance, to the sympathetic bravos of the audience.

A[kim] Volynsky

Zhizn' iskusstvo
September 26, 1922

CALL AN AMBULANCE![10]

The new ballet season begins with the usual circumstances of stage life. The theater has no large choreographic works on the horizon to which one could pin one's hopes. . . .

Wonderful things like *Nutcracker, Raymonda,* and *Corsaire* have been proposed, and such a treasure of imperishable significance as *Sleeping Beauty.* But the question is really tragic and unsolvable given the circumstances of the moment. All these works, the classical creations of Marius Petipa, demand renovation—complete renewal in some places, re-creation and editing in others. Moreover, all of this should be carried out under the leadership of a first-class director, as N. G. Sergeyev was in his day. (Sergeyev has been thrown out in recent years, cast off to some Riga by his self-styled pretentious replacement.) All the variations in *Sleeping Beauty* should be put in their place. The soul must be returned to the corps de ballet numbers, the height of perfection and collective poetry in this choreographic creation, to achieve their harmonic effects. And Aurora's dances? It seems that O. A. Spesivtseva will appear in the role. But after study with Cecchetti in London, and with her own knowledge of classical art, not even to speak of the charming resonance of her individual talent, with whom will this artist rehearse the role in its entirety?

Here I turn to a serious caution. The gifted and outstanding pedagogue N. G. Legat is not in Petrograd now. He did not wish to work in the atmosphere of the current state ballet. Despite a career that smiled on him as the head balletmaster, after a three-year ordeal of not granting him control of the affair, even despite authoritative decrees from the ruling bodies, N. G. Legat preferred to leave our borders. But why? What does this fatal emigration mean, this criminal neglect of primary obligations to the stage and art? Legat is not the only one who functions as an object of excruciating jealousy for various small people, but also E. M. Lyukom and Shavrov—and especially Lyukom—on whom the public and the administration always lavished such praise and compliments. How can this be logically explained? I should certainly repeat: here there is a criminal neglect that can never be adequately stigmatized. But if we speak plainly, face-to-face with the sad state of affairs in the academic ballet, then certainly the larger crime would be the internment of its own talent. And really, what else would it be to work under the humiliating command of phony balletmasters and regisseurs lacking an authoritative voice?

In such conditions, let me ask if the contemporary ballet-theater mechanism works for a foreign enterprise that in Berlin has seized the reserves of our best talent for the enterprises of Diaghilev and other Yellow Devils of his ilk, traveling salesmen of commercial art? If, for one minute, we say that these escapades from Petrograd will continue, that O. A. Spesivtseva will escape to the place Lyukom and Shavrov rushed to, from the happy-go-lucky leadership of the current ballet academies, then very soon our entire choreographic institute will end up abroad. What a tragic prospect for Petrograd: the best talent, the most gifted classical dancers, appearing on European stages under the direction of Cecchetti and Legat!

Caveant Consules!

These are the sad auspices under which our ballet season begins. Of course there's no point in folding one's hands. It's necessary to work. Sharp criticism should be turned on one-self. The curing of the sick organism of the stage must proceed by the natural process of in-ternal healing. Just as experts on literary and social affairs should be at the head of newspa-pers, so people of intelligence and vocation must certainly come forward to head the administrations of theaters—always needful to the nation—to carry culture and to lead, like bonfires on the peoples' squares. There can be no doubt that the state ballet must live through many great catastrophes in this regard. The hopelessly neglected soil of the theater must be weeded in all directions. For exactly this purpose, I. V. Ekskuzovich gathered people of the most diverse qualifications in his Choreographic Council. But the administration in charge of the theater should not forgot one important principle: Great works are not done by means of diplomatic compromises or the well-intentioned smoothing of longstanding and useful conflicts with soothing conciliatory balms. One must hold the lash of criticism in one's hand when the lash of historical *revanche* already whistles over our heads. The moment is too serious, too tragic. It demands will, character, and special action. For ballet is such an asset, such a unique and global pearl of Russia, that no one would ever forgive its loss from the nation's treasury. I speak now as a friend. There is nothing hostile in my words. But as a zealot of classical traditions, I insist on the necessary and immediate cleaning of the Augean stables of the ballet theater. Seeing a falling hero, I call the ambulance.

Caveant consules!

A[kim] Volynsky

Zhizn' iskusstvo

1923, no. 48

BALLET: *SLEEPING BEAUTY*

The Past

It's worth dwelling on the costuming of *Sleeping Beauty*. Here a large space opens before the designer. He isn't restricted to an epoch dictating the character of the costumes and their col-ors. Within the bounds of a fairy tale, he can give free rein to his fantasy and taste. He should nonetheless remember that he is constructing costumes for the ballet. Costumes for dance should be light. Not only light, but obedient to all the demands of the choreography. If an-tique dress, in Goethe's expression, are the one thousandth echo of the human body, then clothing for dance should be the multiple repetition of the peripeteia of its movement. And since these movements are stylized in classical dances, then the dancer's outer covering should possess a corresponding character. But in the stylized costume, the colorful range of tones that enters the audience's field of vision has great significance. A most complete coor-dination of the color of the costume and the type of dance plays a large role here. The importance of this never eluded our wonderful costumer and artist Vsevolozhsky, who once directed the Maryinsky Theater. His costume designs for *Sleeping Beauty* are of enduring interest for the history of this subject. Here was a real director of a ballet theater who knew and understood, down to the last details, exactly what he was directing. Under such a directorate a genius like Marius Petipa, who staged a whole string of works worthy of the world stage of the Russian ballet, could spread his wings. Then the decline began. The short tenure of Volkonsky, the high-society admirer of musical rhythm and adherent of Dalcroze, was marked only by scandals. And after him, V. A. Telyakovsky's era of much work and little glory. He became the systematic liquidator of the celebrated stage's countless resources. Marius Petipa was handed his premature retirement under Telyakovsky, and little by little, one coryphée after another was cast into the shadows. Telyakovsky the Wagnerian understood little about classical dance; his knowledge of it was startling in its poverty. The quasi-innovative and ill-starred experiments of M. M. Fokine began under him, and those led to nothing serious. The neglect of the classical dancers found expression, by the way, in one wonderful fact worth fixing in print since it is so curious and typical. The balletmaster N. G. Legat, who replaced Marius Petipa, was sent an honorable diploma from the French Academy of Dance. The diploma lay for several years among the papers of the office and was passed to the addressee only recently (under I. V. Ekskuzovich), after lying around like some good-for-nothing rag! On the activities of Ekskuzovich, on his administration of the ballet, and on the place he occupies in the story of the ballet's disintegration—it is still early to write. We patiently wait. The truthful and decisive word will be left to the historian of the Petrograd stage, in all phases of its gradual shrinking, impoverishment, and downfall.

Aurora's Costume

We return to the costume question as it applies to *Sleeping Beauty,* beginning with the Prologue. In the Prologue, the costumes are paired and of unusually bright and varied colors. Korovin's tendency, in abolishing Vsevolozhsky's sketches, had only one goal: to dress everyone in faded colors. This was the fundamental and fatal mistake on the part of the artist. One shouldn't use faded colors of an intimate, boudoir rococo pattern for a pure and free fairy tale in the [indecipherable] forest of creative fantasy, for a tale that in spirit so begs for the shining frame of classical dance. The colors should sing, shine, and beckon, inseparable from the body of dances connected to it down to the last detail. With Korovin everything withers and fades. Instead of a living and vivid spring palate for the Lilac Fairy in the Prologue, there is a costume of muted dark green. A grayish lilac-silver wig with a long braid weighs down and ages the whole figure and turns the lighthearted fairy and young dancer Geidenreich into an old woman. The other fairies of the tale wear the same ill-fated wigs with locks hanging almost to their waists that lend these sweet creatures as well a rather corpulent character. The fairy-tale nuances have been eliminated and replaced by a palate of motley colors understandable only with the program in hand. By itself, nothing strikes the eye, nothing expresses itself without the intermediary of commentary. The royal costumes (a male chalmys and a female mantilla) that the king and queen drag along the floor with conventional solemnity simply suffocate with their weight. If to this we add that the decor of the Prologue is painted

in the same faded green color and hung with garlands of lilac, then we have the whole monotone, joyless picture of the opening act. In the orchestra elements of the most wonderful
sound buzz and sway with the clarity of glass; it would seem the easiest thing in the world to
dance to them. Yet on stage everything is taken with grievous realism and moves along
slowly, to the plodding tempos of amphibious creatures. The story is not built around the
Lilac Fairy. But it is Lilac—blooming and fading, with all the corresponding nuances of
spring expiring in the heat of summer—that seizes the dominant role in the ballet and rules
not by right. And that is how it goes from beginning to end.

The grand, complicated waltz in the first act is wonderful not only in the musical sense
but also in the choreographic. The costumes of the corps de ballet are of a pale milky red
color, some darker, others lighter. The cabaret-length little skirts beneath a velvet bodice and
white sleeves with ruffs comprise the dancers outfits. The men are in short pants and velvet
vests. Their stylish hats are trimmed in ostrich feathers. In theory, these are peasants, but
their costumes suggest French *grands seigneurs,* completely out of place in the crowd of simple folk that should accompany the appearance of the king, the queen, and Princess Aurora.
The old democratic festive outfits were so much better in this regard that I recalled them in
all their vivid spectrum! There were white shirts and blue pantalons over the same blue stockings. Their hats were also blue velvet. It was all simple, clean, modest and sufficiently smart,
completely answering the demands of the scene. There was no showy pomp, but a wonderfully poetic background for the appearance of the nobles! Here the amazing sensitivity of
Vsevolozhsky expressed itself, and without the slightest affectation. If the costumes of
Vsevolozhsky were restored during this evolution of morals were are living through, the
artist-dilletante would be in tune with contemporary life to a much greater degree than the
professional artist, who, for all his talent, only succeeded in smearing everything vital and
fantastic in the ballet with monotone pale colors. Korovin sees nothing: neither dance nor
the classical trifles that shine in brilliant colors. He understands nothing in the play of patterns and designs. His whole business is in artificially pompous decorations, heavy costumes,
and red wigs.

Aurora performs a wonderful *hyporchema.*[11] I remind my readers that Greeks used that
word to express all sorts of dramatized dance, in the spirit of the contemporary pas d'action.
Her costume is terribly unsuccessful. Aurora in a red wig and a pink costume. The skirt is
pink, the bodice is pink. With uncovered arms and neck, such a color makes the figure look
tense and rather unvaried. What sort of Aurora is this, the symbolic design of the rising sun,
with all its plenitude of nuances and tones! The heavens are all pink, but the very goddess of
light, carried on a golden chariot, scarcely blends with her background. She is all in the fresh
ardor of bloom, light, of soft morning rays, shooting down from above, in the landscape
awaking to light. Here there can be nothing monotone. And the red wig on Aurora's head
not only weighs her down, but it spoils the whole scene. Once again I must say that with
Vsevolozhsky we once had something wonderful in the artistic and poetic sense here. The
costume was red and bright, with gold sequins strewn over the whole costume, separating
the dancer from the crowd. And the four maids of honor accompanying her in smart black
dresses furnished a deep background for Aurora. Now we see only a noisy and unjustified
riot of color. Plus, the maids of honor have dark wigs. And it must be said that in the first act,

sixteen years after the Prologue, the king and queen remain in the same costumes! The decors don't blaze with originality either: the green arbor, the four columns of the palace with their soft lilac sheen. It feels like paint! Like decors!

I will quickly mention the costume problems in the last acts. In the hunt scene, the long heavy women's costumes with massive trains impede their dancing. And once again, the unavoidable red wigs. The Lilac Fairy, in her next appearance in this act, makes no happy impression in a dress of faded lilac. The Nereids wear poisoned wigs, trailing long locks. And the formerly wonderful panorama, which elicited a unanimous bravo from the entire theater when it was first shown, has finally grown dim. Such is the second act, which, thanks to an unsuccessful selection of costumes, colors, and decors (either faded or worn) against unsuccessful backdrops, leaves the viewer completely cold. There is no fairy tale, no féerie, and therefore no Aurora in the company of the blooming and singing summer surroundings.

In the third and final act, the costumes of all the characters finally change. The queen appears with a white cap on her head. The costumes for the precious stones are not bad at all. The skirts are light and in matching colors and the headpieces are frankly beautiful: Silver and Gold have festive plumage; Diamond and Sapphire have glowing aureoles of soft-bright stones. The White Cat is in a dirty gray wig, a fluff with ears on her head. The princess in "Blue Bird" is in a wig of the same color. The sleeves with puffy frills hide the beauty of the arms. Cinderella wears a completely normal costume, a bit like Gretchen, with a cap on her head. Little Red Riding Hood has almost completely lost her fantastic mien. She wears a tutu, and that's not needed! A white silk blouse under a velvet bodice and round hat of burning spangles, with a tuft of hair. It's too chic for a poor peasant girl with a basket of field flowers under her arm. It's more like a imp from a dark hell than Little Red Riding Hood! With Vsevolozhsky it was all different. There was a real bouquet of happily chosen flowers. A peasant skirt to the knees, a basted white blouse, black bodice with a modest pinafore and a delightful children's hat of cheap cloth on her head. There was no chic, only simplicity, without expensive sparkling! Nor does Aurora's costume satisfy me entirely: I speak of Korovin's designs, not counting any changes added by the caprices of contemporary artists. The pink brocade skirt and the headpiece with white feathers is barely visible against the motley backdrop of the corps de ballet and sometimes falls entirely from vision.

It Didn't Come Off

Now in conclusion I will say a few words about the new Aurora, the young dancer T. A. Troyanovskaya, who replaced Gerdt and Spesivtseva.

Her performance wasn't brilliant. I have a whole list of objections. Her little head and pretty face are a bit heavy, with no daring or decisive shading, though there is as much inclination to soft, insipid poses as you wish. The eyes, and here another objection, though they shine, shine indifferently and for no particular reason, without individual spark. They shine tepidly, with an empty glance to the side lacking in temperament. The smile, and here I especially object, is the same for all the acts, for all moments and situations. It is conventional and sweetly frozen, neither motivating anything nor being motivated by anything from within. It is sunny but in the mists of an inwardly directed existence, both physically and psychologically. I want to say that Troyanovskaya dances only in flat open pictures, not born of any depth. It is everywhere effacé, with no alternation with moments amassed from a deep interior life. Thus there is no life-giving passion beneath the pretty exterior. And such an inwardly structured performance, with plentiful cuts for the sake of ease and lightness of dancing, denuded of any difficult technique, can't for a moment captivate and delight the eye. In the first act of *Sleeping Beauty*, after the protracted and wearisome Prologue, Troyanovskaya doesn't complete whole phrases, or even keep up with the orchestra. The delightful pas de chat in that act were hewn to their barest outlines by the shears of an unacknowledged gardener. One must know how to fill out a musical passage with steps in such a way that it won't be necessary to sacrifice any parts and blend with the next phrase—and not lag behind the numbers. The extended duet with the fiancés (from whom Aurora takes a flower) was as unsuccessful in this regard. She rewards each fiancé with a grateful pirouette, as a sign that her heart is not unfeeling to the gifts of love. Falling behind the music, Troyanovskaya deprived the last fiancé of his share of attention. This offends precisely because one could expect a young dancer keen to rhythm and beat to be able to fully and accurately convey full phrases and monologues of orchestral speech. And then another series of incomplete interpretations in the last parts of the ballet. Her turns weren't firm or secure, with slips that distorted whole phrases. In this sense one couldn't put Troyanovskaya against any of the ballerinas of the past, not Smirnova or Makletsvoa, not even to speak of Gerdt or Spesivtseva. All of these dancers had wonderful turns without the support of a cavalier, they came off dauntlessly clean and firm. Finally, the dancer, who didn't show even one of the dance phrases with bodily or plastic accuracy, suddenly discovered this trait in the last episode of the second act. She fell to the floor, attentively putting one leg over the other, perhaps to hide the wide line of her body from the audience. And here croisé was really not needed, but a generous openness was. I will also add in closing that the artist seems heavy on the hands of the cavalier, and that in partnering, especially in the execution of difficult steps that demand contraposto turns, the stamp of the dancing isn't clean, but weak and utterly lacking in character. One thing is certain: it's external prettiness without an internal face.

Thus, in the main, was T. A. Troyanovskaya examination performance for the rank of ballerina. I noted only the defects because they leapt to the eye, though I don't deny the dancer her feminine charms and obvious talent. That talent will still someday find its form in the course of long, difficult, and untiring work, the price exacted for the right to be called an outstanding ballerina.

A[kim] Volynsky

THE SUNNY COMMUNE, *NOTES OF THE ADMINISTRATION OF THE LENINGRAD ACADEMIC THEATERS (1924) ON THE CREATION OF WORKS OF REVOLUTIONARY CONTENT USING THE LIBRETTOS OF THE OPERAS* LES HUGUENOTS, *AND* LE PROPHÈTE, *OF G. MEYERBEER, R. WAGNER'S* RIENZI, *AND THE BALLET* SLEEPING BEAUTY *OF P. I. TCHAIKOVSKY.*

The General Situation

The proletarian masses firmly demand representations of great emotion and action on the stage of the state opera theaters of the Soviet Republic.

After long and unsuccessful searches for a new revolutionary opera and the libretto of a contemporary author, the directorate of the academic theaters staged several of the most revolutionary of the operas of the old composers on the stage of the Leningrad Academic Theater of Opera and Ballet. But not one of these operas satisfied the contemporary viewer: their revolutionary character was expressed in naive forms and didn't correspond in any way to the approach to historical events.

The ballet is so saturated with rentier-aristocrat culture that not even a grain of the most superficial revolutionary character could be found.

Plans for the 1924–25 Season

. . . The playwright N. Vinogradov, the author of the tragedy *A Russian Prometheus,* well received by the Leningrad press . . . responded to the directorate's call and gave revolutionary plots to the operas *Les Huguenots, Le Prophète, Rienzi,* and the ballet *Sleeping Beauty.* . . .
The ballet *Sleeping Beauty* attracted the attention of the directorate as one of a very few ballets written by a good master-composer, while hundreds of others are musically inadmissible for an academic theater. . . .

Sleeping Beauty—The Sunny Commune

Sleeping Beauty is a brilliant ballet with wonderful music by Tchaikovsky. Unfortunately, Tchaikovsky's music is so "romantic" that it is impossible to contemplate a direct transposition to a bracing revolutionary plot that vividly communicates the proletarian revolution. Therefore it was necessary to insert a certain amount of romanticism in reworking the story, which would be justified by the music and by the general style of ballet art in its present state. To this end, the action of the Prologue has been moved back five hundred years, to the first uprising of the proletariat. A medieval city, the rejoicing of the insurgent artisans. A vivacious, cheerful dance of the men. Led by the young master-leader, they erect the statue of Revolution. Women with flowers and colorful scarves come to meet their brothers and husbands. A dance of freedom, beauty, spring, and labor.

The attack of knights led by a duke. The arrest of the leader. They chain him to the erected statue of Revolution. The duke archly states: "Slaves will never be free."

The leader is in despair. But an astrologer-philosopher dreams of the Sunny Commune on earth. With a wand, he tears the veil of the future and shows the contours of the Sunny Commune on the horizon, lit by the northern lights. The leader—in the haze of visions—sees a future that reveals itself to his medieval imagination in these tones:

Act I. He (the leader) rises, breaks his chains and victoriously leads the masses to a universal uprising. To the palace of the universal duke. The masses destroy the attributes of the duke's power and dance a victory waltz with new symbols of labor.

The statue of Revolution revives, and beautiful Aurora—the scarlet dawn of Worldwide Revolution—comes down to the people. Aurora dances a dance of universal victory with the red banners of the masses to the sound of victorious horns and crowns the leader with a laurel wreath. Following that (the violin solo) she calls the leader to that land where the astrologer showed the Sunny Commune. She opens new vistas, suffused with the radiance of rainbow colors. The masses are ready to go there, and Aurora dances the "marching to battle" dance.

But the universal duke appears with a suite of golden knights and engages in battle with the insurgent masses. Aurora pricks herself on the sword of the duke and falls. The duke carries her off to unknown lands in a boat.

Act II. Against a backdrop of starry space and in search of his beautiful bride, the leader arrives at the tower of the astrologer. He asks the astrologer to show him the path to the Sunny Commune and Aurora. The astrologer shows him scrolls, books, and sketches and then shows the dance of the constellations to the gaze of the leader enlightened by science. Beneath a scarlet veil the most wonderful star dances. She beckons the leader to follow her and asks him to free her from her enemies. He tears the veils and recognizes the form of the scarlet star Aurora. The vision disappears. The leader, with a sword, and the astrologer, with a torch, go to the Sunny Commune. A panorama (a moving decor) opens: a series of pictures of universal labor, interpreted in the romantic fantasy of the medieval leader. Finally they approach the city of the commune in golden riches, the silver flame of electric lighting and the red smoke of factories. They enter the palace. The leader triumphs over the universal duke and his knights. He approaches the scarlet coffin where the fettered Aurora sleeps. The leader ruptures the coffin with a torch, and in scarlet radiance and the flames of red banners Aurora stands: the wonderful dawn of Universal Revolution.

Act III. A celebration in the Sunny Commune. A procession of the guilds of all nations. Dances, apotheosis . . . (quoted in Trabsky 1975, 293–96).

Mariinsky teatr

1999, no. 3-4

SERGEI VIKHAREV, "I MANAGED TO DO WHAT WAS NECESSARY": INTERVIEW WITH MARIA RATANOVA

Maria Ratanova: *A year ago on the rehearsal stage of the theater you showed the Prologue of Sleeping Beauty and convinced the ballet professionals, critics and—most important—the artistic direction of the theater of the necessity of continuing this work. That was your first triumph in your role as a restorer of Petipa's choreographic text. You achieved the main thing then: the sense of authenticity in the reconstructed choreography. But you still had three acts of an enormous ballet before you. Today, on the eve of the premiere, are you happy with the result?*

Sergei Vikharev: I think I managed to do what was necessary. The choreography that was changed in various versions has been returned. The composition of the Prologue has been restored completely. Characters that were taken out have been returned, like the fairie's suites. In Act I the scene with the knitters has been restored, as has the choreography of the dances for Aurora, her maids of honor, the young girls, and the pages with violins. The quantity of dancers in the peasant waltz was returned to the number at the premiere in 1890: now there are forty-eight dancers from the corps de ballet and twenty-four children from the school. In Act II we returned the minuet, the game of blindman's bluff, the farandole, and the mise-en-scène of Aurora's awakening. In Act III, the dances for Cinderella and Fortuné and the combinations for the jewels were lost, there were changes in the pas de deux for Princess Florine and the Blue Bird, the dances for Tom Thumb and his brothers, for Little Red Riding Hood, and in the final mazurka.

What sorts of specific distortions did Petipa's ensembles undergo over time?

The Prologue suffered most of all. In the version that is danced today in the Maryinsky, only a third of the choreography belongs to Petipa. From the moment the curtain is raised to the last scene, only the order of the music corresponds to the original. The direction, the direction of the movements, the musical accents, the choreography—all this was changed by Konstantin Mikhailovich Sergeyev in 1952. It turns out that today the soloists dance the choreography of the corps de ballets, and vice versa. And some choreography has disappeared altogether along with the characters who danced it: the pages who accompany the fairies, for example. Petipa's composition was distorted. The Lilac Fairy's role is considered to have become "dancier." But you can't really call those few arabesques in her entry and the combination soutenu-soutenu-6 chaînés (that Konstantin Mikhailovich made for her in the pas de six of the adagio) dancing. Konstantin Mikhailovich took her native plastic language—pantomime—away from her and gave her nothing in return but those endless pas de bourrées. In Act I we restored the variation for the maids of honor. It was simpler in Petipa than in Konstantin Sergeyev's version, but in that simplicity lies the difficulty. You can't hide in the tours, you have to do thirty-two emboîtés and be so kind as to fly across the whole stage. Petipa's ensemble of nymphs (what we used to call Nereids) is more intimate. There aren't twenty-four dancers, but sixteen. Their number increased in 1914. Their movements remain the same, but the character of the ensemble has changed, its resonance. It's like Tchaikovsky's "Serenade for Strings" played by a full orchestra. Only the pattern of the adagio changed in the choreography for the Nereids.

Why did the theater decide to start with Sleeping Beauty?

Sleeping Beauty is a better candidate for restoration. It is a unique example of a first production of a ballet that was documented. A mass of sketches and photographs were preserved, even the instructions for the stagehands. And finally, Nikolai Sergeyev's notations came from Harvard. For a long time I wondered if we could trust them, but when I analyzed five different versions that are given in theaters around the world and found corresponding fragments of the choreographic texts in Perm, London, and in the manuscripts from the beginning of twentieth century, I didn't have any doubts that these were notations of the original choreography. The composition is archaic—you can sense that in the staging.

Did you stage the whole ballet by yourself?

Yes, I staged the whole thing, with the help of coaches and dancers who are still living and who remember the version danced in the theater before Konstantin Mikhailovich Sergeyev's staging.

Last year, in an interview you gave together with Makhar Vaziev, the director of the Maryinsky Ballet, you said that the revival of Sleeping Beauty *in the Maly Theater got you thinking. What struck you most of all?*

I was struck, for example, by the beautiful moment in the Prologue when each of the fairies does a turn with her pages. But the drama of the Maly's production is limited by the fact that they tried to unite two versions, Konstantin Sergeyev's and Fyodr Lopukhov's. It ended up being neither one, nor the other. And on top of that, the visuals seemed to me less than successful. So for us the question of sets and costumes became very important. But when we looked at the designs for the sets and costumes of the 1890 production, it was clear that their time had come.

Was the restoration of the original design an integral part of the concept of this production?

Absolutely. Vsevolozhsky's costumes and the decors of the academic painters are inseparable from Petipa's original text.

How much improvisation did you have to do in working with Nikolai Sergeyev's notations? We know that they're quite detailed, but there are still some problems. There are places where the music is missing where the choreography is notated.

Stepanov's notation system (in which the ballet is notated) supposes that whoever works with them should have a musical education. The choreography is written in a kind of musical notation that implied that the length of movement would correspond to the length of the beat. In terms of improvisation, do you mean how much of Sergei Vikharev is there?

Well, you're not just an intermediary.

Well, for example, where it says "the guests enter and bow," I show them the kind of bow that would be appropriate to the era and the costumes.

And what happens when there are two variants of one dance combination in the notations. How do you decided between them?

In Nikolai Sergeyev's notations there are two variations for Aurora in Act II, both composed for the music of the Gold Fairy. It's the famous variation Konstantin Sergeyev gave the Lilac Fairy in Act III, the one where she does cabrioles in the second half of the variation. And there's also a variation with turns. And so I say: "Look, girls, whichever you like. There's a more traditional variant, and a more difficult one."

What led you to return the Gold Fairy's music to Aurora in the second act? Lopukhov, for example, felt, that the original music was more suitable here.

The fact that Tchaikovsky was still alive when Petipa carried out these changes and, of course, had a say in them. It would be nice to think that Petipa set Aurora's variation in the vision scene to the music that Tchaikovsky originally composed (the variation in G-flat major with the oboe solo). But when we looked at Tchaikovsky's autographed score in the music library of the theater, it was clear that Petipa refused that music. In the score, after the allegro fragment (the corps de ballet's dance) a sheet is pasted in, and in Drigo's hand (he conducted the premiere) there are four bars written in to shift the tonality to the Gold Fairy's variation (in E-flat major). Of course, one might still wonder when and for what performer this was done, but alongside, also in Drigo's hand, it says in French "Miss Brianza's variation follows." Everything became clear to us then. Miss Brianza danced Aurora from 1890—at the premiere—until 1892.

Who found this?

The conductor Valery Osvyanikov. And these kinds of discoveries were inevitable in the process, because everyone was used to copying the same things from book to book rather than going in to the archives and having a look at the original sources. It's not difficult to copy the same old things from Lopukhov or Fokine. It's more difficult to analyze what they wrote. As an example, everyone collegially cites Lopukhov when they say that Maria Petipa didn't dance in the Prologue. But no one pays any attention to the fact that in one place Lopukhov describes in detail how Maria Petipa couldn't dance, and in another, writes how they forced him to partner the "heavy" Maria Petipa. But if the ballerina came out in the Prologue in heels, who can explain to me why they needed to partner her?

What is the theater's conception of the reconstruction? Is this an "academic" version for the sake of history, or do you think that Petipa's original ballet will seem more contemporary than the last version?

Some people think that it can't last, that it will be seen twice and then disappear. But I think it's going to have a huge success if, of course, the company dances it the way they should. It's a revival: a serious test for the dancers. You have to know how to wear the costume, to mime, to create a dance phrase that corresponds to the music. I try to achieve this in my work, because the things the dancers sometimes do to the music—it's horrible. I try to get the rehearsal pianists and conductors to function as musical dictators.

The reconstruction of Sleeping Beauty *won't be received purely in its historical context. It will have to compete with modern versions of old ballets, like Mats Ek's* Giselle, Swan Lake, *and* Sleeping Beauty *with their ironic, late twentieth-century take on the classics. Do you think that Petipa will look contemporary against this backdrop?*

Well, those are two different things. They are independent works of art, of differing styles and directions. I like Mats Ek's approach, and I like Matthew Bourne's, his "male" *Swan Lake*. But they don't borrow from a different aesthetic. Mats Ek has his own language. And he uses it to create his own work. I have a different task.

Won't it be hard for the dancers of the Maryinsky to dance two Sleeping Beauty*s while the Konstantin Sergeyev version remains in the repertory?*

That's a decision for the artistic direction of the theater. But I think they'll be performed at different times.

Konstantin Sergeyev's Sleeping Beauty *has been performed in the theater for almost half a century. Has anyone insinuated that you're committing blasphemy? That this shows disrespect to the memory of a talented person?*

Yes, that's continuous: "Who's this Vikharev?" No one remembers that when Konstantin Sergeyev staged his *Sleeping Beauty* he was the same age as me. I'm not committing any kind of blasphemy. I'm not changing a single step of Petipa.

But from your opponents' point of view, you're undermining the fundamentals. Until now, many have considered Sergeyev's version maximally close to the original.

That's what they said here, but ballet historians around the world feel that our *Beauty* isn't the real thing. And the same is true of other ballets. Today, in the Petipa repertory, there are four or five ballets, and in each of them, about half of the choreographic text is original. That's still a lot, but no one really knows what is actually Petipa. There are some variations and fragments, but can you really get a sense of the balletmaster's greatness from them? Petipa had his theater and his theatrical ideas. He created a ballet according to his scheme and his laws. We've come to disregard this. And Petipa wasn't just a choreographer, but a talented theatrical director as well. I think *Sleeping Beauty* is ideal in that sense.

Do you agree that the root of many later versions of Petipa lay in an oversimplified understanding of the evolution of his work? A shift from the narrative ballet to danced symphonism? In fact, it seems that this was the shift to an idealized theatrical production, and the zenith of that evolution is Sleeping Beauty.

Yes, and there's also our constant orientation to the West. The serious alterations of the classics began when we began to travel abroad. Western impresarios dictate the number of dancers. You have to cut something. Here's another argument: "That wouldn't be interesting for the Western audience." What does "interesting" or "uninteresting" have to do with anything? It wouldn't occur to anyone to cut a movement of a Beethoven symphony because it might not "interest" someone. You perform the whole thing. And then it starts: "too long, boring." Why is it long? Why is it boring? Maybe it was badly performed? So let's get to work!

How do you react to the main argument of the defenders of the old production: Sergeyev brought the ballet up-to-date. He took out what was old-fashioned, and especially the old-fashioned pantomime of the nineteenth century?

The problem is that the pantomime of the nineteenth century was forgotten long ago and for good. So I have to teach now. I have to teach pantomime to the dancers who don't know how to do it because they stopped teaching it in the school. Certainly at the premiere those pantomime scenes will cause some irritation because the ballet has only begun to live. We need time for the dancers to feel at home in it.

Does the pantomime seem archaic to you?

To me? No. And even if it did, the old-fashioned has its charms. Pantomime is one of the elements of nineteenth-century ballet. It's one of the varieties of the dance language, like character or classical dance.

The Lilac Fairy's role was originally a pantomime role. Have you restored this pantomime entirely?

Yes. But in Petipa, the Lilac Fairy dances where she should dance. She dances at the celebration in honor of Princess Aurora. In Nikolai Sergeyev's notations there are two versions of the Lilac Fairy's variation in the Prologue. One, simpler variation has Maria Petipa written on it. The second, which is much more difficult, isn't attributed to any dancer. And there are photographs of Maria Petipa in the Prologue, in a tutu and on pointe. But for some reason, no one publishes those photographs in books.

For many years we believed Fyodr Lopukhov, who set his famous variation for the Lilac Fairy in the Prologue in 1912 and who maintained that Maria Petipa "hadn't mastered the classical dance"' and therefore didn't dance, but only gestured. What do you think? Why did he have to mislead everyone?

The "nondancing" Maria Petipa is one of the unshakable myths of the history of ballet and was created by Lopukhov himself. You can understand him: he didn't just add something somewhere or another, he allowed himself to redo Petipa's choreography, to take a variation Petipa had created out of the Prologue and put his own in its place. Of course, he had to justify this the rest of his life.

Sleeping Beauty *is a masterwork of two authors, Petipa and Tchaikovsky. All the same, in the literature, Petipa's role is often minimized. There's the idea that the conditions of the nineteenth-century ballet theater sometimes kept Petipa from rising to the level of Tchaikovsky. Did you ever have the sense that Petipa's choreography was not up to the level of the music in places?*

That's some sort of nonsense, that Petipa didn't rise to the level of the music. Everything is absolutely adequate. All the meaningful accents are placed where they should be. Tchaikovsky himself suggested that they write the names of the two authors on the score because Petipa had realized his music so remarkably.

How does this sumptuous féerie—the embodiment of the Imperial Ballet ideal—fit the aesthetic of today's Maryinsky Theater?

Since we've brought back the name of the city and theater reburied the remains of the imperial family, and since we've put the crown back over the tsar's box, it would seem that it's time to return the original repertory of the imperial period.

But there are things that change for good: the school, the technique. Did you have to avoid any steps because they don't dance them anymore?

There was nothing in the Sergeyev notations that the dancers were unaccustomed to dancing. I didn't have to avoid anything. It's just that the rehearsal process stretched out because there was a lot to relearn.

Aren't you afraid that amidst the rich decorations, heavy costumes, and the crowd on the stage, the dances won't be visible?

What Marius Petipa wanted on view will be visible. The dances will be visible where they should be seen. Classical dance will arise only where it will seem miraculous, because classical dance in this ballet is allotted a magical role. Everything else—the pantomime, character, and historical dance—serves as a kind of pedestal for it, creating the effect of contrast and dynamic intensification.

Sleeping Beauty *is unusually complex in structure. There are ensembles that support the choreographic dramaturgy and decors that organize the space. And there is the mythology of the ballet that was constantly simplified in order to make it more accessible to the audience. The names of the fairies in the Prologue are a prime example. What do you think of the names Konstantin Sergeyev gave them?*

Maybe the names of Petipa's fairies weren't understandable to people who happened to wander into the theater. But they don't translate "allegro vivo" for the audience in the Philharmonic. And besides, Konstantin Sergeyev didn't translate them properly. Candide—that not "tenderness," but simpleness, which explains much in the next act. The Lilac Fairy granted her this quality, and as a result, Aurora takes the bad gift, the spindle, quite simply from Carabosse's hands. Aurora had no thought that anyone could bring her evil. They kept her from evil; for twenty years they had protected her from the world. But evil penetrated nonetheless. This is an example of a bad translation that cheapened the story.

In essence, the theater today is rehabilitating Petipa as the creator of brilliant spectacles—grand and monumental in form—that no one today can manage?

The theater is rehabilitating itself first and foremost. Because it must justify its name. I think that only with the reconstruction of *Sleeping Beauty* will we become the Maryinsky Theater once again.

Doesn't the role of Petipa's defender frighten you?

Of course it's a horrible burden. I never prepared myself for this work. I finished the school and tried to take what I could from my teachers. But if you had told me ten years ago that I would stage *Sleeping Beauty* I would have just laughed. I guess it was in the stars.

Notes

1. These writers do not self-identify as balletomanes. They generally speak of the balletomanes in the third person, though they faithfully report the balletomane position and seldom distance themselves from it.
2. Their writing is thus easily distinguishable from that of the "professional" critics who emerged a few decades later. André Levinson and Akim Volynsky covered Russian ballet in its period of early twentieth-century transition. Their reviews reveal a much broader cultural knowledge than is evident in those of the balletomanes.
3. *La Vestale* was something of a *Peterburgskaya gazeta* project: the newspaper's editor, Sergei Khudekhov, wrote the libretto.
4. Ivanov was scarcely alone in promoting his ballet. The *Peterburgskaya gazeta* critic also compared *La Vestale* favorably to *Sleeping Beauty* (16 January 1890).
5. A term best summarized as high-minded bad taste. Vladimir Nabokov's notes on *poshlost'* are reprinted in *Anton Chekhov's Plays* (W. W. Norton, 1977).
6. Roland John Wiley includes a translation of Laroche's "musical letter" in *A Century of Russian Ballet*, 377–84.
7. Slonimsky cites Vladimir Pogozhev, who recalled that the costumes, visuals, and props cost some 42,000 rubles, then a bit more than one-fourth of the yearly production budget of the St. Petersburg theaters (1956, 181).
8. Giannandrea Poesio defines the *ballo grande* this way: "The term . . . is gener-

ally used to indicate the nineteenth century Italian choreographic genre epitomized by the three works—*Excelsior* (1881), *Amor* (1886), and *Sport* (1896)—choreographed by Luigi Manzotti. The term was coined in relation to the extraordinary spectacular character of those productions" (1997). Also: "a vast, spectacular production generally in four, five, six or seven acts, in which the action was mainly mimed, interspersed with incidental dances" (1994).

9. Choreography attributed to Lev Ivanov; the book, to Petipa.

10. The catalog of Petipa's works compiled by Yuri Slonimsky lists four Petipa féeries: *The Magic Pills* (féerie-ballet), 1886; *Sleeping Beauty* (ballet-féerie), 1890; *Nutcracker* (ballet-féerie), 1892; and *Blue Beard* (ballet-féerie), 1896.

11. Petipa augmented the ballet's mass scenes in restaging the work.

12. *Les pilulues du diable,* by Ferdinand Laloue, a "pièce féerie" in three acts and nine scenes, premiered on 16 February 1839 at the Cirque Olympique in Paris.

13. The individual design of the corps de ballets costumes for the ballet precedes this much-heralded innovation of Russia's "new" ballet by several decades.

14. *Excelsior,* for example, was meant to depict the triumph of enlightenment over obscurantism, though the ballet's twelve scenes depicted events as far-ranging as the construction of the Suez Canal and the Brooklyn Bridge.

15. The entrance of the children in the Act I Garland Dance surprised the stagers at the first full-dress rehearsal of the 1999 production: alongside the adults costumed in white and French blue, the appearance of the children in bright red and white costumes recalled the red, white, and blue of the French flag.

16. The term refers to popular Russian carnival shows like the one depicted in the Stravinsky-Fokine ballet *Petrushka.*

CHAPTER 2. LEGENDS OF *SLEEPING BEAUTY*

1. Lincoln Kirstein reports that Alexander III, grateful for the loans from France, allowed the *Marseillaise* to be played before in his presence only in 1889 (1984, 175).

2. Volkonsky records a conversation between the Russian-born Wagnerian singer Felia Litvinne, who wished to sing Isolde in the Maryinsky, and Vsevolozhsky: "Mais, pensez donc, M. le Directeur, cette mort magnifique!" The director's reply: "Oui, mais quelle vie ennuyeuse!" (1992, I, 147).

3. The Grimm version of the tale (from 1812) follows the general contours of Perrault's, with a few alterations (thirteen fairies, rather than eight; gold plates rather than cutlery). The Grimms are also less specific about the fairies' gifts: beauty, virtue, "and so on," though they assure us the gifts are "desirable and magnificent."

4. The precedent for the famous panorama scene in *Sleeping Beauty* was also French: Crosten reports an 1829 Paris production with "a shifting decoration which caused a delightful perspective to unfold before the undulations of a boat" (60).

5. Flashes of choreography in the variations Aurora dances suggest that she has already internalized the fairies' blessings; movement motifs from the fairies' variations echo in hers.

6. Warner speculates that Basile may have adapted his tale from the Italian translation of

the fourteenth-century Arthurian prose legend *Perceforest,* first printed in 1528 (220). *Perceforest* introduces a necrophilic element to the story retained by Basile: unable to rouse the sleeping princess, the hero of the tale consorts with her; she bears a child as a result. The Grimm brother's version of the tale ("Dornröschen") substitutes a kiss, which proves as effective but more palatable.

7. Perrault's evil queen even descends from ogres ("*elle était de race Ogresse*"), though she possesses gourmand tastes: She wishes to eat her son's progeny herself, in a "*sauce Robert,*" then demands to dine on their mother as well.

8. Carabosse's presence or absence in the processionals of Act III of *Sleeping Beauty* has traditionally aroused much debate, though the 1890–91 *Yearbook of the Imperial Theaters* includes Carabosse (in a chariot drawn by rats) on its illustrated list of fairy-tale personages that appear in the ballet's third-act "entrée" (146–47). Vikharev's 1999 staging retained the compromise of the original: Carabosse is borne across the stage in a litter, as is the Lilac Fairy, yet her place in the apotheosis of clouds is a lowly one, and spears held at a threatening angle keep her at bay. Although some among the 1999 St. Petersburg audience were surprised at Carabosse's inclusion in the wedding party, it would seem that not inviting Carabosse—once again—would amount to tempting fate.

9. "Each version of the myth, then, shows the influence of a twofold determinism: one strand links it to a succession of previous versions or to a set of foreign versions, while the other operates as it were transversally, through the constraints arising from the infrastructure which necessitate the modification of some particular element, with the result that the system undergoes reorganization in order to adapt these differences to necessities of an external kind" (1981, 628).

10. Seen from this viewpoint, the Sleeping Beauty legend parallels vampire legends: Lilac's modulation of Aurora's curse places Aurora with those undying immortals who sleep. Fortunately for the princess, Aurora's double act as a procuress, trapping Aurora's prospective prince in the woods.

11. In both works, it is disorder that occasions the sleep: Brunhilde's disobedience and Catalabutte's mistake (which leads to Carabosse's curse).

12. The identification of spinning/knitting with women's tales is underscored in the title of the opening scene of Act I: "Caquets des tricoteuses" or "knitters' chatter."

13. The appearance of Wagner's Loge (fire) to surround Brunhilde's bier with flame furnishes a precedent for the staged scene of the forest in *Beauty.* In Perrault, the forest grows by itself ("in about fifteen minutes"), though bystanders give the young fairy credit. In *Beauty,* as in Wagner, the scene is staged rather than discussed.

14. Lévi-Strauss continues: "One is the reality of being, which man senses at the deepest level as being alone capable of giving a reason and a meaning to his daily activities, his moral and emotional life, his political options, his involvement in the social and the natural worlds, his practical endeavours and his scientific achievements; the other is the reality of non-being, awareness of which inseparably accompanies the sense of being, since man has to live and struggle, think, believe and above all, preserve his courage, although he can never at any moment lose sight of the opposite certainty that he was not present on earth in former times, that he will not always be here in the future and that, with his inevitable disappearance from the surface of a planet which is itself doomed to die, his

labours, his sorrows, his joy, his hopes and his works will be as if they had never existed, since no consciousness will survive to preserve even the memory these ephemeral phenomena, only a few features of which, soon to be erased from the impassive face of the earth, will remain as already cancelled evidence that they once were, and were as nothing" (1981, 694–95).

15. Laroche's essay, with its endorsement of an art form that embraces the "impossible . . . incomprehensible . . . and inexpressible" reveals the influence of symbolist/decadent trends from the West then making inroads into Russian culture. Tolstoy penned *What Is Art?*, his screed against new tendencies in art, in these years.

16. Kshesinskaya first danced *Daughter of the Pharaoh* in 1898 and made her debut in *Esmeralda* in 1899, as did Carlotta Brianza.

17. Here the printed libretto is at odds with the performance traditions and notations. The libretto suggests that Lilac stands by and watches as the prince rushes about the sleeping court. In the 1999 staging, she reminds the prince to kiss Aurora.

18. Konstantinova cites Galina Dobrovolskaya (Lopukhov's biographer), who suggests that this variation was choreographed as early as 1912, but Konstantinova does not cite the source (141).

19. The 1999 production revealed another curiosity of Lopukhov's variation: its relation to Aurora's vision-scene variation, interpolated to the music for the Gold variation from Act III. The music for Gold does not fit in the vision scene. An "old ballet" intrusion (requiring a quick key change), it is discordant as the peasants who crash Giselle's party to dance a pas de deux. Yet the variation was part of the early performance tradition of *Sleeping Beauty.* When asked about this variation, which he returned to the 1999 production, Sergei Vikharev explained: "It would be nice to think that Petipa set the Aurora's variation in the vision scene to the music that Tchaikovsky originally composed (the variation in G-flat major with the oboe solo). But when we looked at Tchaikovsky's autographed score in the music library of the theater, it was clear that Petipa refused that music. In the score, after the allegro fragment (the corps de ballet's dance) a sheet is pasted in, and in Drigo's hand (he conducted the premiere) there are four bars written in to shift the tonality to the Gold Fairy's variation (in E-flat major). Of course, one might still wonder when and for what performer this was done, but alongside, also in Drigo's hand, it says, in French: 'Miss Brianza's variation follows.' Everything became clear to us then. Miss Brianza danced Aurora from 1890—at the premiere—until 1892" (Vikharev)

20. Konstantinova cites a letter she received from Krasovskaya in 1985.

21. Conversation with Sergei Vikharev, 13 February 2001.

22. Leshkov's manuscripts—mostly biographical sketches of dancers—are held in the St. Petersburg Public Library.

23. The attacks on Maria Petipa are not limited to her own biography. In the entry on Sergei Legat, for example, Borisoglebsky writes: "[S. Legat] was so strong, that he could even partner Maria Mariusovna Petipa, who in 1900–1905 was already quite heavy (in the theatrical circles of Petersburg they called her 'the commode'). S. Legat easily lifted her on outstretched arms" (76). The account concludes with Legat's suicide: "after the usual argument with Maria Petipa . . . he grabbed a razor and slit his throat" (ibid.).

CHAPTER 3. ACHIEVING SYMPHONISM

1. The notation of the ballet repertory in the early 1900s represented one conservative response to Petipa's imminent retirement, for example.
2. Mary Grace Swift provides a fine account of the transition from Imperial to State Theaters in the years following the 1917 Revolution in *The Art of Dance in the USSR,* especially as these changes affected the ballet.
3. Lenin generally affirmed the necessity of preserving the cultural legacy of the past, though the theaters were never at the top of his list. According to Fitzpatrick, "In 1919, the short-lived revolutionary government of the Hungarian Soviet Republic nationalized the theatres the day after taking power. Lenin thought this odd, and asked a Hungarian Comintern delegate whether they had no more important business to attend to" (1970, 141).
4. The last of these appeared in 1927.
5. A somewhat different justification takes shape in Lunacharsky's speeches and writings on this issue later. A 1930 speech repeats a familiar refrain from Lunacharsky's later statements on bourgeois culture: "In the course of my work as the director of the theaters and artistic education I always feared destroying this traditional line [here, the art of classical dance], since, having lost it, we might never capture it again" (1958, 415).
6. The theater wing of Proletkult was concerned with the repertories of the state theaters as well as other cultural manifestations they regarded as dangerous: "boulevard" literature, the "yellow" press, and the *café chantant* (Clark 118). In *St. Petersburg: Crucible of Cultural Revolution,* Katerina Clark writes: "It was as if the highbrow intellectuals wanted to eradicate a more successful rival for public attention" (ibid.). Clark traces the perceived threat of the *café chantant* well into the New Economic Policy (NEP) years of the young Soviet republic. In 1922 *The Life of Art* (a publication of NARKOMPROS, Lunacharsky's Commissariat of Enlightenment) announced that NEP art had produced nothing of value (in Schwarz 43).
7. Glaviskussto combined the old functions of Glavpolitprosvet (for political enlightenment) and Glavrepertkom (the repertory committee). The bureau's appearance in 1928 coincided with the start of what Sheila Fitzpatrick and others have termed Russia's Cultural Revolution (1928–31).
8. Sollertinsky discussed the choreography of Michel Fokine and Isadora Duncan in a favorable light in his chapter "Impressionism in Choreography" (1933, 330–45).
9. The critic Akim Volynsky speaks to the problem of emigration in his 26 September 1922 essay in *Zhizn' iskusstva,* "Call an Ambulance!" (see appendix).
10. In his introduction to Lopukhov's first volume of memoirs, written between 1961 and 1963.
11. Yuri Slonimsky and Ivan Sollertinsky were pupils of Gvozdev.
12. The Union of Soviet Writers replaced all independent literary organizations, for example, and the organizational structures of other arts organizations followed suit.
13. Sollertinsky was attacked in the antiformalism debates in 1936 (in the furor over Shostakovich's *Lady Macbeth of Mtsensk*) as the "bard" of formalism (Schwarz 127).

14. Here, "bourgeois" carries a favorable connotation, as it refers to an enlightened, progressive bourgeoisie of the prerevolutionary period.

15. The "Ukranian Week" was the first of a series of *dekadas,* ten-day festivals of arts of the Soviet republics that were shown in Moscow from 1936 to 1941 (Schwarz 132).

16. Derived from *kul'tura*—culture.

17. "The dramatic reversal of the mid 1930s has been attributed to a general process of 'embourgeoisement' of the Stalinist regime and repudiation of revolutionary values. This is probably true, but we should remember that contemporaries often saw it differently. Communists who had moved up from the lower classes were particularly inclined to see their assumption of distinctions modeled on those of the old regime as simply a proof that the Revolution had finally triumphed: they now had what the old bosses used to have" (Fitzpatrick 1999, 107).

18. The article is adapted from the Petipa chapters of Krasovskaya's 1963 volume *Russian Ballet Theater in the Second Half of the Nineteenth Century* (211–336). I will cite the more accessible English-language version of the article in most cases, though I occasionally refer to the lengthier 1963 version.

19. Marina Konstantinova's book *Sleeping Beauty* (1990), in the "Masterworks of the Ballet" series, is altogether more thoughtful than much of the Soviet scholarship and criticism that preceded it. She incorporates the writings of Vadim Gaevsky, for example, at a time when Gaevsky was only emerging from his persona non grata status following the publication of his book *Divertissement* eight years earlier.

20. Even though Krasovskaya later identifies *Sleeping Beauty* as the "acme of the nineteenth-century symphonic ballet" (1972, 20), the ballets of Petipa are only seeds of the "sturdy tree" that matured later (conveniently, in Krasovskaya's lifetime).

21. The 1922 article, Asafiev's most extensive writing on *Sleeping Beauty,* was originally published in the *Ezhenedel'nik petrogradskikh gosudarstvesnnikh teatrov* [Weekly of the Petrograd State Theaters] (vol. 5, pp. 28–36) and coincided with Lopukhov's 1922 restaging of *Beauty.* The article was republished in 1954 in the second volume of Asafiev's *Selected Works.* Asafiev also wrote under the pen name Igor Glebov.

22. Bogdanov-Berezovsky's quote appeared in G. Orlov's *Russkii Sovetskii Symfonizm* [Russian-Soviet Symphonism], 1966, p. 80.

23. Opinions of the music of Petipa's frequent collaborators, Ludwig Minkus, Cesare Pugni, and Ricardo Drigo, have changed little since Musorgsky's time. In a delicate summary of the situation in *Tchaikovsky's Ballets,* Roland John Wiley echoes the appraisal of Rozanova and others: "Petipa's composers were prolific, often facile, yet provided the choreographer a tuneful, rhythmic 'floor' on which to base dances" (1–10).

Gennady Rozhdestvensky marked the assumption of his very brief artistic directorship of the Bolshoi Theater in Moscow in August 2000 with an anti-Pugni campaign. As evidence for the dire artistic state of the Bolshoi Theater, he cited the seven scheduled performances of Pierre Lacotte's version of Pugni's *Daughter of the Pharaoh* when only two performances of Musorgsky's *Boris Godunov* were listed on the season roster. Rozhdestvensky then opened the Bolshoi season with a performance of *Boris* (rather than the traditional opener, Glinka's *Life for the Tsar*) and reduced scheduled performances of

Daughter of the Pharaoh to the two performances the theater was obliged to give by contract (Andronov, Kuznetsova).

24. Vanslov's entry was reprinted in the 1997 *Russian Ballet Encyclopedia* (Moscow) with only minor changes.

25. It is difficult to understand how one could speak of the dance in *Beauty* as pas d'action from Rozanova's description. Like most of the Soviet writers of her generation, Rozanova exaggerates the role of narrative—at the expense of the pantomime. Like Krasovskaya, she treats *Beauty* as an evolving entity rather than a series of different productions.

26. The Great Patriotic War of the Soviet people against fascism (World War II) not only failed to interrupt the scientific research work of Asafiev, it stimulated it. According to Protopopov, Asafiev considered untiring work for the cause of Soviet musical culture his patriotic duty (12).

27. "But how to symphonize dance? No one, and especially those who insist on it, ever says" (54).

28. Rozanova published a second book on Tchaikovsky's symphonism in 1976: *Simfonicheskie printsipy baletov Chaikovskogo* [Symphonic principles in Tchaikovsky's ballets] (Moscow).

29. Petipa is thus "perfected," as his ballets were in the Soviet period.

30. Krasovskaya's writing reflects the often extreme anti-Western bias of the *zhdanovshchina* of the postwar Stalin era.

31. In his original production for St. Petersburg's Bolshoi Theater, Petipa used sixty-four dancers; that number was halved when the ballet moved to the Maryinsky Theater with its shallower stage (Gaevsky 1981, 70).

32. The remainder of Krasovskaya's discussion of the actual ballet recounts its action in poetic, general terms with no indication of the production to which Krasovskaya refers: 1952, 1922, 1914, or 1890: "After this came the majestic, luminous peace of the waltz of the Lilac Fairy. A fragrant bush flowered in its flowing tempos as the dancer's arms swung open. Covering the stage with a clear, calm pattern of movements, the Lilac Fairy crowned with her dance the abundant gifts of her friends" (1972, 27). Krasovskaya writes of the Lilac Fairy's variation in the ballet's Prologue but describes the variation choreographed by Fyodr Lopukhov and included in Konstantin Sergeyev's 1952 version for the Kirov Ballet. In other words, she describes the choreography of Lopukhov in her discussion of Petipa's choreography. The difficulty of describing dances that exist in variant productions or have been lost vexes every dance historian, but the conflation of the work of various choreographers in an article that seeks to evaluate the choreography of a particular choreographer is troubling indeed.

CHAPTER 4. RED AURORAS

Epigraph: From *How Russians Speak,* 1978–79, Collection of Dansmuseet, Stockholm.

1. Murray Frame gives the following statistics: *Sleeping Beauty,* twenty performances; *Le Corsaire, Raymonda,* and *Esmeralda,* seventeen performances each; *Swan Lake* and *The Humpbacked Horse,* sixteen each (169). These figures correspond to those given in two

Soviet sources (Yufit and Khrushevich), though the latter sources calculate differently: Yufit by season; Khrushevich by year.

2. Leonid Leontiev, who would later become the head of the ballet troupe, discussed the problems hunger posed to the ballet in a 1918 interview: "Undernourishment is felt in the troupe terribly. The lack of fats and sugar weakens the organism, and the artists literally lack the strength to work. Even such a strong partner as Vladimirov complains that it's difficult to support a ballerina. And if the adagio goes well, then in the variation, the artists' legs give out and turn into some sort of mush. And this is natural, since you can't fill up on one potato. With chronic malnutrition come leg injuries, dislocations, strained tendons, etc. A whole rank of ballerinas who carry the repertory, like Gerdt, Vill, Lyukom, Spesivtseva, and others, have become invalids" (in Yufit 198).

3. Schwarz reports the "re-writing of operatic libretti while leaving the music intact" as a by-product of the revolution: "Thus, *Tosca* became 'The Battle for the Commune,' *Les Huguenots* was transformed into 'The Decembrists,' *A Life for the Tsar* emerged as 'Hammer and Sickle.' New texts were also provided for *Rienzi* and *Don Giovanni*. More creative was a new version of *Carmen* under the name 'Carmencita and the Soldier' (1924) staged by Nerirovich-Danchenko; it proved very popular" (64).

4. The Leningrad theater administrators made their recommendation in 1924, the year after Lopukhov completed his new staging of *Sleeping Beauty* and at roughly the same time Asafiev penned his first essays on Tchaikovsky.

5. I include the Diaghilev ballet's 1921 staging of the ballet in London among these Petersburg productions. Staged primarily by Nikolai Sergeyev (who supervised the 1914 Petersburg version) and others still identified with the St. Petersburg ballet, this first émigré production should be discussed in light of other Petersburg stagings.

6. Benois discounts the possibility of reviving the work: "No reconstruction could save it. All the conventions, all the technical devices change, or are forgotten, even despite what seems to be the pious observance of traditions" (1993, I, 606).

7. Benois contradicted himself later (in a pattern typical of former World of Art artists writing in the West). In 1939, Benois recalled Korovin's sets as surpassing the "rather timid work" of the 1890 painters and Korovin's costumes as "better still and in colouring, incomparably superior to Vsevolojsky's somewhat dilettante and tasteless inventions" (1941, 132).

8. Lopukhov also indicts the "untalented hand" of Nikolai Sergeyev, then the company's regisseur, in changing some of the ballet's mises-en-scene in the newly decorated 1914 production (1972, 81).

9. Volynsky, (1861–1926), a pseudonym of Khaim Flekser, was a writer and literary critic whose attentions turned to dance in the 1910s. Volynsky's 1923 review of the ballet repeats much he had already written of the same production in 1914, but it is the most complete of his reviews of *Sleeping Beauty*.

10. Denis Ivanovich Leshkov (1883–1933), sometimes spelled "Lyashkov."

11. The Bibienas were a family of Italian architects and theater designers active from the 1680s to the 1780s, notably in Vienna.

12. The visual style of the eighteenth century had long been a hobbyhorse of the World of Art artists. Alexander Golovin's decors for Vsevolod Meyerhold's production of the Ler-

montov play *Masquerade,* an extravagantly stylized production in eighteenth-century style, premiered on the eve of the February 1917 Revolution.

13. Lopukhov's revisions to *Sleeping Beauty* actually came in two phases. Nosilov reports that during the 1923–24 season, Lopukhov "enlivened the scene with the spinners, returned the old French dances, the entr'acte, created a new scene for Carabosse and mice in the awakening, used the fairies as an introduction to the Act III grand pas de deux, and returned the sarabande" (320).

14. Nosilov's attitude typifies the Soviet view of the bourgeois inheritance: the classics are not capable of living in the repertory as they are; there is always curatorial work to be done.

15. Even today in Russia—on theater affiches and programs, in reference works and conversation—the authorship of a ballet is still routinely assigned to its composer, not its choreographer, as is generally the case in the West.

16. Natalia Roslavleva asserts that the volume was written as early as 1916 (1966, 203).

17. Stephanie Jordan summarizes the main arguments for and against this musically motivated form of dance as articulated in Europe in the 1930s. Those opposed to staging dances to concert music argued that the music was already self-sufficient and too sophisticated for dancing; dance enthusiasts cited the desirability of bringing great music to a broader public and also of using musical structures to organize the choreography (52).

18. The critic Georgi Khubov attacked the encyclopedia entry's "mechanical leveling" at the Second All-Union Congress of Composers in 1957 (Schwarz 303–4).

19. A leading Leningrad music critic, Bogdanov-Berezovsky (1903–71) was among those censured in 1948 for "cosmopolite errors," "groveling before Western music," and ignoring Russian music (Schwarz 250).

20. As Harold Segel demonstrates in *Body Ascendant* (1998), modernism had long mistrusted words.

21. The respective heydays of the ballet (1830s to 1840s in Paris, early twentieth-century Russia) coincided with romantic eras in poetry. At both junctures, intellectuals from the visual arts and literature venerated the dance as a medium capable of expression without recourse to realism, prose, or even words.

22. We should recall that Bogdanov-Berezovsky declared symphonism "a means of musical representation and of concrete reality in the highest philosophical categories" (in Schwarz 159).

23. These gestures were not unique to the ballet but shared much in common with gestures then used on opera and dramatic theater stages (see Poesio, 1994, 1995, 1999).

24. Balanchine's *Nutcracker* (1954) includes a mime sequence attributed to Ivanov that Balanchine himself performed as a child in the Maryinsky (Balanchine 1983, 211). In the interview with Volkov, Balanchine discusses the pantomime he retained in his 1965 production of *Harlequinade* (an adaptation of Petipa's *Les Milions d'Arlequins,* from 1900).

25. In fact, the majority of new viewers to make their way to the Maryinsky/Kirov became part of the audience after the revolution, not World War II, a fact that numerous early Soviet sources proudly cite.

26. Lopukhov continues: "There were also tacky details in the monologues, like 'from there (shown with the hand), will come one soldier with a sword (once again showing, with

the hand, the place where the sword should be), in a hat with a feather (again, the gesture with the hand, though perhaps a more natural one), he will see, kiss, and she—Aurora—will rise up.' Maria Mariusovna repeated this very same monologue twice, once in the future tense, in the Prologue, and the second time in the present tense, before the last act, though there was no difference of any sort in these gesticulations" (91–92).

27. The Moscow production was revived by V. Monakhov, though it included choreography from previous Moscow versions of the ballet, including that of Gorsky and Tikhomirov (Konstantinova 180).

28. Sergeyev restaged *Raymonda* in 1948 and *Swan Lake* in 1950. *Sleeping Beauty* thus functioned as the culmination of this postwar restoration of the Petipa classics.

29. Still Lopukhov's staging but with the Korovin designs.

30. Sergeyev's *Sleeping Beauty* held its place in the Kirov/Maryinsky repertory until 1999, when Vikharev's staging replaced it. Sergeyev's version is still performed in Japan. The production is well documented. The catalog of the New York Public Library's Dance Collection lists three filmed versions of the ballet, from the 1960s to the 1990s. Unfortunately, the earliest recorded version, which features Natalia Dudinskaya (Sergeyev's wife and the Aurora of the 1952 production) as Carabosse, is the most condensed (at only eighty-four minutes long) and most ruinously adapted for filming.

31. Bogdanov-Berezovsky had good reason to praise Sergeyev's achievements: he had been implicated in the censure of Soviet musicologists in 1949 (see Schwarz 249–50).

32. Arkady Sokolov (b. 1937), St. Petersburg ballet critic and historian. In post-Soviet times known as Sokolov-Kaminsky.

33. Ballet historian, critic, and poet (b. 1925).

34. Typically grouped with the terms *partiinost* (party spirit) and *narodnost* (national character). The Soviet ballet encyclopedia gives the following definition: "Idea-ness in art is an understanding referring to the artist's adherence to a particularly system of ideas corresponding to social, moral, and aesthetic ideals, and the embodiment of these ideals in art" (Vanslov 1981).

35. Another loaded term: "The Soviet ballet represented a new stage in the evolution of realism, when realism was joined together with the ideas of socialism in the interest of the truthful reflection of new social realities (see socialist realism)" (Vanslov 1981).

36. Sergeyev's staging premiered on 11 March 1992; Sergeyev died in St. Petersburg on 1 April 1992.

37. Grigorovich replaced Sergeyev's *Corsaire* with his own "new stage version" (based on Sergeyev's staging) on 16 February 1994.

CHAPTER 5. BRINGING *BEAUTY* BACK

1. Alan Confino defines collective memory as "the representation of the past and the making of it into a shared cultural knowledge by successive generations in 'vehicles of memory' such as books, films, museums, commemorations, and others" (1997, 1386).

2. Institutional internecine rivalries among the ballet school, the conservatory, and the theater proved enormously useful in stirring up trouble as well, as representatives of each in-

stitution were anxious to present their institutions as somehow purer and more faithful to the nineteenth-century legacy or, at very least, less tainted than the others.

3. Spelled "Sergejev" at Harvard.

4. Unfortunately, Vikharev and his team deemed the variation undanceable as notated—it lacked the usual (and necessary) pauses between phrases of virtuoso dancing. Instead, Prince Désiré danced the 1952 Sergeyev variation in its place, the only instance where a set piece from the 1952 choreography was used.

5. The restoration of architectural monuments in the Soviet era was nonetheless selective. In *Mythmaking in the New Russia,* Smith discusses the subversive potential of campaigns to save buildings and monuments whose conservation the state did not sanction: "Long before perestroika, Russian nationalists of various stripes had embraced the cause of saving Russia's endangered patrimony. Indeed, support for historically significant buildings was one of the few catalysts of civic activism in the USSR before 1989. To defend decaying estates and abandoned churches was in effect to criticize the Soviet regime, which had done so much to transform the landscape by destroying or neglecting the architectural legacies of the imperial period and by devastating traditional Russian village life with inept policies. Yet some scholars, history buffs, and writers risked offending the government because they saw conservation of Russian architecture and the natural landscape as means of expressing love for their native land and culture" (119–20).

Smith speaks of conservation that goes well beyond the restoration of Romanov palaces—those long attracted foreign tourists and hard currency—but more ordinary and ideologically problematic structures: the manor homes of local gentry, village churches, etc. As Smith suggest, the restoration of other structures could be subversive.

6. In *The Imaginary Museum of Musical Works,* Lydia Goehr writes: "The ideal of *Werktreue* pervaded every aspect of practice in and after 1800 with full regulative force. Following from the central conception of a musical work as a self-sufficiently formed unity, expressive in its synthesized form and content of a genius' idea, was the general submission of all associated concepts. Concepts and ideals having to do with notation, performance, and reception acquired their meaning as concepts subsidiary to that of a work. In a certain sense this had had to be the case, for these subsidiary concepts had served to give a highly abstract concept concrete expression. Without their development, in other words, the abstract work-concept developed and articulated with the romantic, aesthetic theory of fine art would never have found its regulative force in practice" (242).

7. Gorsky staged his Moscow production of *Sleeping Beauty* from Stepanov notations already in 1898 (Gorsky 82–83).

8. To our earlier questions (to restore or not to restore? and how?) we could add: What to restore? And who should carry out the restoration? A calling card of the Maryinsky Ballet, *Sleeping Beauty* represented an obvious a candidate for restoration. Yet attention began to fix on the second parts of both sets of questions once the theater had answered the first ones. Once the decision to restore (and to restore *Sleeping Beauty*) was taken, attention shifted to the means of reconstruction and the person in charge of that restoration.

9. Putin won the March 2000 election handily. Racism, like xenophobia and homosexuality, did not officially exist in the Soviet Union, though each managed to thrive, and the

ascension of non-Russians to positions of power and authority in the "national" theater has long distressed local bigots. Valery Gergiev's rise to the top of the Maryinsky hierarchy was greeted with a slanderous, thinly veiled roman à clef depicting the conductor as one Abdullah Bcsnovatogo (the raving), whose faulty Russian is punctuated with interjections praising Allah.

10. Krasovskaya died months later, in August 1999.

11. Benois never designed a *Sleeping Beauty* in Russia, though he did advise Lopukhov on the staging of the 1922–23 production in which Krasovskaya danced. The slip is telling: As one writer put it, "in the ballet, Benois and his comrades are still indisputable authorities" (Dolinina 1999b).

12. His interview, with Vaziev and Gershenzon, first appeared in *Russian Telegraph*, 11 April 1998 (Vaziev et al.).

13. For Arlene Croce, the ballet's main idea is less obvious: "The moral substance of *The Sleeping Beauty* is porous; you can find anything in it you like: a defense of monarchy, a myth about the earth's renewal, a love story, the Incarnation."

14. This split paralleled the sharp differences in opinion between dance and music critics in 1890.

15. Ippolitov's statement closely parallels the musicological festishization of the *Werktreue,* discussed earlier. Indeed, those who question music's quest for authenticity as a means of communing with the author's original intent (notably Goehr and Taruskin) only seek to question the relevance of this object-oriented approach for a time-based art form.

16. Our mythic reading of the ballet's libretto suggests that Aurora's characterization lacked such layers of meaning, that reflection and meditation lie beyond her.

17. Although friends and colleagues understood that my interest in their response was, in part, professional, strangers who spoke with me about the production were only aware that I was foreign.

18. Oushakine asked Siberian students to describe (1) the Soviet man/woman, (2) the "new" Russian man/woman, and (3) the post-Soviet man/woman.

19. According to Annette Fern, research and reference librarian of the Harvard Theatre Collection, the Kirov Ballet had contacted the collection concerning the Sergeyev documents in the 1980s, but nothing came of the brief correspondence.

20. The irony of a wordless national hymn became more apparent in the year following the premiere of *Sleeping Beauty* and the publication of Oushakine's article as the anthem of the Soviet Union was reinstated as the national hymn of Russia in late 2000. For the second time in less than a decade of statehood, Russia's national anthem was wordless or possessed words entirely inappropriate to the present situation ("In the victory of Communism's deathless ideal, / We see the future of our dear land"). The new, still wordless anthem became a source of fun for countless media commentators as it also encapsulated the wordlessness Oushakine and other social scientists had observed.

The decision to reinstate the Soviet anthem was part of President Putin's campaign to fix Russia's state symbols. The reinstatement of the Soviet anthem and red flag (for the armed forces) represented a revanche to some, but Putin appealed, predictably, to a different layer of national history to effect the compromise: "If we agree that the symbols of the preceding epochs, including the Soviet epoch, must not be used at all, we will have to admit then that our mothers' and fathers' lives were useless and meaningless, that their lives were in vain" (quoted in Kathleen Smith 182).

APPENDIX

1. The author omits Fleur de Farine and Canari.
2. In Russian, the form of these two words is the same: *dukhami.*
3. Another play on words. In Russian, *takt* refers to a measure of music as well as to "tact."
4. A reference to a character from Krylov's fables who patched his caftan with pieces from other parts of it.
5. *La Vestale* was something of a *Peterburgskaya gazeta* project: the newspaper's editor, Sergei Khudekhov, wrote the libretto (see Wiley 1985, 2).
6. The *Novoe vremya* reviewer added a note here: "We use the word 'variation' here in the choreographic rather than the musical sense."
7. The music critic of *Novoe vremya,* Mikhail Mikhailovich Ivanov (1849–1927) was a student of Tchaikovsky who composed the score of Petipa's 1888 ballet *La Vestale.*
8. A note here by the *Nuvelist* reviewer stated: "We don't wish to make any kind of comparison of the music of these two ballets and only speak of commonality of their general direction. We owe an appraisal of the music of *La Vestale* to our readers."
9. A term best summarized as high-minded bad taste. Vladimir Nabokov's notes on *poshlust'* are reprinted in *Anton Chekhov's Plays* (W. W. Norton, 1977).
10. Volynsky's title "Kareta skoroj pomoshchi" translates literally as "ambulance," though he uses a slightly antiquated term to evoke a horse-drawn conveyance.
11. According to Lillian B. Lawler, *hyporchema* designated a dance native to Crete combining "instrumental music, song, dance, and pantomime, to the music of lyre or flute, or even both together" (101).

Works Cited

Abbate, Carolyn. 1989. "Opera as Sympohny, a Wagnerian Myth." *Analyzing Opera: Verdi and Wagner.* Berkeley: University of California Press.

Acocella, Joan. 1999. "Lost and Found: The Kirov Looks Forward by Looking Back." *New Yorker* 75.20 (26 July): 88–91.

Andreeva, Ekaterina. 1999. "Chudesnoe obretenie basic values romantizma v Mariinskom teatre" [The miraculous acquisition of the basic values of romanticism in the Maryinsky Theater]. *Mariinskij teatr* 3–4: 5.

Andronov, Nikita. 2000. "Bolshoi sezon" [A big ("Bolshoi") season]. *Kommersant Daily,* 16 September: 9.

Asafiev, Boris V. (Igor Glebov). 1922. *Instrumental'noe tvorchestvo Chaikovskogo.* [Chaikovsky's instrumental works]. Moscow: Devyataya gosudarstvennaya tipografiya.

———. 1954. *Akademik B. V. Asaf'ev: Izbrannye trudy* [Academic B. V. Asafiev: Selected works]. Vol. 2. Moscow: Izdatel'stvo akademii nauk SSSR.

Bakhrushin, Yu[ri]. 1940. "Balety Chaikovskogo i ikh tsenicheskaya istoriya" [Chaikovsky's ballets and their stage history]. In *Chaikovsky i teatr* [Chaikovsky and the theater]. Moscow: Iskusstvo.

Banes, Sally. 1998. *Dancing Women: Female Bodies on Stage.* London: Routledge.

Bartlett, Rosamund. 1995. *Wagner and Russia.* Cambridge: Cambridge University Press.

Basile, Giambatista. 1932. *The Pentamerone of Giambattista Basile.* Ed. N. M. Penzer. Vol. 2. New York: Dutton.

Benois, Alexandre. 1922. "Pietet ili koshchunstvo?" [An homage or blasphemy?]. In *Ezhene-delnik gosudarstvennikh petrogradskikh akademicheskikh teatrov* [Weekly of the State Academic Theaters] 11:31–35.

———. 1941 *Reminiscences of the Russian Ballet.* Trans. Mary Britnietva. London: Putnam.

———. 1993. *Moi vosponimaniya* [My reminiscences]. Moscow: Nauka.

Bezpalov, Vasily. 1927. *Teatry v dni revoluyutsii 1917* [Theaters in the days of the 1917 Revolution]. Ed. Evgeny Kuznetsov. Leningrad: Academia.

Bland, Alexander. 1981. *The Royal Ballet: The First Fifty Years.* Garden City, N.Y.: Doubleday.

Bogdanov-Berezovsky, V. 1941. "Muzykal'naya dramaturiya baletov P. I. Chaikovskogo" [The musical dramaturgy of P. I. Chaikovsky's ballets]. In *P. I. Chaikovsky na tsene teatra opery i baleta imeni S. M. Kirova (b. Mariinsky)* [P. I. Chaikovsky on the stage of the Theater of Opera and Ballet named for S. M. Kirov (the former Maryinsky)]. Leningrad: Kirov Theater. 239–84.

———. 1959. *Leningradkii gosudarstvennyj akademicheskii ordena Lenina teatr opery i baleta imeni S. M. Kirova* [The Leningrad State Academic Order of Lenin Theater of Opera and Ballet named for S. M. Kirov]. Leningrad: Iskusstvo.

———. 1962. *Stat'i o balete* [Essays on ballet]. Moscow: Sovetsky kompozitor.

Borisoglebsky, M[ikhail], ed. 1939. *Materialy po istorii russkogo baleta* [Materials for a history of Russian ballet]. Vol. 2. Leningrad: Izdatel'stvo Leningradskogo gosudarstvennogo khoreograficheskogo uchilishcha.

Buckle, Richard. 1988. *George Balanchine, Ballet Master.* London: Hamilton.

Byock, Jesse, trans. 1990. *The Saga of the Volsungs: The Norse Epic of Sigurd the Dragon Slayer.* Berkeley: University of California Press.

Carnaghan, Ellen. 1996. "Alienation, Apathy, or Ambivalence? 'Don't Knows' and Democracy in Russia." *Slavic Review* 55.2: 361–62.

Cherepnin, A. 1927. "Dialektika baleta" [The dialectic of the ballet]. *Zhizn' iskusstvo* [The life of art], Pt. 1, 34: 6–7; pt. 2, 35: 4–5.

Cherkassky, Dmitry. 1994. *Zapiski baletomana* [Notes of a balletomane]. Moscow: ART.

Clark, Katerina. 1995. *Petersburg, Crucible of Cultural Revolution.* Cambridge: Harvard University Press.

Clément, Catherine. 1988. *Opera, or the Undoing of Women.* Trans. Betsy Wing. Minneapolis: University of Minnesota Press.

Confino, Alan. 1997. "Collective Memory and Cultural History: Problems of Method." *American Historical Review* 102.5 (December): 1386–1403.

Croce, Arlene. 1999. "On *Beauty* Bare." *New York Review of Books.* 12 August.

Degen, Arsen. 1999. "*Spyashchaya krasavitsa:* Mneniya o premére" [Sleeping Beauty: Thoughts on the premiere]. *Mariinskij teatr* 3–4: 4.

Dobrovolskaya, Galina N. 1977. "B. V. Asafiev i I. I. Sollertinskij o balete" [B. V. Asafiev and I. I. Sollertinsky on ballet]. In *Muzyka i khoreografiya sovremennogo baleta* [Music and choreography in contemporary ballet]. Leningrad: Muzyko. 234–39.

———. 1998. "Fedor Lopukhov." *International Encyclopedia of Dance.* New York: Oxford University Press.

Dolinina, Kira. 1999a. "Pora, Krasavica!" [Wake up, Sleeping Beauty!]. *Kommersant vlast'* 18 May.

————. 1999b. "*Spyashchaya krasavitsa:* Mneniya o prem'ere" [*Sleeping Beauty:* Thoughts on the premiere]. *Mariinskij teatr* 3–4: 16.

Dudinskaya, Natalia. 1993. "We Must Preserve the Heritage of Petipa's Genius." *Balet,* special English-language edition: 7–8.

Dunning, Jennifer. 1999. "Vera Krasovskaya, 83, Historian and Critic of the Russian Ballet." *New York Times.* 21 August.

Ezhegodnik imperatorskikh teatrov [Yearbook of the Imperial Theaters]. 1892–1920. St. Petersburg: Izdanie direktsiya imperatorskikh teatrov.

Fitzpatrick, Sheila. 1971. "The Emergence of Glaviskusstvo: Class War on the Cultural Front, Moscow 1928–29." *Soviet Studies* 23.2: 236–53.

————. 1992. *The Cultural Front: Power and Culture in Revolutionary Russia.* Ithaca: Cornell University Press.

————. 1999. *Everyday Stalinism. Ordinary Life in Extraordinary Times: Soviet Russia in the 1930s.* New York: Oxford University Press.

Frame, Murray. 2000. *The St. Petersburg Imperial Theaters: Stage and State in Revolutionary Russia, 1900–1920.* London: McFarland.

Gaevsky, V[adim]. 1981. *Divertisment: Sud"by klassicheskogo baleta* [Divertissement: The fate of classical ballet]. Moscow: Iskusstvo.

————. 1999. "Dyagilevskaya epopeya mariinskogo teatra" [The Maryinsky's Theater's Diaghilev epic]. *Mariinskij teatr* 3–4: 3.

————. 2000. "Zaveshchanie mastera. K 90-letniyu so dnya rozhdeniya Konstantina Sergeeva." [The master's last will: On the ninetieth anniversary of Konstantin Sergeyev's birth]. *Mariinskij teatr* 3–4: 11.

Galaida, Anna. 1999. "Mariinka khochet v proshloe" [The Maryinsky wishes for the past]. *Novye Izvestiya.* 13 May.

Genné, Beth. 2000. "Creating the Canon, Creating the 'Classics' in Twentieth-Century British Ballet." *Dance Research* 18.2: 132–62.

Gershenzon, Pavel. 1999. "Dom Petipa, ili zdanie imeni Petipa?" [The house of Petipa? Or a building named for him?]. *Pulse.* Summer.

Goehr, Lydia. 1992. *The Imaginary Museum of Musical Works.* Oxford: Oxford University Press.

Gordeeva, Anna. 1999. "Kraski ne poblekli za 100 let" [The colors haven't faded in 100 years]. *Obshchaya gazeta,* 13 May.

Gosudarev, Aleksei. 1999. "*Spyashchaya krasavitsa:* Mneniya o prem'ere" [*Sleeping Beauty:* Thoughts on the premiere]. *Mariinskij teatr* 3–4: 4.

Grimm, Jacob and Wilhelm. 1987. *The Complete Fairy Tales of the Brothers Grimm.* Trans. Jack Zipes. New York: Bantam.

Gronow, Jukka. 1997. *The Sociology of Taste.* London: Routledge.

Guest, Ann Hutchinson. 1998. "Stepanov Notation." *International Encyclopedia of Dance.* New York: Oxford University Press.

Guest, Ivor. 1986. *Gautier on Dance.* London: Dance Books.

Gvozdev, A. 1928. "O reforme baleta" [On ballet reform]. *Zhizn' iskusstvo* [The life of art] 1: 5–6.

Ippolitov, Arkady. 1999. "*Spyashchaya krasavitsa:* Mneniya o prem'ere" [*Sleeping Beauty:* Thoughts on the premiere]. *Mariinskij teatr* 3–4: 4–5.

Ivanov, M[ikhail]. 1890. "Musical Sketches." *Novoe vremya.* 22 January: 2.

Jacobs, Laura. 1999. "Tchaikovsky at the Millennium." *New Criterion* 18.1 (September): 21–28.

Karp, Poel. 2000. "Novaya staraya *Spyashchaya. Spyashchaya krasavitsa* v Kovent Gardene." [The new-old *Beauty: Sleeping Beauty* in Covent Garden]. *Mariinskij teatr* 3–4, sec. 2:2.

Kelly, Catriona, and Vadim Volkov. 1998. "Directed Desires: Kul'turnost' and Consumption." In *Constructing Russian Culture in the Age of Revolution: 1881–1940*. Ed. Catriona Kelly and David Shepherd. Oxford: Oxford University Press.

Kemp-Welch, A. 1991. *Stalin and the Literary Intelligentsia, 1928–39*. New York: St. Martin's Press.

Kendall, Elizabeth. 1992. "Reflections: The Kirov." *New Yorker* 68.16 (8 June): 77–89.

Kennan, George F. 1984. *The Fateful Alliance: France, Russia, and the Coming of the First World War*. New York: Pantheon Books.

Kennedy, Janet. 1998. "Line of Succession: Three Productions of Tchaikovsky's *Sleeping Beauty*." In *Tchaikovsky and His World*. Ed. Leslie Kearney. Princeton: Princeton University Press.

Khrushevich, I. P., ed. 1957. *Gosudarstveny ordena Lenina akademichesky teatr opery i baleta imeni S. M. Kirova* [Kirov State Order of Lenin Academic Opera and Ballet Theater]. Leningrad: Gosudarstvennoe muzykalnoe izdanie.

Khudekov, S[ergei]. 1890. "The Balletomane's Grief." *Peterburgskaya gazeta*, 5 January.

Kirstein, Lincoln. 1984. *Four Centuries of Ballet: Fifty Masterworks*. New York: Dover.

Konstantinova, M[arina Evgenievna]. 1990. *Spyashchaya krasavitsa* [*Sleeping Beauty*]. Shedevry baleta [Masterworks of the Ballet]. Moscow: Iskusstvo.

Korovyakov, Dmitry Dmitrievich ["N"]. 1890. "Novyj balet" [The new ballet] *Novosti i birzhevaya gazeta*, 5 January: 3.

Krasovskaya, Vera Mikhailovna. 1963. *Russky baletnyj teatr vtoroj poloviny 19 veka* [Russian ballet theater in the second half of the nineteenth century]. Leningrad: Iskusstvo.

———. 1972. "Marius Petipa and 'The Sleeping Beauty.'" Trans. Cynthia Read. *Dance Perspectives* 49: 6–56.

———. 1999. "Balet ne mozhet zamarinovat'sya" [A ballet can't be conserved]. *Kommersant Daily*, 6 May: 10.

Kshesinskaya, Matilda. 1961. *Dancing in Petersburg: The Memoirs of Kshessinska, H.S.H. the Princess Romanovsky-Krassinsky*. Trans. Arnold Haskell. Garden City, N.Y.: Doubleday.

Kuznetsova, Tatyana. 1999. "Spyashchaya, na kotoroj ne zasnesh'" [A Beauty that won't put you to sleep]. *Kommersant Daily*, 6 May: 10.

———. 2000. "Balety v Bol'shom vybirayut na slukh" [Ballets in the Bolshoi are chosen by ear]. *Kommersant Daily*, 20 September: 13.

Laroche, H. [Larosh, G.]. 1890. "Muzykal'noe pis'mo iz Peterburga" [A musical letter from St. Petersburg]. *Moskovskie vedemosti*, 17 January: 3–4.

———. 1895. *P. I. Chaikovsky kak dramatichesky kompozitor* [P. I. Chaikovsky as a dramatic composer]. St. Petersburg: Imperial Theaters.

Lawler, Lillian B. 1964. *The Dance in Ancient Greece*. Middletown, Conn.: Wesleyan University Press.

Lenin, V. I. 1980. *V. I. Lenin o kul'ture* [V. I. Lenin on culture]. Moscow: Politizdat.

Lévi-Strauss, Claude. 1981. *The Naked Man*. Trans. John and Doreen Weightman. New York: Harper and Row.

————. 1991. *Conversations with Claude Lévi-Strauss.* Didier Eribon. Trans. Paula Wissing. Chicago: University of Chicago Press.

Levinson, André. 1913. "O starom I novom balete" [On the old and new ballet]. In *Ezhegodnik imperatorskikh teatrov* [Yearbook of the Imperial Theaters]. 1:1–20.

————. 1915. *Rech* 268:15.

Lopukhov, Fyodr. 1925. *Puti baletmejstera* [Paths of a balletmaster]. Berlin: Petropolis.

————. 1966. *Shestdesyat let v balete* [Sixty years in ballet]. Moscow: Iskusstvo.

————. 1971. Annotations. In *Marius Petipa: Materialy, vospominaniya, stat'i* [Marius Petipa: Materials, reminiscences, articles]. Leningrad: Iskusstvo.

————. 1972. *Khoreographicheskie otkrovennosti* [Choreographic revelations]. Moscow: Iskusstvo.

Lunacharsky, A. V. 1922. "Sovetskoe gosudarstvo i iskusstvo" [The Soviet government and art]. *Izvestiya,* 19 February.

————. 1924. *Teatr i revolyutsiya* [Theater and revolution]. Moscow.

————. 1958. *V mire muzyki* [In the world of music]. Moscow: Sovetsky kompozitor.

————. 1964. *Sobranie sochinenij* [Collected works]. Moscow: Khudozhestvennaya literature.

Macauley. Alastair. 2000. "*The Sleeping Beauty*—The British Connection." *Dancing Times* (September): 1051–57.

Malkov, N. ["Islamei"]. 1928. "Simfoniya tanca" [The symphony of dance]. *Zhizn' iskusstvo* [The life of art] 27: 4.

Michon, George. 1929. *The Franco-Russian Alliance.* New York: Macmillan.

Naumova, Nina. 1999. "Molchanie kak golos surovogo zhiznennogo opyta" [Silence as the voice of hard life experience]. In *Retsidiviruyushchaya a modernizatsiya v Rossii: beda, vina ili resurs chelovechestva* [Recidivism and modernization in Russia: Misfortune, guilt, or human resource]. Moscow: Editorial URSS.

Nosilov, N. I. 1941. "Balety P. I. Chaikovskogo na scene teatra opery i baleta im. S. M. Kirova" [The ballets of P. I. Chaikovsky on the stage of the Theater of Opera and Ballet named for S. M. Kirov]. In *P. I. Chaikovsky na scene teatra opery i baleta imeni S. M. Kirova (b. Mariinsky)* [P. I. Chaikovsky on the stage of the Theater of Opera and Ballet named for S. M. Kirov (the former Maryinsky)]. Leningrad: Kirov Theater, 287–336.

Ostrovsky, A. N. 1958. *Polnoe sobranie sochinenij* [Complete collected works]. Vol. 16. Moscow: State Publishing House of Artistic Literature.

Oushakine, Serguei. 2000. "In the State of Post-Soviet Aphasia: Symbolic Development in Contemporary Russia." *Europe-Asia Studies* 52.6: 991–1016.

Perrault, Charles. 1967. *Contes de fées.* Ed. Gilbert Rouger. Paris, Garnier.

"Petrogradskie teatry v sezon 1922–23 goda" [Petrograd theaters in the 1922–23 season]. *Ezhenedelnik petrogradskikh gosudarstvennykh akademicheskikh teatrov* [Weekly of the Petrograd State Academic Theaters] 1922. 3:56.

Petipa, Marius. 1971. *Marius Petipa: Materialy, vospominaniya, stat'i* [Marius Petipa: Materials, reminiscences, articles]. Ed. A. Nekhendzi. Leningrad: Iskusstvo.

P. I. Chaikovsky na tsene teatra opery i baleta imeni S. M. Kirova (b. Mariinsky) [P. I. Chaikovsky on the stage of the Theater of Opera and Ballet named for S. M. Kirov (the former Maryinsky)]. 1941. Ed. N. A. Shuvalov. Leningrad: Kirov Theater.

Pleshcheev, Aleksandr. 1896. *Nash balet, 1673–1896* [Our ballet]. St. Petersburg: Benke.

Poesio, Giannandrea. 1994. "Enrico Cecchetti: The Influence of Tradition." *Dance History.* Ed. J. Adshead and J. Layson. London: Routledge.

———. 1995. "The Origins of Ballet Mime. Parts 2 and 3." *Dancing Times* 24–25: 155–57.

———. 1997. "Gender and Politics in the Italian Ballo Grande." Paper presented at the annual meetings of the Society of Dance History Scholars. Barnard College, New York City.

———. 1999. "Mime Acting in *The Sleeping Beauty.*" *Dancing Times* 89.1065: 839–42.

Poznansky, Alexander. 1991. *Tchaikovsky, the Quest for the Inner Man.* New York: Schirmer.

Protopopov, Vl. 1954. "Raboty B. V. Asafe'eva o Chaikovskom" [B. V. Asafiev's work on Chaikovsky]. In *Akademik B. V. Asaf'ev: Izbrannye trudy* [Academic B. V. Asafiev: Selected works]. Vol. 2. Moscow: Izdatel'stvo akademii nauk SSSR. 5–16.

Ratanova, Maria. 1999. "*Spyashchaya krasavitsa:* Mneniya o prem'ere" [*Sleeping Beauty:* Thoughts on the premiere]. *Mariinskij teatr* 3–4: 5, 16.

Roslavleva, Natalia. 1964. "Balanchine's Choreo-Symphonies." *The Ballet Annual and Year Book.* London: Adam and Charles Black.

———. 1966. *Era of the Russian Ballet.* London: Gollancz.

Rozanova, Olga. 1999. "*Spyashchaya krasavitsa:* Mneniya o prem'ere" [*Sleeping Beauty:* Thoughts on the premiere]. *Mariinskij teatr* 3–4: 16.

Rozanova, Yu[lia]. 1965. *O Simfonizme v balete Chaikovskogo "Spyashchaya krasavitsa"* [On symphonism in Chaikovsky's ballet *Sleeping Beauty*]. Moscow: Muzyka.

Sankt-Peterburg/Petrograd/Leningrad. Enciklopedicheskij spravochnik [Encyclopedic reference work]. 1992. Ed. B. B. Piotrovsky. Moscow: Bol'shaya Rossijskaya entsiklopediya.

Sedov, Yaroslav. 1999. "Spi, moya krasavica" [Sleep, my beauty]. *Itogi* 6 (July): 59–61.

Scholl, Tim. 1994. *From Petipa to Balanchine: Classical Revival and the Modernization of Ballet.* London: Routledge.

———. 1999. "Conveying a Classic Back to Its Lavish Origins." *New York Times.* 27 June, 28–29.

Schwarz, Boris. 1983. *Music and Musical Life in Soviet Russia.* Bloomington: Indiana University Press.

Shumilova, Emiliya Ivanovna. 1976. *Pravda baleta* [The truth of ballet]. Moscow: Iskusstvo.

Skalkovsky, Konstantin. 1890. *Novoe vremya,* 5 January. Quoted in Roland John Wiley, *A Century of Russian Ballet.* Oxford: Oxford University Press, 1990, 373–76.

Slonimsky, Yu[ri]. 1937. *Mastera baleta* [Masters of the ballet]. Leningrad: Iskusstvo.

———. 1956. *P. I. Chaikovsky i baletnyj teatr ego vremeni* [P. I. Chaikovsky and the ballet theater of his time]. Moscow: Muzgiz.

———. 1966. Introduction to *Shestdesyat let v balete* [Sixty years in ballet]. Moscow: Iskusstvo.

Slonimsky, Yu[ri], ed. 1971. *Marius Petipa: Materialy, vospominaniya, stat'i.* [Marius Petipa: Materials, reminiscences, articles]. Leningrad: Iskusstvo.

Smith, Kathleen E. 2002. *Mythmaking in the New Russia: Politics and Memory during the Yeltsin Era.* Ithaca: Cornell University Press.

Smith, Marian. 2000. *Ballet and Opera in the Age of Giselle.* Princeton: Princeton University Press.

Sollertinsky, Ivan. 1928. "V sporakh o tancoval'nom teatre" [The debate over dance theater]. *Zhizn' iskusstvo* [The life of art] 27: 5.

———. 1929. "Kakoj balet nam v sushchnosti nuzhen?" [What sort of ballet do we really need?]. *Zhizn' iskusstvo* [The life of art] 40: 5.

————. 1930. "Vlevo ot sphagata" [Further left than the splits] *Rabochij i teatr* 8: 8.

————. 1933. "Muzykal'nyj teatr na poroge oktyabrya i problema operno-baletnogo nas-lediya v epokhu voennogo kommunizma" [The musical theater on the eve of October and the problem of the opera and ballet legacy in the era of war communism]. In *Istoriya sovet-skogo teatra* [The history of Soviet theater]. Vol. 1. Leningrad: Khudozhestvennaya lit. 291–356.

Stanislavsky, Konstantin. 1924. *My Life in Art,* Boston: Little, Brown.

Stites, Richard. 1992. *Russian Popular Culture: Entertainment and Society since 1900.* New York: Cambridge University Press.

Stolyarova, Galina. 1998. "Reawakening Petipa's Real *Sleeping Beauty.*" *St. Petersburg Times.* 20–26 April.

Surits, E[lizaveta]. [also "Souritz" and "Suritz," "Elizabeth"]. 1979. *Khoreograficheskoe iskusstvo dvadtsatykh godov: Tendentsii, razvitiia* [Choreography of the 1920s: Tendencies, develop-ments]. Moscow: Iskusstvo.

————. 1990. *Soviet Choreographers in the 1920s.* Trans. Lynn Visson. Durham: Duke Uni-versity Press.

————. 2000. "Gorsky i moskovsky balet" [Gorsky and the Moscow ballet]. In *Baletmejster A. A. Gorsky* [Balletmaster A. A. Gorsky]. St. Petersburg: Dmitry Bulanin.

Surits, E., and E. Belova, eds. 2000. *Baletmejster A. A. Gorsky* [Balletmaster A. A. Gorsky]. 2000. St. Petersburg: Dmitry Bulanin.

Svetlov, Valerian. 1908. "Ballet." *Peterburskaya gazeta.* 18 February: 5.

Swift, Mary Grace. 1968. *The Art of the Dance in the U.S.S.R.* South Bend: Notre Dame Uni-versity Press.

Taruskin, Richard. 1995a. *Text and Act; Essays on Music and Performance.* New York: Oxford University Press.

————. 1995b. "Pathetic Symphonist." *New Republic* 212.6 (6 February): 26–40.

Third Youth: Marius Petipa in Petersburg [Tret'ya molodost': Marius Petipa v Peterburge]. 1965. Dir. Jean Dreville. Screenplay by Aleksandr Galich and Pol Andreotta. Videocas-sette. Lenfilm, 2000.

Trabsky, A. Ya., ed. 1975. *Russkij sovetskij teatr, 1921–26* [Russian Soviet theater, 1921–26]. Leningrad: Iskusstvo.

————. 1982. *Russkij sovetskij teatr, 1926–32* [Russian Soviet theater, 1926–32]. Vol. 1 Len-ingrad: Iskusstvo.

Vanslov, Viktor. 1977. "Balet v ryadu drugikh iskusstv" [Ballet among the other arts]. *Muzyka i khoreografiya sovremennogo baleta* [Music and choreography in contemporary ballet]. 5–32.

————. 1981a. "Formalizm." *Balet entsiklopediya.* Moscow: Sovetskaya entsikopediya.

————. 1981b. "Idejnost'" [Idea-ness]. *Balet entsiklopediya.* Moscow: Sovetskaya entsikopediya.

————. 1981c. "Modernizm" [Modernism]. *Balet entsiklopediya.* Moscow: Sovetskaya entsi-kopediya.

————. 1981d. "Realizm" [Realism]. *Balet entsiklopediya.* Moscow: Sovetskaya entsikopediya.

————. 1981e. "Soderzhanie i forma" [Content and form]. *Balet entsiklopediya.* Moscow: Sovetskaya entsikopediya.

————. 1981f. "Symfonichesky tanets." *Balet entsiklopediya.* Moscow: Sovetskaya entsiko-pediya.

———. 1993. "Marius Petipa—Still Current." *Balet,* special English-language edition: 3–4.

———. 1998. "Russia: Theatrical Dance since 1917." Trans. and ed. Elizaveta Surits. *International Encyclopedia of Dance.* New York: Oxford University Press.

Vasilevsky, I. F. ["Bukva"]. 1886. "Roskosh′ i velikolepie novykh teatral′ nykh postanovok: Feeriya 'Volshebnye pilyuli' i balet 'Prikaz korolya'" [Splendor and magnificence in new theatrical productions: The féerie *The Magic Pills* and the ballet *The King's Command*] *Russkie vedemosti.* 26 February: 2–3.

———. 1890. "Novyj balet *Spyashchaya krasavitse*" [The new ballet *Sleeping Beauty*]. *Russkie vedemosti.* 14 January: 2.

———. 1891. "Feeriya i balet" [The féerie and the ballet]. *Russkie vedemosti.* 8 December: 3.

Vaughan, William. 1996. "Vienna: Historismus in Europa." *Burlington Magazine* 138 (December): 846–48.

Vaziev, Makhar, and Sergei Vikharev. 1999. "A Sleeping *Beauty.*" Interview with Pavel Gershenzon. *Ballet Review* 27.1: 15–21. [Originally published as "Mariinskii teatr pristupil k restavracii baleta *Spyashchaya krasavitsa*" [The Maryinsky Theater begins work on a reconstruction of *Sleeping Beauty*]. *Russkij telegraf,* 11 April 1998: 8.]

Vikharev, Sergei. 1999. "Mne udalos′ sdelat′ to, chto neobkhodimo bylo sdelat′" [I managed to do what was necessary]. Interview with Maria Ratanova. *Mariinskij teatr* 3–4: 2.

Vinogradov, Nikolai Glebovich. 1924. "Solnechnaya kommuna" [The Sunny Commune]. In *Russkij sovetskij teatr, 1921–26* [Russian Soviet theater]. Ed. A. Ya. Trabsky. Leningrad: Iskusstvo. 295–96.

Volkonsky, Prince Sergei. 1992. *Moi vospominaniya* [My reminiscences]. 2 vols. Moscow: Iskusstvo.

Volkov, Solomon. 1985. *Balanchine's Tchaikovsky: Conversations with Balanchine on His Life, Ballet and Music.* New York: Doubleday.

Volynsky, Akim ["Flekser"]. 1914a. "Korovin I Vsevolozhsky" [Korovin and Vsevolozhsky]. *Birzhevye vedemosti,* 18 February.

———. 1914b. "Tancy v *Spyashchej krasavice*" [The Dances in *Sleeping Beauty*]. *Birzhevye vedemosti,* 22 March.

———. 1922. "Kareta skoroj pomoshchi" [An ambulance!], *Zhizn'ikusstva* [The life of art]. 38: 3.

———. 1923. "Spyashchaya krasavitsa" [*Sleeping Beauty*]. *Zhizn'ikusstva* [The life of art]. vol. 48.

Warner, Marina. 1994. *From the Beast to the Blonde: On Fairy Tales and Their Tellers.* London: Chatto and Windus.

Wiley, Roland John. 1976. "Dances from Russia: An Introduction to the Sergejev Collection." *Harvard Library Bulletin* 24: 96–112.

———. 1985. *Tchaikovsky's Ballets:* Swan Lake, Sleeping Beauty, Nutcracker. Oxford: Oxford University Press.

———. 1990. *A Century of Russian Ballet: Documents and Accounts, 1810–1910.* Oxford: Oxford University Press.

Yufit, A. Z., ed. 1968. *Russkij sovetskij teatr, 1917–21* [Russian Soviet theater, 1917–21]. Leningrad: Iskusstvo.

"Znamenatel′noe pyatiletie" [A momentous five years]. 1937. Editorial. *Teatr* 1: 3–8.

Index

Asafiev, Boris (Igor Glebov), 83, 84, 88, 90

Bakst, Leon, 105–6
Balanchine, George, 116–17
Balletomanes, 2
Basile, Giambattista, 38, 40
Bayadère, I, 94–95
Benois, Alexandre, 104, 105, 106, 110
Borisoglebsky, Mikhail, 33, 58–62

Cherepnin, Alexander, 74–75
Clément, Catherine, 40–44

Diaghilev, Sergei, 71–73, 105–6
drambalet, 103, 120, 122

Franco-Russian alliance, 32

Gershenzon, Pavel, 144

Ivanov, Mikhail, 3, 5–7

Kennan, George, 32–33
Khudekov, Sergei, 4, 11, 23
Kirstein, Lincoln, 32
Konstantinova, Marina, 36, 53–54
Korovin, Konstantin, 104–6
Korovyakov, Dmitry, 13, 21
Krasovskaya, Vera, 82, 84, 92–94
Kul'turnost', 80–82

Laroche, Herman, 7, 8, 12, 27–28, 46–47
Lenin, Vladimir Ilyich, 67, 69
Lévi-Strauss, Claude, 45
Lopukhov, Fyodr, viii, 91–92, 106–14, 120, 121; choreography of the Lilac Fairy's variation, 55–58
Lunacharsky, Anatoly, 67–69, 72

Manzotti, Luigi, 22, 23

Ostrovsky, Alexander, 27

Perrault, Charles, 38, 40
Petipa, Maria, 49–59, 62, 121
Petipa, Marius, 92–98; and the féerie, 23–25
Proletkult, 69
Propp, Vladimir, 42

Schwarz, Boris, 83, 85
Sergeyev, Konstantin, viii; 1952 production, 122–30
Sergeyev, Nikolai, viii, 49, 59–63
Skalkovsky, Konstantin, 4
Sollertinsky, Ivan, 72, 75–78, 83
Stepanov, Vladimir, viii, 136–43
"symphonism," 82–89, 90–92, 94–100

Tchaikovsky, Pyotr Ilyich, 80, 85, 87–89; and Wagner, 37

Vaziev, Makhar, 136
Vikharev, Sergei, 136–45
Vsevolozhsky, Ivan, viii, 98; libretto of *Sleeping Beauty,* 38

Wagner, Richard, 34, 90
Warner, Marina, 38, 40, 42
Wiley, Roland John, viii

Zakharov, Rostislav, 79
Zucchi, Virginia, 46